Palgrave Socio-Legal Studies

Series Editor
Dave Cowan
School of Law
University of Bristol
Bristol, UK

The Palgrave Socio-Legal Studies series is a developing series of monographs and textbooks featuring cutting edge work which, in the best tradition of socio-legal studies, reach out to a wide international audience.

More information about this series at
http://www.palgrave.com/gp/series/14679

Antonia Porter

Prosecuting Domestic Abuse in Neoliberal Times

Amplifying the Survivor's Voice

palgrave
macmillan

Antonia Porter
Kent Law School
University of Kent
Canterbury, Kent, UK

Palgrave Socio-Legal Studies
ISBN 978-3-030-61368-6 ISBN 978-3-030-61369-3 (eBook)
https://doi.org/10.1007/978-3-030-61369-3

Cover illustration: Contributor: Islandstock/Alamy Stock Photo

This Palgrave Macmillan imprint is published by the registered company Springer Nature Switzerland AG
The registered company address is: Gewerbestrasse 11, 6330 Cham, Switzerland

Acknowledgements

This book could not have been completed without the funding that I received from the University of Kent's 50th-anniversary bursary or from the postdoctoral fellowship awarded by the Economic and Social Research Council (in the guise of the South East Network for Social Sciences). I am ever grateful for being given the opportunity.

From the outset, Dr. Sinéad Ring inspired and encouraged me. Her hard work and her support has been unwavering and her passion for the wider feminist legal project motivated me on countless occasions. This monograph would not have been possible without her. Thanks also to Prof. Donatella Allessandrini for providing her brilliant 'eureka' moments during our reading groups and for considering the first completed draft with such enthusiasm. Prof. Emily Grabham, Dr. Emily Haslam, Prof. Helen Carr, Prof. Judy Fudge, Prof. Rosemary Auchmuty, Prof. Vanessa Munro and Prof. Dermot Walsh have all provided much-appreciated feedback on my work at earlier stages. I have been humbled by the generous way you have all given your time. Particular and special thanks go to Prof. Rosemary Hunter who carefully invested her time, energy and knowledgeable insight to provide incisive analysis and stylistic advice.

I am grateful to the prosecutors and support workers who agreed to speak to me as part of the project and who were so open and frank during interviews. Thanks go especially to the survivors I interviewed and to whom this monograph is dedicated. Your stories are moving and provoking and I hope this work contributes in some way to advancing the best interests of women who have or who are experiencing domestic abuse.

Outside of the academy, I am so lucky to have great friends and a wonderful family who have all supported me, kept me grounded and injected fun into the day to day (even, and especially, during lockdown). Mum and dad, you are essentially the best parents in the world and my brother Joe, thanks for always having my back. Arlo and Flora, you make me so proud and you bring me immeasurable amounts of happiness every day. And finally, to Dan, I am so fortunate to have you—your wisdom, your perspective and your brilliant humour!

About this Book

Criminal prosecutions are key to the UK government's strategy to end violence against women and girls. Crown Prosecution Service policy affirms that domestic abuse offences are 'particularly serious' and prosecutors are reminded that it will be rare that the 'public interest' will not require pursuance of such offences through the criminal courts. The book argues that past inattentive treatment by state criminal justice agencies in relation to domestic abuse is now being self-consciously reversed by neoliberal governing agendas intent on denouncing crime and holding offenders to account.

Seeking to unpick some of the discourses and perspectives that may have contributed to the current prosecutorial commitment, the book considers its emergence within the context of the women's movement, feminist scholarship and an era of neoliberalism. Three empirical chapters explore the prosecution commitment, on the one hand, and the impact on women's lives, on the other. The book's final substantive chapter offers a distinctive normative conceptual framework through which practitioners may think about women who have experienced domestic abuse that will have both intellectual appeal and practical application.

Contents

About the Author

Dr. Antonia Porter is a lecturer at the University of Kent where she teaches Criminal Law, Evidence and Legal Ethics. Her research interests lie at the intersection between feminist legal scholarship and criminal justice. Qualifying as a solicitor in 2004, she has practised as a criminal defence lawyer and as a Senior Crown Prosecutor. She continues to be instructed by the Crown Prosecution Service as a trial advocate.

1
Introduction

1. Motivations and Objectives

As a practising criminal prosecutor, I find intimate partner abuse cases notably prevalent and the predominance of female victims striking. In fact according to Crown Prosecution Service (CPS) figures, domestic abuse accounts for nearly one in five CPS prosecutions and women are the victim in 83% of such cases.[1] Having previously been a defence advocate, I joined the CPS in 2007 at a time when new domestic violence policy and guidance, paired with mandatory training across the service was being implemented.[2] It marked the service's henceforth commitment to dealing with domestic abuse 'within a gendered framework' and as a 'particularly serious'

[1]Use of the term 'victim' in the book reflects its usage in the criminal justice system. In no way do I intend to totalise women's experiences or overlook the empowered agency of women who have experienced domestic abuse. Crown Prosecution Service, 'Violence Against Women and Girls Report 2018–20 19' (2019 CPS) A13 available at https://www.cps.gov.uk/sites/default/files/documents/publications/cps-vawg-report-2019.pdf accessed 28 January 2020.

[2]Here, I use the term 'domestic violence' and not 'domestic abuse' because this reflects CPS terminology in 2007. Crown Prosecution Service, 'Policy for Prosecuting Cases of Domestic Violence' (CPS HQ 2005); Crown Prosecution Service, 'Domestic Violence: Good Practice Guidance' (CPS HQ 2005) available at http://webarchive.nationalarchives.gov.uk/, http://www.crimereduction.homeoffice.gov.uk/domesticviolence/domesticviolence51.pdf; and Crown Prosecution Service, 'Evaluation of the National Domestic Violence Training Programme 2005–2008' (2008) available at https://www.cps.gov.uk/publications/equality/evaluation_of_national_domestic_violence_training_programme.html accessed 29 June 2017.

A. Porter, *Prosecuting Domestic Abuse in Neoliberal Times*, Palgrave Socio-Legal Studies,
https://doi.org/10.1007/978-3-030-61369-3_1

crime.[3] Improving the conviction rate and bringing 'more perpetrators to justice'[4] became the organisation's priority.

This book is inspired by my experience of that policy implementation and the subsequent delivery of the prosecution of intimate partner abuse, particularly at the point a woman withdraws her support for the criminal prosecution. On the one hand, I have observed CPS policy and guidance that ostensibly sets out to serve the state's self-consciously feminist agendas and, on the other, execution of the policy which bows to neoliberal stratagems and New Public Managerial demands.[5]

In this book, I want to probe and excavate the narratives and discourses that underpin the CPS priority contained in both CPS policy and the daily working practices of prosecutors. Specifically, I consider domestic abuse prosecutions in the context of two key discourses located in the state treatment of violence against women; 'feminism' and 'neoliberalism'. Against the backdrop of their potentially strained union, I set the vocalised concerns and exigencies of women, noting the occasions when contemporary criminal justice responses do not serve women as intended.

2. Prosecuting Domestic Abuse at the CPS

Victims of domestic abuse[6] are considerably more likely to retract their support for the criminal prosecution, or fail to attend trial to give evidence, as compared to victims of other criminal offences. One in three domestic

---

[3]Crown Prosecution Service, 'A Consultation on the CPS Violence Against Women Strategy and Action Plans—A Response to Consultations' (2012) available at https://www.cps.gov.uk/publication/consultation-cps-violence-against-women-strategy-and-action-plans-response-consultation accessed 6 February 2020; Crown Prosecution Service, 'Domestic Abuse Guidelines for Prosecutors' available at https://www.cps.gov.uk/legal-guidance/domestic-abuse-guidelines-prosecutors accessed 9 February 2020.

[4]Crown Prosecution Service, 'Delivering Justice: Violence Against Women and Girls Report, 10th Edition' (2017) 1 available at https://www.cps.gov.uk/sites/default/files/documents/publications/cps-vawg-report-2017.pdf accessed 28 January 2020.

[5]Vanessa Munro, 'Violence Against Women, "Victimhood" and the (Neo)Liberal State' in Margaret Davies and Vanessa Munro (eds), *The Ashgate Research Companion to Feminist Legal Theory* (Ashgate 2013) 234. What I mean by New Public Managerialism is described in Chapters 3 and 4. Succinctly, it describes an ideology usually associated with the private business sector (here the public sector) that strives for systems efficiency and economy, typically overseen by an expanded management structure.

[6]Domestic abuse, or domestic violence, is defined across government as, 'any incident of controlling, coercive or threatening behaviour, violence or abuse between those aged 16 or over who are or have been intimate partners ... regardless of their gender or sexuality' and covers a range of types of abuse, 'including, but not limited to, psychological, physical, sexual, financial or emotional abuse' in Crown Prosecution Service, 'Domestic Abuse Guidelines for Prosecutors' (CPS 2014) available at https://www.cps.gov.uk/legal-guidance/domestic-abuse-guidelines-prosecutors accessed 2 March 2020.

abuse prosecutions fails in this way, [7] accounting for over 7500 cases annually.[8] This compares to one in ten prosecutions generally.[9] The reasons that women request the termination of proceedings against their current or former partner are myriad and diverse. They will include both material and relational considerations that do not apply to other general offences.[10] Prosecutors must therefore regularly confront the sensitive question of how to proceed in these circumstances.

Tasked with implementing the prosecutive power of the state, prosecutors act on behalf of the 'public' and not individual victims.[11] The Code for Prosecutors (The Code) sets out the two-stage test that must be met before prosecutions are pursued; the first is to consider whether there is a 'realistic prospect of conviction' on the available evidence—the 'evidential test'—the second is to ask whether the public interest will be best served by bringing the prosecution—the 'public interest test'.[12] Where a victim of domestic abuse is supportive of criminalisation and, evidentially, there is a realistic prospect of conviction, the prosecutor's decision to charge or proceed is straightforward; the victim's wants align with the 'public interest' which almost invariably expects domestic abuse to be prosecuted. Indeed, CPS policy confirms that, '[i]t will be rare for the public interest not to be met' in domestic abuse cases.[13]

---

[7]Crown Prosecution Service, 'Violence Against Women and Girls Crime Report 2015–16' (CPS 2016) 31 available at https://www.cps.gov.uk/sites/default/files/documents/publications/cps_vawg_report_2016.pdf accessed 17 April 2018.

[8]Crown Prosecution Service, 'Violence Against Women and Girls Crime Report 2010–2011' (CPS 2011).

[9]Crown Prosecution Service, 'Violence Against Women and Girls Crime Report 2015–16' (CPS 2016) 31 available at https://www.cps.gov.uk/sites/default/files/documents/publications/cps_vawg_report_2016.pdf accessed 17 April 2018.

[10]Women may withdraw support for the prosecution due to, inter alia, fear of retaliation by the perpetrator/his associates; concerns about the court process or outcome; or ongoing proceedings creating problems in their continued intimate relationship. See Lisa Goodman and Deborah Epstein, *Listening to Battered Women: A Survivor Centred Approach to Advocacy, Mental Health and Justice* (American Psychological Association 2009) 97.

[11]Francis Bennion, 'The New Prosecution Arrangements' (1986) *Criminal Law Review* 3–15, 3; Crown Prosecution Service, 'The Decision to Charge' available at https://www.cps.gov.uk/cps-page/decision-charge accessed 1 March 2020.

[12]The 'realistic prospect of conviction' or 'evidential' test is met when impartial assessment of all admissible evidence concludes that a court would be 'more likely than not to convict the defendant of the charge alleged'. Crown Prosecution Service, 'The Code for Prosecutors' (2018) available at https://www.cps.gov.uk/sites/default/files/documents/publications/Code-for-Crown-Prosecutors-October-2018.pdf accessed 1 March 2020.

[13]Crown Prosecution Service, 'Domestic Abuse Guidelines for Prosecutors' (CPS 2014) available at https://www.cps.gov.uk/legal-guidance/domestic-abuse-guidelines-prosecutors accessed 2 March 2020.

Where a victim is unsupportive, prosecutors can either accede to her request to discontinue proceedings or decide to pursue the prosecution, absent her support.[14] 'Victimless' prosecutions can be achieved where a realistic prospect of conviction exists without requiring the victim to give evidence. This might be feasible if additional corroborative evidence such as police 999 calls, third-party testimony, medical evidence of her injuries or police body-worn video footage is available. It might also be possible, exceptionally, to make a successful hearsay application to have the complainant's written statement read at trial.[15] However, the opportunity to prosecute intimate partner abuse absent the victim, relying on third-party evidence, is an uphill challenge. So, alternatively, as a 'last resort',[16] prosecutors may request the court to issue a summons to secure the victim's attendance at trial against her stated wishes.[17]

It is clear that the CPS is committed to taking domestic abuse 'seriously'.[18] The current approach to intimate partner abuse was triggered in 2005 by revised policy and guidelines, and mandatory service wide training which was rolled out and completed by 2008 (training which I undertook). My own anecdotal observation in practice was that the commitment to taking the offence seriously was manifesting as a tendency on the part of prosecutors to summons unsupportive victims to trial. My in-depth interviews with prosecutors, conducted in 2017, do not contradict that perception. However, the primary research in Chapter 4 indicates that, following further training which was delivered by the service in 2016–2017, the preference for summons may be beginning to wane in favour of evidence-led (or victimless) prosecutions.[19] Where the victim is no longer supportive, victimless

[14]A Crown Prosecutor has discretion to discontinue a case under s23 Prosecution of Offences Act 1985 or apply to withdraw the charge or offer no evidence in court. In the Crown Court, alternatively, the prosecutor may ask that the count be left to lie on the indictment, apply for a motion to quash the count or invite the Attorney General to enter *nolle prosequi.*

[15]A hearsay application may be made as follows: s116(2)e Criminal Justice Act 2003 if the victim is in fear; s114(1)d if it is considered 'in the interests of justice' to do so; s118/common law if it falls under the principles of res gestae.

[16]Crown Prosecution Service, 'Domestic Abuse Guidelines for Prosecutors' (n 13).

[17]The court has power to issue a summons under Serious Organised Crime and Police Act 2005, s169 where the court deems it is in the interests of justice to secure the material evidence of the witness at trial.

[18]Crown Prosecution Service, 'Policy for Prosecuting Cases of Domestic Violence: 2005' (n 2).

[19]In spring 2017, the CPS introduced four new mandatory domestic abuse e-learning modules. Crown Prosecution Service, 'Crown Prosecution Service Annual Report and Accounts 2016–2017' (2017) available at https://www.gov.uk/government/uploads/system/uploads/attachment_data/file/628968/CPS_annual_report_2016_17.pdf accessed 13 February 2020.

prosecutions are arguably less controversial than summons because the victim is not coerced into physical court attendance but they are not without implications for women's autonomy. I refer collectively to these two preferred approaches—summons and evidence-led—as the emergence of 'tenacious prosecutions' at the CPS.

'Tenacious prosecutions' are traceable to CPS domestic abuse policy and the CPS training emphasis. They are evidenced in my primary research and in CPS performance statistics that have reported year on year increases to the domestic abuse conviction rate between 2010 and 2019.[20] If a tenacious prosecutorial approach has emerged, I am concerned in this book to answer the question *how* it has done so, specifically in the context of the violence against women movement and an era of neoliberalism. I also explore the *consequences* that arise for women from the state's commitment to criminalisation and the CPS drive to achieve convictions in matters of intimate partner abuse. In the light of these consequences, the book also contemplates how prosecutors might think about making decisions in domestic abuse cases where the victim is reluctant, in ways that might best support her 'thrivership' (a concept I discuss in Chapter 6).

The remainder of this introductory chapter proceeds by looking at three possible prosecutorial approaches when a woman indicates her preference for case discontinuance and draws out the consequences of each. It then outlines some of the central themes found in the literature pertaining to the state treatment of violence against women and explains why the two theoretical frames—feminism and neoliberalism—have been chosen. I reflect on the advantages and disadvantages of prioritising a criminal justice response to domestic abuse and draw out the paradoxical 'successes' of feminism's cooperation with the neoliberal state. I note, on the one hand, the potential of the law to validate women's account and the pivotal role law can play in moving women towards living abuse free, yet the union has also been signalled as 'a betrayal of … emancipatory [feminist] roots'[21] and as deeply flawed because 'the law is simply not a one size fits all solution'.[22]

---

[20]Crown Prosecution Service, 'Delivering Justice: Violence Against Women and Girls' Report 2018–19' (CPS 2019) available at https://www.cps.gov.uk/sites/default/files/documents/publications/cps-vawg-report-2019.pdf accessed 28 January 2020.

[21]Mimi Kim, 'Challenging the Pursuit of Criminalisation in an Era of Mass Incarceration: The Limitations of the Social Work Response to Domestic Violence in the USA' (2013) 43 *British Journal of Social Work* 1276.

[22]Leigh Goodmark, *A Troubled Marriage: Domestic Violence and the Legal System* (New York University Press 2013).

3. Prosecutorial Discretion in Domestic Abuse Cases: Three Approaches

The first approach a prosecuting authority might take when discontinuance is requested by a victim of domestic abuse, is to simply accede to the request, or what has been called 'automatic drop'.[23] This appears to have been the CPS approach prior to 2008 when complainant retraction in the context of prosecuting domestic abuse appeared to have 'an almost singular effect; namely, discontinuance'.[24] Secondly, there is pursuance of the prosecution irrespective of the woman's request or whether her personal interests are best met by that course. Nichols has called this 'no-drop' approach to prosecution a 'social change' approach because of its potential to challenge the social structures that permit violence against women.[25] This was the approach operating in CPS practice in 2009 immediately following revised guidelines, policy and mandatory training aimed at addressing the preceding praxis of 'automatic drop'.[26] Or thirdly, prosecutors may weigh up factors to determine whether the woman's safety and/or sense of autonomy might be best met through either course. This third approach has variously been called a 'victim-informed',[27] 'survivor-defined'[28] or 'victim empowerment'[29] approach. The CPS has never named the approach but current domestic abuse policy most closely advocates prosecutors emulate this 'survivor-defined' way (whilst the primary research in this book explores to what extent the policy plays out in working practice).

---

[23]Lisa Goodman and Deborah Epstein, *Listening to Battered Women: A Survivor-Centered Approach to Advocacy, Mental Health, and Justice* (American Psychological Association 2008).

[24]Antonia Cretney and Gwynn Davis, 'Prosecuting "Domestic" Assault' (1996) *Criminal Law Review* 162; Louise Ellison, 'Prosecuting Domestic Violence Without Victim Participation' *The Modern Law Review* (2002) 834, 834.

[25]Andrea Nichols, 'No-Drop Prosecution in Domestic Violence Cases: Survivor-Defined and Social Change Approaches to Victim Advocacy' (2014) 29(11) *Journal of Interpersonal Violence* 2114.

[26]Matthew Hall, *Victims of Crime: Policy and Practice in Criminal Justice* (Willan Publishing 2009) 143–146.

[27]Lauren Cattaneo et al., 'The Victim-Informed Prosecution Project: A Quasi-Experimental Test of a Collaborative Model for Cases of Intimate Partner Violence' (2009) 15(10) *Violence Against Women* 1227.

[28]Lisa Goodman, Kristie Thomas, Lauren Bennett Cattaneo, Deborah Heimel, Julie Woulfe and Siu Kwan Chong, 'Survivor-Defined Practice in Domestic Violence Work: Measure Development and Preliminary Evidence of Link to Empowerment' (2016) 31(1) *Journal of Interpersonal Violence* 163.

[29]Carolyn Hoyle and Andrew Sanders, 'Police Response to Domestic Violence: From Victim Choice to Victim Empowerment' (2000) 40(1) *British Journal of Criminology* 14.

(i) 'Automatic Drop': Discontinuing Cases on Victim Request

The first approach, routinely acceding to a reluctant victim's wishes and dropping the case accordingly, can be advantageous to the extent that it demonstrates that the criminal justice system is responsive. Winick, founder of the therapeutic jurisprudence movement, has argued that 'being heard' in this way is 'vital to an individual's sense of her own locus of control [and] emotional well-being'.[30] She may withdraw from the prosecution because arrest alone achieved cessation of the immediate behaviour as intended or she may have weighed up that the costs of prosecution (breakdown of the family structure, loss of financial support, increased risk of violent retaliation) outweigh the potential benefit of prosecution outcomes (where the legal process is stressful, probation sentences might be ineffective, fines impact the family as a whole or custody would take him away from childcare or earning responsibilities). Having her wishes actioned is likely to instil a sense that the criminal justice system is not impersonal, impervious or even coercive, rather it is sensitive and respectful to the victim. Moreover, being victim reactive might forge a sense of trust in the victim to call on the criminal justice system in the future in the knowledge that victim preference is recognised and that her autonomy (or self-governance) is valued.[31]

Unquestioningly acceding to the victim's request, however, is not without notable shortcomings. If victim withdrawal is habitually assented, there is a risk of a transfer of power to the abuser. He (or his associates) may pursue violence or intimidating tactics in an effort to coerce the victim into retracting. Or he may make 'apologetic manipulations' which minimise his abusive behaviour and maximise the intensity of their bond to persuade the victim into retracting, knowing that her retraction will have the effect of terminating his prosecution.[32] The risk that her stated request is not actually her preferred choice is therefore real. The automatic drop approach also engenders in police, prosecutors and other agents of the criminal justice system an impatience and cynicism about the victim's reliability and even her credibility.

[30]Bruce Winick, 'Applying the Law Therapeutically in Domestic Violence Cases' (2000) 69 *UMKC Law Review* 33, 64.

[31]Eve Buzawa and Carl Buzawa, *Domestic Violence: The Criminal Justice Response* (3rd edn, Sage 2003).

[32]Nichols, 'No-Drop Prosecution in Domestic Violence Cases' (n 25).

(ii) 'No-Drop' Prosecution: Refusal to Discontinue Cases on Request

Advocates of no-drop prosecutions cite that the approach averts the potential for the transfer of power to the perpetrator, ensuring that the burden of whether or not to prosecute is taken out of the victim's (and indirectly the perpetrator's) hands.[33] No-drop prosecutions which remove, or largely remove, the prosecutor's exercise of discretion to discontinue the case also recognise that, often, victims cannot be relied upon to bring offenders to account; retracting or failing to attend court because they wrongly minimise the perpetartor's behaviour or blame themselves. The psychological consequences of a coercively controlling relationship can contribute to a woman's loss of self-confidence, self-esteem and a failure to believe in her own capacity for agency to bring about change in what Lenore Walker has called 'learned helplessness'.[34] The effects of gaslighting (where a perpetrator's behaviours might include lying about events or the victim's abilities, manipulating the victim's decision-making and choices and minimising or denying his own abusive behaviours) can undermine a victim's perception, judgement or even memory. As a consequence, victims can be reluctant to cooperate with a prosecution because they 'fail to see that criminal intervention can assist in the shared goal of getting their abuser to stop the violence'.[35] *Requiring* criminal intervention through a no-drop approach ensures that any benefit that the victim might receive from the criminal process is facilitated.

However, if the state wishes to help keep women safe, no-drop prosecutions can contradict the effort. Inflexibly pursuing the prosecution has disadvantages. First, in the absence of protections such as safe housing or the defendant's remand into custody, the victim is at (increased) risk of violence whilst being involved in proceedings.[36] This is because of the potential for retaliatory abuse. Especially in the context of a survivor asserting themselves by invoking the law, a perpetrator may attack as a means of trying to reassert

---

[33]Donna Wills, 'Domestic Violence: The Case for Aggressive Prosecution' (1997) *University California Los Angeles Women's Law Journal* 173; Evan Stark, 'Mandatory Arrest of Batterers: A Reply to Its Critics' (1993) 36(5) *American Behavioral Scientist* 651; and Dennis Saccuzzo, 'How Should Police Respond to Domestic Violence: A Therapeutic Jurisprudence Analysis of Mandatory Arrest' (1998) 39 *Santa Clara Law Review* 765.

[34]Lenore Walker, *The Battered Woman Syndrome* (4th edn, Springer 2016).

[35]Wills (n 33) 178.

[36]Linda Mills, 'Killing Her Softly: Intimate Abuse and the Violence of State Intervention' (1999) *Harvard Law Review* 550, 585.

control in the relationship.[37] Second, if the victim's situation and stated wishes are ignored it can cause victims to lose confidence in criminal justice agents' ability to act in their best interests, instilling in them reluctance to call police in an emergency in the future.[38] Third, no-drop prosecutions can have the effect of overlooking women's agency, leaving them with a reduced sense of personal control over their lives, confirming messages that a perpetrator may have instilled throughout the relationship about her self-efficacy. The approach runs the risk of replacing perpetrator coercion with state coercion.

(iii) Survivor-Defined Approach: Balancing Interests

The third strategy, the 'survivor-defined' approach, endeavours to combine the advantages of the other two approaches. It therefore recognises that whilst a woman's decision may not be entirely free because it is formed in coerced circumstances, the decision might still be entirely considered. For that reason, a woman's wishes ought not to be immediately discounted as arising from perpetrator manipulations on the one hand or 'learned helplessness' on the other. The decision may be formed by someone acting with astute awareness or wisely in the circumstances bearing in mind personal, material or safety factors, particularly if she intends to maintain the relationship. The victim's request and reasons should therefore, ordinarily, form part of the prosecutor's determination, bearing in mind the autonomy enhancing potential of effecting them.

As the 'survivor-defined' approach encourages prosecutors to make their decision being cognisant of women's individual situations and needs, this may also require prosecutors to proceed with the case despite a woman's stated wishes. The approach encourages prosecutors to obtain as full information about the situation as possible—from risk assessments, Independent Domestic Violence Advocates engaged with the victim in the community and by insisting that the police take comprehensive retraction statements from the victim to explore her reluctance. Where the danger posed

---

[37]See, for example, Martha Mahoney 'Victimization or Oppression? Women's Lives, Violence, and Agency' in Martha Fineman and Roxanne Mykitiuk (eds), *The public Nature of Private Violence: The Discovery of Domestic Abuse* (Routledge 1994) 59–92.

[38]Lauren Catteneo, Lisa Goodman, Deborah Epstein, 'The Victim-Informed Prosecution Project: A Quasi-Experimental Test of a Collaborative Model for Cases of Intimate Partner Violence' (2009) *Violence Against Women* 1227, 1229–1230; Eve Buzawa and Carl Buzawa, *Domestic Violence: The Criminal Justice Response* (3rd edn, Sage 2003).

by the perpetrator presents a high risk of further harm to the victim, the potential of a remand into custody or a rehabilitative sentencing outcome might merit ongoing prosecution. If the decision is taken out of the victim's hands, the possibility that the perpetrator will pursue retaliatory violence is reduced, though not extinguished. A 'survivor-centred' approach ought to trigger open communication between the victim and prosecuting authority to explain the decision being made on her behalf and why. This open communication might also include signposting her to other agencies that can support her. A 'survivor-defined' approach can yield positive outcomes for victims, such as higher satisfaction with the justice system, greater physical and emotional well-being and a willingness to use the justice system in the future.[39]

This third way or 'victim-informed' approach, which takes each offence on a case-by-case basis (once a presumption to prosecute has been made), is what the CPS ostensibly adopts in its policy and guidelines.[40] CPS guidelines for Prosecutors confirm that before deciding whether or not to summons an unsupportive victim, '[f]ull consideration should be given to the specific facts of the case and impact on the complainant's safety and well-being'.[41] I examine the extent to which this is deployed in practice in Chapter 4, bearing in mind the influences on prosecutors of both feminist expectations and the present neoliberal climate.

4. The Gendered Nature of Domestic Abuse: Feminist Explanations

In this section, I argue that domestic abuse is experienced predominantly by women and that the CPS have, accordingly, adopted feminist accounts of the crime's aetiology based in gender inequality. These feminist accounts have laid the groundwork for the CPS commitment to 'tenacious prosecutions'.

Gender is a significant causal pathway to the commission of domestic abuse and, since 2009, its prevalence in England and Wales has remained

[39]Nichols, 'No-Drop Prosecution in Domestic Violence Cases' (n 25).

[40]See Crown Prosecution Service, 'Violence Against Women and Girls' Report' (2017) available at http://www.cps.gov.uk/publications/docs/cps-vawg-report-2017.pdf accessed 1 March 2020; and Crown Prosecution Service, 'Domestic Abuse Guidelines for Prosecutors' (n 13).

[41]Ibid.

broadly unchanged.[42] Women are the predominant victims of intimate partner abuse with 26% of women and 15% of men having experienced 'some form of domestic abuse' on at least one occasion since the age of 16.[43] Yet, the gendered nature of abuse becomes more marked when one considers who is most frequently abused. Of those who have experienced four or more incidents of intimate partner abuse, the overwhelming majority are women; 89% compared to only 11% of men.[44] Moreover, not only is men's abuse likely to be more recurrent, it is also likely to be more physically injurious.[45] Even Murray Straus, the controversial 'family violence' sociologist whose work has sought to expose the extent of violence perpetrated by women in intimate relationships, concedes that 'because of the greater physical, financial and emotional injury suffered by women, they are the predominant victims'.[46] Marianne Hester's longitudinal study confirms that men are significantly more likely to be repeat offenders and that the intensity and severity of violence they use is much more extreme.[47]

Some scholars particularly in the field of men and masculinities have, nonetheless, asserted equivalent rates of men's and women's violence in intimate relationships. Kimmel suggests this may have been 'motivated by a desire to undermine or dismantle initiatives that administer to female victims [of domestic abuse]'.[48] The gender symmetrists' contention has invariably been based on the 'Conflict Tactics Scale' (CTS), a questionnaire designed by 'family violence scholar', Murray Straus, to assess both

[42]Sylvia Walby, Jude Towers and Brian Francis, 'The Decline in the Rate of Domestic Violence Has Stopped: Removing the Cap on Repeat Victimisation Reveals More Violence' (2014) *Violence and Society* 1. Walby et al.'s report reveals that once the Crime Survey for England and Wales cap of 5 repeat incidents is removed, rates of victimisation have not incrementally reduced as headlined in the ONS report year ending March 2017; Office for National Statistics, 'Domestic Abuse: Findings from the Crime Survey of England and Wales' (2017) available at https://www.ons.gov.uk/peoplepopulationandcommunity/crimeandjustice/articles/domesticabusefindingsfromthecrimesurveyforenglandandwales/yearendingmarch2017 accessed 26 February 2018.

[43]Office for National Statistics (n 42).

[44]Sylvia Walby and Jonathan Allen, 'Domestic Violence, Sexual Assault and Stalking: Findings from the British Crime Survey' (Home Office 2004) vii.

[45]Michael Kimmel, '"Gender Symmetry" in Domestic Violence: A Substantive and Methodological Review' (2002) *Violence Against Women* 1332, 1348.

[46]Murray Straus, 'Yes, Physical Assaults by Women Partners: A Major Social Problem' in Mary Walsh (ed), *Women, Men and Gender: Ongoing Debates* (Yale University Press 1997) 204, 219.

[47]Marianne Hester, 'Who Does What to Whom? Gender and Domestic Violence Perpetrators in English Police Records' (2013) 10(5) *European Journal of Criminology* 623.

[48]Kimmel (n 45) 1332.

men's and women's perpetration of physical violence. Yet the scale has been roundly criticised for its methodological problems.[49]

The CPS guidance for prosecutors describes that, 'domestic abuse is rarely a one-off incident' and that it includes 'cumulative and interlinked physical, psychological, sexual, emotional or financial' abuses that can have a 'particularly damaging effect on the victim'.[50] The CPS recognises that when domestic abuse is committed within a pattern of coercion, power or control it is primarily, but not exclusively, committed by men against women.[51] Whilst still acknowledging that domestic abuse victims can be men and that the perpetrators can be women, given the overall gender asymmetry of the behaviour, particularly when it comes to repeated abuse, the CPS adopts the United Nations position. This describes 'domestic abuse' as:

> A manifestation of historically unequal power relations between men and women, which have led to domination over and discrimination against women by men and to the prevention of the full advancement of women, and … violence against women is one of the crucial social mechanisms by which women are forced into a subordinate position compared with men.[52]

It is not surprising that feminists took on the subject and uncovered explanations about both its causes and solutions. Houston describes that the dominant feminist account has been the 'radical' feminist thesis that was initially used to theorise rape. In this conception, domestic abuse in the home was considered both reflective and reinforcing of both individual and systemic male domination in society. Houston describes this account as an

[49]Murray Straus, 'Measuring Intrafamily Conflict and Violence: The Conflict Tactics (CT) Scales' (1979) *Journal of Marriage and the Family* 75. The Scale draws on participant recollections of violence from the preceding 12 months only; it does not consider context, such as whether the person was acting defensively; and it does not distinguish between levels of violence deployed—so a slap carries the same weight as a serious wounding. It has been contended that if gender symmetry is to be asserted at all it would be more accurate to suggest it clustered at the very lowest levels of violence (see Rebecca Dobash, Russel Dobash, Kate Cavanagh and Ruth Lewis, 'Separate and Intersecting Realities: A Comparison of Men's and Women's Accounts of Violence Against Women' (1998) 4(4) *Violence Against Women* 382).

[50]Crown Prosecution Service, 'Domestic Abuse Guidelines for Prosecutors' (2014) available at https://www.cps.gov.uk/legal-guidance/domestic-abuse-guidelines-prosecutors accessed 9 February 2018.

[51]Crown Prosecution Service, 'Violence Against Women and Girls Report 2016–2017' (CPS 2017) available at https://www.cps.gov.uk/sites/default/files/documents/publications/cps-vawg-report-2017_1.pdf accessed 27 April 2018.

[52]Resolution adopted by the General Assembly 48/104. Declaration on the Elimination of Violence against Women (1993).

understanding of domestic abuse as 'patriarchal force'.[53] Studies support this account and reveal that impulsive men, generally accepting of violence, frequently engage in domestic abuse where their behaviour is buoyed by traditionally held attitudes towards women (e.g. attachment to gender roles) or feelings of hostility towards women generally.[54]

As outlined, the CPS violence against women strategy now plainly adopts this feminist understanding of the dynamic of abuse as 'patriarchal force' and references the work of feminist Michelle Madden-Dempsey to urge prosecutorial pursuit to combat intimate partner abuse as a means of 'characteris[ing] the state as having values that lessen patriarchy'.[55] Such a commitment to prosecutions speaks to the 'intrinsic' (expressive or symbolic denouncement) and 'consequential' (actual behaviour changing) value of prosecutions and their potential to render society less patriarchal by setting and evolving norms.

The government's reliance on the criminal law as a means to address and to end domestic abuse has also given rise to s76 Serious Crime Act 2015 which criminalises, for the first time, coercive and controlling behaviours which may or may not include physical assault. Moreover, the commitment to end VAWG paved the way for Clare's Law[56] (which gives any member of the public the right to request information contained in police records regarding their partner's potential risk to them) and Domestic Violence Protection Orders[57] (which allows the police to apply for a magistrates' court 'non-contact' order to obtain short-term protection for an alleged victim).

Noting how recent governmental policy and legislation appears to reflect certain demands made by certain feminist groups, Halley and others have been quick to claim that 'feminism' has come to 'walk the halls of power' by virtue of a breed of 'governance feminist' who has effectively engaged in our

---

[53]Claire Houston, 'How Feminist Theory Became (Criminal) Law: Tracing the Path to Mandatory Criminal Intervention in Domestic Violence Cases' (2014) *Modern Law Review* 217.

[54]Michael Johnson, *A Typology of Domestic Violence: Intimate Terrorism, Violent Resistance and Situational Couple Violence* (Northeastern University Press 2008) 32.

[55]United Nations, '15 of the United Nations Special Rapporteur on Violence Against Women, Its Causes and Consequences: A Critical Review (1994–2009)' (2009) 27 available at http://www.ohchr.org/Documents/Issues/Women/15YearReviewofVAWMandate.pdf cited in Crown Prosecution Service, 'Violence Against Women and Girls Report, 10th Edition, 2016–17' (2017) A1 available at https://www.cps.gov.uk/sites/default/files/documents/publications/cps-vawg-report-2017_0.pdf accessed 23 March 2020. See Chapter 2 for a fuller discussion on Madden-Dempsey's work.

[56]The Domestic Abuse Disclosure Scheme was introduced in March 2014.

[57]Domestic Violence Protection Orders were introduced in March 2014.

governing power structures.[58] 'Governance feminists', according to Halley, combine the ostensibly liberal feminist strategy of targeting state institutions and legal reform to achieve equality, with the highly emotive and charged discourse of radical and/or dominance feminism (in which women are depicted as oppressed, victimised and vulnerable to men's violence in the home as a result of male tyranny).[59] This recipe, Halley asserts, has proved highly influential in the violence against women field because feminists have found successive neoliberal governments particularly hospitable to their account and demands.[60] In part, she posits this is due to neoliberalism's commitment to shoring up individual freedoms and, more specifically, victims' rights (as discussed further in Chapter 3). A less benevolent explanation might be that it is convenient for neoliberal governments to harness a criminal justice response; the radical feminist thesis is easily deployed to both justify and facilitate the 'expressive justice'[61] and 'penal populism' that plays well with the electorate. For, when 'brutish' men oppress and mistreat their 'vulnerable' women, the government's deployment of a 'law and order' agenda garners approval as a means of protecting victims and punishing offenders thereby controlling the risk of the crime.

The notion that the feminist movement has collaborated with the neoliberal state's 'penal turn' has fuelled Halley's concerns that feminism is no longer in total command of the violence against women agenda. Halley has therefore urged that feminists must 'strive toward an ethic of responsibility in confronting the[ir] punitive [and carceral] ambitions'.[62] Yet, Halley's portrayal of the strategic 'governance feminist' motivated by so-called dominance feminism with access to the institutions of state, state-like and state affiliated power is, I suggest, overly simplistic. Her account defines feminism by the outcome rather than recognising feminism as a political process.[63]

[58]Janet Halley, Prabha Kotiswaran, Rachel Rebouché and Hila Shamir, *Governance Feminism: An Introduction* (University of Minnesota Press 2018) 31.

[59]'Radical' and 'dominance' feminisms both describe structural male domination as causational to women's oppression.

[60]If feminists can be shown to have successfully influenced the UK government's VAWG strategy, then the most transparent way that this is likely to have been achieved is through feminist engagement with the frequently deployed mechanism of government consultations with interested parties.

[61]See, for example, Kristin Bumiller, *In an Abusive State: How Neoliberalism Appropriated the Feminist Movement Against Sexual Violence* (Duke University Press 2008). See my Chapter 3 for an exploration of what is meant here by 'expressive justice'.

[62]Halley (n 58) 31.

[63]Serena Natile and Silvana Tapia, 'Governance Feminism: An Introduction' (2018) 52(4) *Law and Society* 1106, 1110.

Feminism takes place (as Halley herself acknowledges) both in the everyday, the micro-struggles and the indiscernible and also at a macro, transnational level spurred by social and political activism and ideology. The neat academic argument that Halley makes about highly influential 'dominance feminists' (even if this is taken only as a heuristic) 'seeking to wield governmental power' by accessing the 'modes of power they seek to master'[64] overstates feminism's presence and influence on governmental direction. Halley's account overlooks members of the 'women's movement' who do not share carceral ambition but who have been directly consulted by government, who have openly campaigned for alternative legal and institutional change and who have championed post-modern and socialist feminist discourses and thought. Indeed, whether feminists in the UK have been able to take part in constructive policymaking that steers the government response is restricted by the need for any advocacy group to present themselves and their organisations to neoliberal government departments and funding bodies primarily in terms of how they can offer value for money and cost savings.[65] I argue that Halley's account underplays neoliberalism's dominant ideology and pre-disposition to attend to social problems with penal solutions. Halley's account therefore exaggerates (dominance) feminist input and minimises neoliberal governments' strategic adoption of radical feminist theory to propel their own popular 'law and order' agenda.

Nonetheless, the 'patriarchal force' thesis is visible in the CPS VAWG strategy, despite the theory receiving criticism from many feminists about its 'heavy determinism' and for 'being over-prescriptive in its claims about causes and solutions'.[66] Hoyle observes that the use of radical feminism's discourse in the government response to violence against women has become an 'ideological straitjacket'.[67] It suggests that patriarchy is the only or primary way to understand the aetiology of domestic abuse thereby marginalising alternative or complementary explanations about perpetrator offending. Post-modern or 'third-wave' feminists urge us to recognise that the 'patriarchal force' thesis ignores the non-homogeneity of either the abused or the abuser based in terms of, amongst other things, class, race or sexuality.[68]

[64]Halley (n 58) 13.

[65]Armine Ishkanian, 'Neoliberalism and Violence: The Big Society and the Changing Politics of Domestic Violence in England' (2014) 34(3) *Critical Social Policy* 333, 333.

[66]Carolyn Hoyle, 'Feminism, Victimology and Domestic Violence' in Sandra Walklate (ed), *Handbook of Victims and Victimology* (Taylor and Frances 2012) 146.

[67]Ibid., 162.

[68]Ibid., 162.

Whilst male domination will always form a socio-cultural backdrop which explains why domestic abuse is asymmetric and why men are more likely to resort to violence and coercive control, as a single factor explanation it does not explain why some men are and some men are not abusive. Rather, we might recognise that there are factors operating on multiple levels which trigger domestic abuse in their interplay. Not only do these factors include those operating at the macrolevel (cultural, attitudinal and structural norms that perpetuate gender inequality and condone male violence) but they also include 'trigger factors' at a situational level (such as unemployment related stress, social learning or personal histories and networks) and at an individual level (an abuser's pathology, psychiatry or substance misuse).[69]

The danger is that, when the state adopts the radical feminist account, a universal male oppressor is conceived, together with an essentialist female victim, which fails to allow for intersectional or post-intersectional accounts of what it is to be someone experiencing domestic abuse.[70] This has paved the way, I argue, for feminist theories of domestic abuse as 'patriarchal force' to become interpreted by the state as a need for tenacious and committed criminal justice interventions (where criminalisation carries the symbolic and expressive value of condemning male power, dominance and control over women). In this book, I contemplate the consequences of the state adoption of feminist explanations and expose how the state may itself be accused of perpetrating coercive practices in the pursuit of protecting women and advancing their freedoms.[71] Crucially, I advocate that an understanding of domestic abuse as 'patriarchal force' need not occlude 'the various ways in which violence is structured along axes other than gender'[72] whilst accepting that intimate partner abuse always exists within broader, structural conditions of power means that the phenomenon will never be reducible to an interpersonal level alone.

[69]Lori Heise, 'Violence Against Women: An Integrated, Ecological Framework' (1998) 4(3) *Violence Against Women* 262.

[70]See also *Goodmark* (n 22) 3 in which Goodmark suggests that in the United States the dominance feminism 'portrait of a subordinated woman in need of salvation anchor[s] laws and policies'.

[71]An accusation Mills makes about the state in the United States in Linda Mills, *Insult to Injury: Rethinking our Responses to Intimate Abuse* (Princeton University Press 2003).

[72]Munro, 'Violence Against Women, "Victimhood" and the (Neo)Liberal State' (n 5) 238.

5. Neoliberalism: The 'Hegemonic Discourse of Our Times'

Neoliberalism, as an 'art of governance',[73] permeates multiple strata of the state apparatus. 'Governance' here signals the Foucauldian understanding that legal power is fragmented and dispersed, where agents of the state, such as the Crown Prosecutor, are complicit in (and necessary to) the carrying out of the tactics of government. As neoliberalism has been heralded as the 'hegemonic discourse of our times',[74] its nostrums and logics weave themselves into all areas of life, configuring it economic terms. Our vocabularies, habits, principles of justice and practices of rule are all framed in ideology that understands the market as the source of human freedom and where privatisation and profit-making is fundamental. Thus, even in the absence of specific government directives, the CPS will be mediated by the discursive influence of neoliberalism.[75]

Neoliberal politics became the dominant political ideology in the United Kingdom from the late 1970s. The post-war period had been associated with the full state and Keynesian welfarism. Governments had been expected to spend heavily on public infrastructure and welfare benefits so that consumer spending, growth and job creation were stimulated. Thatcher's incoming 1979 Conservative government, however, no longer articulated this economic rationality, and Thatcher spoke not of collective interests but of the responsibility of the individual to make the most of the free market conditions the government was now offering. Those that faltered were considered to have done so due to individual defectiveness or through choice. The neoliberal rationale justified the hollowing out of social democratic state welfarism because underperforming citizens were labelled 'undeserving'.

As well as experiencing recession, the UK in the 1970s faced steadily rising rates of crime. The issue of crime and 'law and order' therefore garnered attention during the 1979 election campaigns. The incoming 1979 Conservative government took the opportunity to suggest that welfarism had failed and that post-war penal-welfare criminology—which had largely understood criminal activity to be the result of collective, social and structural failures for which the state had a responsibility to improve—did not

[73]Michel Foucault, in Michel Senellart (ed), *The Birth of Biopolitics: Lectures at the College de France 1978–79* (Picador 2004) 131.

[74]Robert Reiner, *Law and Order: An Honest Citizen's Guide to Crime Control* (Polity 2007) 1–2.

[75]Margaret Davies, 'Feminism and Flat Law Theory' (2008) 16(3) *Feminist Legal Studies* 281, 282.

work. Penal-welfarist confidence in the potential for offenders to be rehabilitated through social support was replaced by the neoliberal 'volitional' theory of criminology.[76] This understood that crime was committed as a result of individually situated opportunities available to rationally choosing actors. As criminals were now considered to be acting out of 'rational choice', punitive responses and incarceration were pursued by governments to disincentivise and deter potential offenders. Probation officers were directed by government to 'manage' offenders to reduce recidivism, whilst their rehabilitation and welfare role was downgraded.[77] Successive neoliberal governments preferred the tough rhetoric of 'law and order' because 'penal populism' played well to the electorate.

As neoliberals considered the post-war public sector as bloated and inefficient they advocated the rolling back of state control in relation to public services, preferring privatisation. Yet, where services remained under state control, they became heavily regulated spaces where the ideas and practices of managerialism, together with its cost/benefit analyses took hold. Already familiar to the private sector and competitive markets, the criminal justice system was also encouraged to streamline procedures, reduce expenditure and measure it outcomes. 'New Public Managerialism', as managerialism become known in the public sector, strives for economy in the criminal justice system through the efficient conclusion of cases. The practical dissemination of neoliberal approaches, markedly via New Public Managerial priorities, is present within the CPS and has implications for the delivery of tenacious domestic abuse prosecutions as I explore in Chapter 4.

Harvey has argued that any popular social movement that advances individual freedoms is liable to absorption by neoliberalism.[78] Neoliberalism's apparent embrace of the violence against women movement is also typical of the way neoliberalism strategically navigates for retention of power, often irrespective of adherence to dogmatic neoliberal orthodoxy. Neoliberal governments gain political advantage through their apparent embrace of feminism; enabling them to effect penal toughness 'in a benevolent feminist guise'.[79] The feminist campaign concerning domestic abuse has therefore served the neoliberal evolution of criminal justice as an apparatus to manage

---

[76]Malcolm Feeley, 'Crime, Social Order and the Rise of Neo-conservative Politics' (2003) *Theoretical Criminology* 111, 112.

[77]Emma Bell, *Criminal Justice and Neoliberalism* (Palgrave Macmillan 2011) 90–91.

[78]David Harvey, *A Brief History of Neoliberalism* (Oxford University Press 2005) 41.

[79]Elizabeth Bernstein, 'Carceral Politics as Gender Justice? The "Traffic in Women" and Neoliberal Circuits of Crime, Sex and Rights' (2012) 41 *Theoretical Society* 233, 235.

risk and control offenders. I argue that feminist ideological concepts such as 'patriarchal force' have been swept up in and immersed by neoliberal punitive ambitions as they serve neoliberalism's emphases of responsibilisation and risk management.[80]

6. Criminal Versus Non-criminal Justice Responses

Feminists endorsing criminal justice involvement in abusive intimate relationships recognise the value of criminal justice's condemnatory power and legitimacy in seeking justice for victims.[81] When a perpetrator is convicted it means that a victim is believed and can represent an important milestone in her journey towards living abuse free. Habituated prosecutorial action and achieving convictions also address a sense of historic inadequacy, sending the important message that violence against women is wrong. Liberal feminist, Michelle Madden-Dempsey, for example, has confidence in the criminal justice system to create a gender-just and equal society and fends off critique that criminal justice is a 'blunt instrument'.[82] Her confidence in prosecutorial pursuit lies in her confidence in the ability of legal rules to guide societal norms and conduct, and she consequently urges us to treat committed criminal prosecutions as a viable feminist project to end intimate partner abuse and, indeed, patriarchy generally.[83]

By contrast, feminists such as Aya Gruber and Leigh Goodmark propose that preferring a criminal justice response to intimate partner abuse absolves the state from having to confront the underpinning structural arrangements that incubate the offending behaviour.[84] If criminalisation is the primary state reaction to domestic abuse, they argue that already marginalised women are disproportionately and negatively affected (immigrants and 'women of color', for example, are less likely to voluntarily engage the criminal justice system). Criminalisation does little to prevent domestic violence

---

[80]See also Munro, 'Violence Against Women, "Victimhood" and the (Neo)Liberal State' (n 5).

[81]Elizabeth Schneider, *Battered Women and Feminist Lawmaking* (Yale University Press 2000).

[82]Michelle Madden-Dempsey, *Prosecuting Domestic Violence: A Philosophical Analysis* (Oxford University Press 2009) 215.

[83]Ibid., 222.

[84]Leigh Goodmark, *Decriminalizing Domestic Violence: A Balanced Policy Approach to Intimate Partner Violence* (University of California Press 2018); Aya Gruber, *The Feminist War on Crime: The Unexpected Role of Women's Liberation in Mass Incarceration* (University of California Press 2020).

and, despite its huge costs, it affords little protection to the intended beneficiaries. Moreover, in making criminalisation the default response, alternatives to it remain underdeveloped.

The alternative to having total faith in a criminal justice response on the one hand or pushing for decriminalisation of intimate partner abuse is the 'survivor defined' approach which sits in Elizabeth Schneider's so-called murky middle ground.[85] Just as this project, Schneider's 'feminist law-making' project interrogates the widely assumed benefit of a criminal justice response. Whilst acknowledging that criminalisation is likely to be an appropriate strategy in many contexts, 'it is only one of many strategies we ought to be considering'.[86] I share this reticence in over-relying on criminalisation. Until we know the real effect of current practices that emphasise criminal responsiveness, or until effectively functioning alternatives are developed, there is value in drawing attention to the pitfalls of engaging the penal state, acknowledging its limitations, proposing ameliorations to the system and flagging up the opportunities that may be lost by treating the social problem of domestic abuse primarily as crime.

Writing some thirty years ago, Carol Smart urged feminists not to go to law as if it were a panacea and instead to de-centre law as *the* solution to women's oppression.[87] Querying law's claim to be able to find the truth of things and law's failure to transform the quality of women's lives, Smart called on feminists engaged in both policy production and scholarship to consider non-legal strategies.[88] In the intervening years, her approach has softened as she has observed that law has had a 'positive capacity to adapt to social change and to offer recognition and affirmation' for some women.[89] Law's response to feminism, Smart notes, has included progressive change, and her post-modern feminist project of de-centring law was never intended, she reflects, to mean that feminists and women should ignore law or write it off.[90] Smart maintains that feminists critique the law as it manifests in practice and to expose the way in which law has the power to

[85]Elizabeth Schneider, *Battered Women and Feminist Lawmaking* (Yale University Press 2000) as referred to in Holly Maguigan, 'Wading into Professor Schneider's "Murky Middle Ground" Between Acceptance and Rejection of Criminal Justice Responses to Domestic Violence' (2002) 11 *American University Journal Gender Society Policy and Law* 427.

[86]Elizabeth Schneider, *Battered Women and Feminist Lawmaking* (n 81) 5.

[87]Carol Smart, *Feminism and the Power of the Law* (Routledge 1989) 5.

[88]Ibid., 5.

[89]Rosemary Auchmuty and Karin Van Marle, 'Special Issue: Carol Smart's Feminism and the Power of Law' (2012) 20 *Feminist Legal Studies* 65–69.

[90]Carol Smart, 'Reflection' (2012) 20 *Feminist Legal Studies* 161, 162.

define women's subjectivities in ways that do not serve them individually or collectively.[91]

Answering Smart's appeal, this book interrogates both the working practices of prosecutors in intimate partner abuse cases and the way that women experience the law and 'tenacious prosecutions'; it identifies the occasions when law meets women's needs, falls short or even merits abandonment, highlighting when victories won in the criminal justice system may not be worth the price paid.[92] The book therefore challenges criminal law as the pre-eminent solution to intimate partner abuse.

Ambivalence about criminal justice is not unique to feminists. The traditional liberal adversarial model of criminal justice can be a cause of dissatisfaction for critical legal scholars generally. Though not writing explicitly as a feminist legal scholar, Norrie, just as Schneider and Smart, expresses reticence in embracing the criminal justice system. His unease is associated with the neoliberal 'penal equation', a formula which requires that 'crime plus responsibility equals punishment'.[93] Norrie observes that if criminal justice fails to deliver a reduction in crime, society appears to call for more of the same as part of the 'law and order' paradigm. Criminal justice is criticised by Norrie as part of society's set of 'stock responses' to social problems where 'justice', 'responsibility' and 'desert'[94] sidle up to regressive-looking notions of revenge and payback,[95] the likes of which are unpalatable to left-leaning critical and feminist legal scholars alike.

In addition to concerns about the 'penal equation', feminists who express reticence in entrusting the state to end domestic abuse do so for a range of reasons. The first might be due to the grass-roots nature of the original violence against women movement which achieved dynamism precisely because it worked through informal networks without state involvement. In that vein, Martha Fineman has suggested that a renewed era of feminism might begin 'with the realization that mounting fundamental challenges to systems of social control means working outside of the existing institutional

[91]Carol Smart, *Feminism and the Power of the Law* (Routledge 1989) 25.

[92]Donna Coker, 'Crime Control and Feminist Law Reform in Domestic Violence Law: A Critical Review' (2001) 4 *Criminal Law Review* 801; Ruth Lewis, 'Making Justice Work: Effective Legal Interventions for Domestic Violence' (2004) 44 *The British Journal of Criminology* 204; and Heather Douglas, 'Battered Women's Experiences of the Criminal Justice System: Decentring Law' (2012) 20 *Feminist Legal Studies* 121.

[93]Alan Norrie, *Law and the Beautiful Soul* (Glasshouse 2005) 75.

[94]'Desert', meaning to receive appropriate and deserved punishment for one's behaviour.

[95]Norrie (n 93) 75.

structures of the state'.[96] Connectedly, by treating social problems as crime, domestic abuse campaigners unwittingly participate in the depoliticisation of a social movement, crowding out not only alternative potentially effective practical responses but also conceptual reimaginings that might overhaul the structural status quo to end violence against women.[97] A second reason feminists might be reticent about relying on criminal justice is due to a cautious regard some feminists have for the potential of the criminal law to deliver impartial justice. For these feminists, calling upon the criminal law supports and legitimates a legal tradition steeped in precisely the sort of social ordering they seek to eradicate. For them, law is not considered gender-free or neutral[98]; law itself might even be characterised as violent or abusive.[99]

My focus on the prosecutorial treatment of domestic abuse inherently requires me to engage with the criminal law and the criminal process. My critical approach is not intended to discredit criminal law's moral strength, to dismiss its potential to set and evolve norms and its potential to produce beneficial outcomes for many women.[100] Rather, my intention is to reflect on the unintended consequences of the current prosecutorial approach and to suggest improvements for the survivor of abuse. I do this by exposing any shortcomings of the current prosecutorial approach bearing in mind its situation in the wider criminal justice process and by drawing attention to any limiting discourses.

Therein lies the shared aims and methods of feminist, socio-legal and critical legal scholarship of the type the book emulates; the disruption of the legal positivist account of law as emanating from a superior source, delivering coherent reasoning that benefits everyone.[101] I want to reposition survivors not as passive recipients of law but as active participants in law creation. I explore the potential for women's thrivership with or without the criminal law's help and suggest that women's non-essentialist, polycentric and intersubjective characteristics and experiences lend themselves to case-by-case

[96]Martha Fineman, book endorsement at the rear of Kristin Bumiller, *In an Abusive State: How Neoliberalism Appropriated the Feminist Movement Against Sexual Violence* (Duke University Pres 2008).

[97]Mimi Kim, 'Challenging the Pursuit of Criminalisation in an Era of Mass Incarceration: The Limitations of the Social Work Response to Domestic Violence in the USA' (2013) *43 British Journal of Social Work* 1276.

[98]Joanne Conaghan, *Law and Gender* (Oxford University Press 2013).

[99]Linda Mills, 'Killing Her Softly: Intimate Abuse and the Violence of State Intervention' (1999) *Harvard Law Review* 550, 585.

[100]Cass Sunstein, 'Social Norms and Social Roles' (1996) *Columbia Law Review* 903, 909.

[101]Margaret Davies, 'Feminism and the Flat Theory of Law' (n 75) 281.

assessment about what is in their best interests.[102] I want therefore to play a part in the discursive unsettling of the (neoliberal) penal equation and any notion that the criminal law singlehandedly has the tools, reach and power to effect the best outcomes for women and, ultimately, to end domestic abuse.

7. Methodology

(i) Socio-Legal Research

In the legal positivist account, law claims to be separated from society and is therefore able to provide 'natural', 'rational' or 'objective' outcomes and determinations. This has been the dominant mode of understanding the nature of law. Socio-legal scholars, however, recognise that legal ideas and practices can be understood as the effect of social, historical, cultural, political or professional consequences and conditions.[103] If domestic abuse perpetrators can now expect to be prosecuted and convicted, positivists might argue this reflects the legitimacy and authority of the law to pursue them. For socio-legal scholars, the same practice of tenacious prosecutions may also cause them to reflect upon how factors external to law and legal procedure might have brought about the practice; for example socio-legal scholars might reflect on how feminists in the late modern political and cultural era demanded state responsiveness and how neoliberal governments have promoted the expansion of criminalisation.[104]

By using a socio-legal perspective of law, I want to show how 'law is produced by society' whilst examining ways in which '"society" is produced by law'.[105] Whilst 'socio-legal' may imply that I use sociology as method, in fact 'socio-legal' scholarship is not confined to sociological theory. A socio-legal orientation signals a *transdisciplinary* understanding of law and legal practices that includes, inter alia, psychology, criminology, political economy and history.[106] By using socio-legal method, I show how prosecutorial

---

[102]Ibid., 288.

[103]Roger Cotterrell, 'Why Must Legal Ideas Be Interpreted Sociologically?' (1998) *Journal of Law and Society* 171, 173.

[104]David Garland, *The Culture of Control: Crime and Social Order in Contemporary Society* (Oxford University Press 2001).

[105]Cotterrell (n 103) 175.

[106]Ibid., 175.

decision-making is affected by forces external to legal doctrine, statutory offence considerations and the available evidence.

The area of criminal prosecutions and the role of the criminal prosecutor remains a 'relatively under researched' field.[107] The comparative lack of scholarly attention in this area stands in contrast to the pivotal role that prosecutors play:

> Important boundaries are crossed with the decision to prosecute. Private troubles become public affairs... the mode of law enforcement switches abruptly from private ... in which compromise outcomes are... possible ... to public adversarial debate in which legal justice is delivered in a binary verdict of guilty or not guilty.[108]

When prosecutors exercise their discretion in domestic abuse cases, they consult specific CPS guidance and policy. It is here that the overlap between public opinion, shifting societal expectations and decisions of legal professionals is plain. CPS policy and guidance is imbued with sociological influence because the CPS openly carries out consultation exercises with interested parties in the formative stages of policy production, prior to publication and as an ongoing process. The CPS must take into account a range of people, business and voluntary bodies affected by the policy and may contact specific groups affected by the policy if appropriate.[109] The former Director of Public Prosecutions, Sir David Calvert Smith (1998–2003), opened lines of communication with the academic community and academics may still take part in consultation exercises.[110] In the case of domestic abuse policy for example, consultation took place with feminist groups such as the Fawcett Society, Women's Aid, Refuge and the UK Network of Sexwork Projects as well as other groups not purporting to be feminist such as London Probation and the British Association of Social Workers. Herein lies the most direct way that current public, expert and feminist discourses affect the direction of CPS working practices and also where the value of socio-legal method for the topic under consideration in this book is patent.

---

[107]Lucia Zedner, *Criminal Justice* (2nd edn, Oxford University Press 2010) 146.

[108]Keith Hawkins, *Law as Last Resort: Prosecution Decision-Making in a Regulatory Agency* (Oxford University Press 2002) 422.

[109]'CPS Consultation Principles 2015' emailed to the author by CPS Policy Directorate.

[110]Andrew Ashworth, 'Developments in the Public Prosecutor's Office in England and Wales' (2000) *European Journal of Crime, Criminal Law and Criminal Justice* 257, 261. Calvert-Smith was DPP in 1998–2003.

Further evidence that the CPS does not function within a vacuum and must be sensitive to cultural-societal changes is that the Director of Public Prosecutions is accountable to parliament for CPS performance each year when she or he appears before the Justice Select Committee.[111] In this way, the CPS openly interacts with and is responsive to public opinion. So, whilst Crown Prosecutors must act on individual cases fairly, independently and objectively in the interests of justice,[112] it would be a foolhardy prosecution service that failed to reflect in policy shifting societal opinions and political priorities lest it lead, ultimately, to undermining the legitimacy of this public service.

In Chapter 5, I use a tributary of socio-legal scholarship—legal consciousness—as a means of analysing the in-depth interviews I conducted with survivors. Marking a move away from simply extracting women's *attitude* towards the law, legal consciousness enables us to see the variant and contradictory ways women position themselves in relation to the criminal law through their engagement with it, their understanding of it and the way they imagine the law operates. In so doing, the empirical research in Chapter 5 evidences the ways in which 'legality is a social structure actively and constantly produced in what people say and in what they do'.[113] This method signals a disruption to thinking about law as a 'superior norm'.[114] It reveals how people make sense of their experiences of law, showing how law and justice has or does not have legitimacy for the people whose lives it touches. The method necessarily, therefore, invites normative reflection.

In evaluating women's legal consciousness, I reveal aspects of the criminal justice system's gendered nature, its role in perpetuating women's disadvantage and its part in 'gendering subjectivity'.[115] Feminist legal theory has always sought to expose law's implication in the production and perpetuation of gendered power; in this instance, I highlight this through the lens of criminal law's treatment of abused women.

This book is not concerned, therefore, with an examination of the discretionary decision-making of prosecutors in practice through a closed analysis

---

[111] The 'independence' of the CPS is discussed more fully in Chapter 3.

[112] Crown Prosecution Service, 'The Code for Prosecutors' (n 12).

[113] Patricia Ewick and Susan Silbey, *The Common Place of Law: Stories from Everyday Life* (University of Chicago Press 1998) 223.

[114] Davies, 'Feminism and the Flat Theory of Law' (n 75) 289.

[115] Joanne Conaghan, 'Reassessing the Feminist Theoretical Project in Law' (2000) 27(3) *Journal of Law and Society* 351, 363.

of the laws[116] or rules and policies[117] set up to guide the prosecutor. Rather it recognises that feminist and neoliberal discourses are disseminated to prosecutors through various means including political agendas, institutional imperatives and practice rationalities. I want also to show that prosecutorial domestic abuse decision-making is constitutive of survivors' identities and stories. By highlighting the experiences of those women, I hope to encourage prosecutors to equip themselves with the fullest information so that they can make considered decisions in ways that might best support survivor 'thrivership'.

(ii) Qualitative Research and Thematic Analysis

Having conducted a review of the literature into the existing concepts, controversies and key figures in the area of feminist legal studies generally and domestic abuse more specifically, I also completed a literature review into the key concepts and theories applying to 'neoliberalism'. I familiarised myself with government strategy and policy direction in the area of violence against women and closely analysed the CPS policies and guidance. My subsequent qualitative research took the form of nine semi-structured interviews with prosecutors (2017), eleven with survivors of domestic abuse (2017) and five focus groups with domestic abuse support workers, comprising seventeen participants (2019).

As far as recruiting prosecutors was concerned, I sent individual letters to named prosecutors inviting them to take part, anonymously, in the research. As the project became known locally, prosecutors I had not approached directly volunteered themselves and gave me contact details of other potential interviewees. The sample was thus built from my initial local knowledge of prosecutors, networking and the effect of 'snowballing'. The sample drew from one CPS area in the South of England; a region comprising rural areas and urban and coastal conurbations. Three men and six women participated, eight white and one black, with a spread of experience ranging from associate prosecutors to senior prosecutors with management experience.

Survivors volunteered to take part following my email and telephone approaches to a number of domestic abuse support charities in the South of

[116] For example the Criminal Procedure Rules 2015, Prosecution of Offences Act 1985 or case law concerning judicial review of prosecutorial decision-making.

[117] For example Crown Prosecution Service, 'Domestic Abuse Guidelines for Prosecutors' (n 13) and Crown Prosecution Service, 'The Code for Prosecutors' (n 12).

England (one woman approached me directly having heard about the project independently of the charities I had approached). I also attended one charity in person and spoke at their staff meeting to promote the project and my need for volunteers. The survivors in my sample were all women; nine were white, one was black and one was Asian; all were able bodied. Half of the interviews took place in the women's homes and the other half at the offices of the charities that were supporting them.

The seventeen support workers that took part in five focus groups (of sizes ranging from three to five participants) drew from five different charities that I approached via email or telephone across Essex, London and Kent. All were white women. I travelled to their offices to facilitate the focus groups in person (on one occasion I secured an independent office space in a mutually convenient location).

I obtained ethical approval from Kent Law School; all the participants consented to have their testimonies recorded and transcribed and I gave reassurance that their anonymity would be preserved. All empirical work took place face to face in person and was guided by the use of separate semi-structured interview schedules/focus group prompts. Flexible schedules acted as a topic guide, prompting me to cover the target areas of enquiry but allowing flexibility in terms of sequencing the questions. This method also allowed latitude to explore topics in depth where responses were felt to be significant.[118] The questions were largely open questions which invited extended or 'rich'[119] responses from participants, permitting respondents to answer in their own terms and reducing direction or influence from me.

Interviews with prosecutors employed, what Roulston has called, a neo-positive[120] approach. A neo-positivist conception of the semi-structured interview technique assumes that the prosecutor being interviewed 'has an inner or authentic self, not necessarily publicly visible, which may be revealed through careful questioning by an attentive and sensitive interviewer who contributes minimally to the talk'.[121] I used 'open' and 'non-leading' questions to uncover the prosecutors' perspectives, opinions and experiences and adopted a neutral role (by not expressing my own perspective on the research topic). In so doing, I endeavoured to minimise the risk of bias and researcher influence during the collection of data.

---

[118]Alan Bryman, *Social Research Methods* (4th edn, Oxford University Press 2012) 212.

[119]Karl Weick, 'The Generative Properties of Richness' (2007) 50 *Academy of Management Journal* 14.

[120]Kathryn Roulston, 'Considering Quality in Qualitative Interviewing' (2010) *Qualitative Research* 199, 205.

[121]Ibid., 204.

Conversely, when interviewing women survivors, I adopted Roulston's 'romantic'[122] approach to interviewing. This meant that I expressed empathy or interest in what was being said so that 'genuine rapport and trust'[123] could be built between myself and the participant. I felt that such an approach was important because of the sensitive nature of the stories they were telling and the need for the women to feel supported and not judged. I hope that the approach also facilitated the women to feel like they could be open with me.

Central to the project is this perspective of the women affected. My intention has always been to 'unsilence' these women and highlighting their perspective forms part of feminist 'consciousness raising'.[124] By telling their stories, it becomes possible to notice not only differences between them but also their shared perspectives and experiences. By taking women's standpoint—that is by using women's knowledge and social reality as the point of departure—I try to expose the narratives of survivors as they have encountered the law. Chapter 5's exploration of legal consciousness reinforces the *variety* of ways these women use and think about law in their daily lives[125] thereby calling into question any prosecutorial approach that tends to uniformity.

As an active researcher, I acknowledge my own theoretical and lived position in relation to the data,[126] particularly as a former employee and current freelance agent of the CPS and as a white, middle-class, heterosexual woman. Reflexivity is essential as it forefronts not only the biases that may guide and motivate me, but it also draws out what I may be inhibited from seeing.[127] My own assumptions, motives and pre-existing hypotheses may never be shaken off, but by recognising them and making my personal experience known, I hope they might become an asset for my research.[128] For example, I sensed that prosecutors felt able to speak candidly with me because they assumed that I would understand their perspective. I therefore

---

[122]Ibid., 206. The approach is equated with 'emotionalist' approaches.

[123]Ibid., 205.

[124]Hilaire Barnett, *Introduction to Feminist Jurisprudence* (Cavendish 1998) 19.

[125]Rosie Harding, '"Dogs Are 'Registered', People Shouldn't Be": Legal Consciousness and Lesbian and Gay Rights' (2006) 15(4) *Social and Legal Studies* 511, 512.

[126]Virginia Braun and Victoria Clarke, 'Using Thematic Analysis in Psychology' (2006) 3(2) *Qualitative Research in Psychology* 77.

[127]Diane Watt, 'On Becoming a Qualitative Researcher: The Value of Reflexivity' (2007) 12(1) *The Qualitative Report* 82, 82.

[128]Ibid., 94.

acknowledge that my own 'political and intellectual autobiograph[y]'[129] will have shaped the interview design (which questions to ask and how I was able to recruit prosecutors for example) and the interview process (which questions I asked and which answers I probed) and, ultimately, the end product (the identification of recurrent and pertinent themes and the interpretation of these). Despite this, throughout the data gathering process, thematic coding and interpretative analysis, I have endeavoured to apply objectivity to uncover the themes' qualities, meanings and implications.[130]

8. Argument Overview and Chapter Outline

Past inattentive treatment by state criminal justice agencies in relation to domestic abuse is now being self-consciously reversed by neoliberal governing agendas intent on denouncing crime and holding offenders to account. Governing neoliberals have endorsed radical feminism's 'patriarchal force' thesis, which provides them additional political fuel and theoretical justification for the apparent reliance on criminal justice as a primary means of addressing domestic abuse. In response to feminist calls—to eradicate differing treatment of public and private violence and to understand abused women as vulnerable subjects in need of protection—a 'tenacious' commitment to achieving prosecutions has emerged.

The consequences of the current approach are that prosecutors invariably consider achieving convictions in these cases as success. In the context of a prosecution service that is efficiency driven, prosecutors' readily conceive of the abused legal subject as 'at-risk' or 'vulnerable'. But this can have the effect of requiring prosecution in all cases rather than prompting a genuine survivor-defined, case-by-case approach at the point a woman expresses her wish for case discontinuance. Criminal justice priorities and ways of working can also have the effect of foreclosing alternative ways of conceiving her agency and the ways she can navigate her safety. Reliance on criminal justice as the antidote to domestic abuse renders law and legal processes the pre-eminent 'solution', when in fact women can be frequently disappointed or failed by criminal justice outcomes. At the same time, other strategies to

129Natasha Mauthner and Andrea Doucet, 'Reflections on a Voice-Centred Relational Method' in Jane Ribbens and Rosalind Edwards (eds), *Feminist Dilemmas in Qualitative Research: Public Knowledge and Private Lives* (Sage 1998).

130Simon Watts, 'User Skills for Qualitative Analysis: Perspective, Interpretation and the Delivery of Impact' (2014) 11(1) *Qualitative Research in Psychology* 1–14.

support women in the community to effect their safety become ancillary (such as providing adequate housing, access to an income and to childcare), whilst alternative discourses about the structural causes of and solutions to gendered intimate violence receive insufficient attention.

Chapter 2 summarises some of the key moments in women's history in respect of domestic abuse. It reveals how feminism and its closely associated activist sister, the women's movement, uncovered intimate partner abuse and rendered it an undeniable social problem. The chapter interrogates the public/private divide as a means of understanding the production of gender inequality (in society and in law) said be at the root of domestic abuse. 'Privacy' was previously used to justify a lack of state intervention in abusive relationships but now the notion garners little rhetorical support and contemporary approaches to domestic abuse advocate that prosecutions ought to be pursued in the same way as publicly occurring violence. I ask whether a careful engagement with the affirmative potential of women's 'privacy' might assist prosecutorial decision-making when a woman withdraws her support for the prosecution.

If domestic abuse is considered first and foremost as crime, Chapter 2 also considers the criminal law itself to be a legitimate target for scrutiny particularly in regard to the claim that it is a 'gender-free zone'[131] where neutrality, fairness and truth prevail. Prior to the current commitment to prosecutions, when female domestic abuse victims retracted their support for a prosecution, cases were almost inevitably dropped.[132] These women were considered unreliable and non-credible as witnesses[133] as they were failing to behave in the ways expected from legal subjects; self-interested, measured and 'rational'.[134] More recently (I argue since training took place between 2005 and 2008) in re-assessing women's decisions to retract, prosecutors make an assessment of what is in the best interest of the victim bearing in mind her 'particular vulnerability'.[135] No longer dismissing unsupportive victims as unknowing irrational actors, prosecutors make an assessment of how far short of expected 'norms' she has fallen and how in need of protection she

[131]Joanne Conaghan, 'Reassessing the Feminist Theoretical Project in Law' (2000) 27 *Journal of Law and Society* 351, 359–363.

[132]Louise Ellison, 'Prosecuting Domestic Violence Without Victim Participation' (2002) 65(6) *The Modern Law Review* 834.

[133]Antonia Cretney and Gwynn Davis, 'Prosecuting Domestic Assault: Victims Failing Courts, or Courts Failing Victims?' (1997) 36(2) *The Howard Journal of Crime and Justice* 146.

[134]Nagaire Naffine, *Sexing the Subject (of Law)* (Oxford University Press 1995).

[135]Crown Prosecution Service, 'Domestic Abuse Guidelines for Prosecutors' (n 13).

is. I suggest that 'tenacious prosecutions' are the CPS response to re-assessing the legal subject, motivated by a need to show understanding of her vulnerability and consequently to 'protect' her from further harm.

Chapter 3 sketches the values, strategies and practices of neoliberalism. It notes the deployment of notions of 'freedom', 'individualism' and 'responsibilisation' in the service of increased criminalisation and punitiveness. Neoliberalism's logics also extend to techniques of New Public Managerialism which, I suggest, are evident at the Crown Prosecution Service. If 'neoliberalism', broadly conceived, has been the dominant political ideology of recent times, Chapter 3 shows how its constraining logic pervades state responses to domestic abuse and stifles non-penal solutions that might tackle structural inequality in line with materialist and early radical 'outsider' feminist goals.

Neoliberalism strategically navigates for retention of power. Its embrace of feminist demands for a criminal justice response to domestic abuse at once bolsters its public credentials yet has the effect of depoliticising and suppressing discordant feminist voices. By treating the social problem of domestic abuse as crime,[136] the state and criminal justice priority becomes one of ensuring individuals are both deterred from committing crime on the one hand—through consistent and committed prosecutions and sentencing—and of protecting victims from the risk of future crime on the other. This rationale has built a crime control culture in which, I argue, the prosecution of domestic abuse is part.

The book turns its focus in Chapter 4 away from factors that may have led to the recent turn to criminalisation towards consideration of the consequences; specifically in this chapter Crown Prosecutors' handling of intimate partner abuse cases. Through analysis of in-depth interviews with prosecutors, Chapter 4 shows that in the CPS the neoliberal technique of New Public Managerialism shapes everyday conduct and 'working practice'. Managerialism frames prosecutorial practices in terms of administrative outcomes and organisational targets, specifically in the CPS by expecting increased conviction rates. The chapter shows how the tendency towards 'tenacious prosecutions' can be attributed, at least in part, to features of New Public Managerialism. The chapter concludes by discussing prosecutors' failure to articulate the gendered nature of domestic abuse (save to acknowledge

[136]Mimi Kim, 'Challenging the Pursuit of Criminalisation in an Era of Mass Incarceration: The Limitations of the Social Work Response to Domestic Violence in the USA' (2013) 43 *British Journal of Social Work* 1276.

that victims are usually women). The findings from Chapter 4 lend some support to those feminists who have been reticent to harness the criminal justice system for fear, inter alia, that it fails to sensitively deliver nuanced, survivor-defined outcomes.

Chapter 5 uses empirical research conducted with women who have experienced intimate partner abuse, to assess the consequences for women from 'tenacious prosecutions'. I use legal consciousness—Ewick and Silbey's toxonomy of being 'before', 'with' or 'against' the law—as a lens to analyse how this group of women consider, behave and relate to criminal law in daily life.[137] The qualitative interviews in Chapter 5 reveal how law may not be a site of refuge or resolution for women survivors and confirm that the criminal process may not always facilitate wholly positive outcomes. Nonetheless, the chapter's use of legal consciousness identifies the justice possible, if not consistently attained, through legal intervention. The chapter therefore raises a number of factors and lessons that merit prosecutorial attention. These are explored further in Chapter 6.

Chapter 6 builds on the observation that the common use of the term 'vulnerable' in CPS policy has an 'othering' effect, in which the 'helpless' victim is perceived to require state intervention in the form of tenacious penal solutions. The depiction of the vulnerable victim, whilst well-intended, is overly simplistic and the victim/agent dichotomy that underpins it wrongly presupposes that one precludes the other. This final substantive chapter theorises an alternative way of thinking about women who have been abused—as potential 'thrivers'—and uses primary data gathered from focus groups with domestic abuse support workers to reflect on my theoretical observations and proposals and suggest practical ways that prosecutors might improve outcomes for women survivors.

Firstly, I propose that prosecutors recognise that we are all ontologically vulnerable, and that, as such, the state bears responsibility to support us to be resilient.[138] As far as the criminal justice system is concerned, the presumption to prosecute domestic abuse (per CPS policy) meets the state responsibility to the extent that consistent prosecutions of abusers have the potential to challenge existing patriarchal structures and ideologies.[139] Thus,

[137]Patricia Ewick and Susan Silbey, *The Common Place of Law: Stories from Everyday Life* (University of Chicago Press 1998).

[138]Martha Fineman, 'The Vulnerable Subject: Anchoring Equality in the Human Condition' (2008) 20 *Yale Journal of Law and Feminism* 1.

[139]See, e.g., Michelle Madden-Dempsey, *Prosecuting Domestic Violence A Philosophical Analysis* (Oxford University Press 2009); Cass Sunstein, 'Social Norms and Social Roles' (1996) *Columbia Law Review* 903, 909.

the state begins to address the conditions said to be at the heart of much intimate partner abuse. However, this leaves the question open as to how a prosecutor should be guided when faced with a woman who no longer supports a prosecution through the courts.

Secondly, building on the presumption to prosecute as a foundation to domestic abuse prosecutorial decision-making, I urge prosecutors to make tailored decisions at the point a woman expresses her wish for case termination. I argue that prosecutors should make decisions that are focused on enhancing survivors' chances of 'thriving'[140] and argue that this focus is not necessarily incompatible with prosecutors' managerial priorities. 'Thriving' is characterised by safety, a positive outlook, improved health and well-being and by a reclamation of the self.[141] 'Thriving' means that survivors are functioning well and are able to make decisions from a range of options. Using techniques advocated by scholars in the field of therapeutic jurisprudence[142]—such as displaying kindness and empathy to demonstrate sensitivity to victims' needs, and being trauma-informed—prosecutors should strive for the best 'therapeutic' (mental health and emotional) outcomes so that victims are supported to thrive. Prosecutors might be given training in counselling and interpersonal skills, be encouraged to liaise with domestic abuse support workers more freely and even to discuss the matter with the woman directly. Guided in this way, and taken together, a theoretically informed survivor-defined praxis can emerge. Working with a presumption to prosecute yet considering how to support a survivor to thrive would sharpen prosecutors' regard for occasions when prosecution may not be preferable.

Finally, the book's Conclusion notes prosecutors easily justify 'tenacious prosecutions' because the approach expresses state condemnation of domestic abuse as required by policy objectives on the one hand and because it aims for 'justice' for victims and the public on the other. Such prosecutorial pursuit has the potential to be part of public education about domestic abuse, to punish and rehabilitate offenders through sentencing and to support victims by holding perpetrators to account. Yet criminalisation heralds the depletion of other practical and conceptual remedies to end intimate partner abuse. Crucially, neoliberalism's penal response to domestic abuse has the potential to misjudge abused women's subjectivities and fails

[140]Isobel Heywood, Dana Sammut and Caroline Bradbury-Jones, 'A Qualitative Exploration of "Thrivership" Among Women Who Have experienced Domestic Violence and Abuse: Development of a New Model' (2019) 19 *British Medical Council Women's Health* 106.

[141]Ibid.

[142]David Wexler, 'Applying the Law Therapeutically' (1996) 5(3) *Applied and Preventive Psychology* 179.

to conceive them as potential 'thrivers'. The conclusion also steps back and reflects upon the gains and losses of feminism's collaboration with the neoliberal state and, moreover, makes observations about how the findings presented here contribute to the feminist legal project's exposure of the inherent masculinity of law and legal processes.

References

Ashworth A, 'Developments in the Public Prosecutor's Office in England and Wales' (2000) *European Journal of Crime, Criminal Law and Criminal Justice* 257.

Auchmuty R and Van Marle K, 'Special Issue: Carol Smart's Feminism and the Power of Law' (2012) 20 *Feminist Legal Studies* 65.

Barnett H, *Introduction to Feminist Jurisprudence* (Cavendish 1998).

Baxter P and Jack S, 'Qualitative Case Study Methodology: Study Design and Implementation for Novice Researchers' (2008) *The Qualitative Report* 544.

Bell E, *Criminal Justice and Neoliberalism* (Palgrave Macmillan 2011).

Bennion F, 'The New Prosecution Arrangements' (1986) *Criminal Law Review* 3.

Bernstein E, 'Carceral Politics as Gender Justice? The "Traffic in Women" and Neoliberal Circuits of Crime, Sex and Rights' (2012) 41 *Theoretical Society* 233.

Braun V and Clarke V, 'Using Thematic Analysis in Psychology' (2006) 3(2) *Qualitative Research in Psychology* 77.

Bumiller K, *In an Abusive State: How Neoliberalism Appropriated the Feminist Movement Against Sexual Violence* (Duke University Press 2008).

Buzawa E and Buzawa C, *Domestic Violence: The Criminal Justice Response* (3rd edn, Sage 2003).

Cattaneo L et al, 'The Victim-Informed Prosecution Project: A Quasi-Experimental Test of a Collaborative Model for Cases of Intimate Partner Violence' (2009) 15(10) *Violence Against Women* 1227.

Coker D, 'Crime Control and Feminist Law Reform in Domestic Violence Law: A Critical Review' (2001) 4 *Criminal Law Review* 801.

Conaghan J, *Law and Gender* (Oxford University Press 2013).

Conaghan J, 'Reassessing the Feminist Theoretical Project in Law' (2000) 27(3) *Journal of Law and Society* 351.

Cotterrell R, 'Why Must Legal Ideas Be Interpreted Sociologically?' (1998) *Journal of Law and Society* 171.

Cretney A and Davis G, 'Prosecuting "Domestic' Assault" (1996) *Criminal Law Review* 162.

———, 'Prosecuting Domestic Assault: Victims Failing Courts, or Courts Failing Victims?' (1997) 36(2) *The Howard Journal of Crime and Justice* 146.

Crown Prosecution Service, 'A Consultation on the CPS Violence Against Women Strategy and Action Plans—A Response to Consultations' (CPS 2012) available at https://www.cps.gov.uk/publication/consultation-cps-violence-against-women-strategy-and-action-plans-response-consultation accessed 10 February 2020.

———, 'Crown Prosecution Service Annual Report and Accounts 2016–2017' (2017) available at https://www.gov.uk/government/uploads/system/uploads/attachment_data/file/628968/CPS_annual_report_2016_17.pdf accessed 13 February 2020.

———, 'Delivering Justice: Violence Against Women and Girls Report, 10th Edition' (CPS 2017) available at https://www.cps.gov.uk/sites/default/files/documents/publications/cps-vawg-report-2017.pdf accessed 28 January 2020.

———, 'Domestic Abuse Guidelines for Prosecutors' (CPS 2014) available at https://www.cps.gov.uk/legal-guidance/domestic-abuse-guidelines-prosecutors accessed 9 February 2020.

———, 'Domestic Violence: Good Practice Guidance' (CPS HQ 2005) available at http://webarchive.nationalarchives.gov.uk/, http://www.crimereduction.homeoffice.gov.uk/domesticviolence/domesticviolence51.pdf accessed 29 June 2017.

———, 'Evaluation of the National Domestic Violence Training Programme 2005–2008' (CPS 2008) available at https://www.cps.gov.uk/publications/equality/evaluation_of_national_domestic_violence_training_programme.html accessed 29 June 2017.

———, 'Policy for Prosecuting Cases of Domestic Violence' (CPS HQ 2005) available at http://webarchive.nationalarchives.gov.uk/, http://www.crimereduction.homeoffice.gov.uk/domesticviolence/domesticviolence51.pdf accessed 29 June 2017.

———, 'The Code for Prosecutors' (CPS 2018) available at https://www.cps.gov.uk/sites/default/files/documents/publications/Code-for-Crown-Prosecutors-October-2018.pdf accessed 1 March 2020.

———, 'Violence Against Women and Girls Crime Report 2010–2011' (CPS 2011).

———, 'Violence Against Women and Girls Crime Report 2015–16' (CPS 2016) available at https://www.cps.gov.uk/sites/default/files/documents/publications/cps_vawg_report_2016.pdf accessed 9 February 2020.

———, 'Violence Against Women and Girls Report 2018–2019' (CPS 2019) available at https://www.cps.gov.uk/sites/default/files/documents/publications/cps-vawg-report-2019.pdf accessed 28 January 2020.

Davies M, 'Feminism and Flat Law Theory' (2008) 16(3) *Feminist Legal Studies* 281.

Davies M and Munro V (eds), *The Ashgate Research Companion to Feminist Legal Theory* (Ashgate 2013).

Dobash R, Dobash RE, Cavanagh K and Lewis R, 'Separate and Intersecting Realities: A Comparison of Men's and Women's Accounts of Violence Against Women' (1998) 4(4) *Violence Against Women* 382.

Douglas H, 'Battered Women's Experiences of the Criminal Justice System: Decentring Law' (2012) 20 *Feminist Legal Studies* 121.

Ellison L, 'Prosecuting Domestic Violence without Victim Participation' (2002) *The Modern Law Review* 834.

Ewick P and Silbey S, *The Common Place of Law: Stories from Everyday Life* (University of Chicago Press 1998).

Feeley M, 'Crime, Social Order and the Rise of Neo-conservative Politics' (2003) *Theoretical Criminology* 111.

Fineman M, 'The Vulnerable Subject: Anchoring Equality in the Human Condition' (2008) 20 *Yale Journal of Law and Feminism* 1.

Fineman M and Mykitiuk R (eds), *The public Nature of Private Violence: The Discovery of Domestic Abuse* (Routledge 1994).

Foucault M, in Senellart M (ed), *The Birth of Biopolitics: Lectures at the College de France 1978–79* (Picador 2004).

Garland D, *The Culture of Control: Crime and Social Order in Contemporary Society* (Oxford University Press 2001).

Goodmark L, *A Troubled Marriage: Domestic Violence and the Legal System* (New York University Press 2013).

———, *Decriminalizing Domestic Violence: A Balanced Policy Approach to Intimate Partner Violence* (University of California Press 2018).

Goodman L and Epstein D, *Listening to Battered Women: A Survivor Centred Approach to Advocacy, Mental Health and Justice* (American Psychological Association 2009) 97.

Goodman L et al., 'Survivor-Defined Practice in Domestic Violence Work: Measure Development and Preliminary Evidence of Link to Empowerment' (2016) 31(1) *Journal of Interpersonal Violence* 163.

Hall M, *Victims of Crime: Policy and Practice in Criminal Justice* (Willan Publishing 2009).

Halley J, Kotiswaran P, Rebouché R and Shamir H, *Governance Feminism: An Introduction* (University of Minnesota Press 2018).

Harding R, '"Dogs Are 'Registered', People Shouldn't Be": Legal Consciousness and Lesbian and Gay Rights' (2006) 15(4) *Social and Legal Studies* 511.

Harvey D, *A Brief History of Neoliberalism* (Oxford University Press 2005).

Hawkins K, *Law as Last Resort: Prosecution Decision-Making in a Regulatory Agency* (Oxford University Press 2002) 422.

Heise L, 'Violence Against Women: An Integrated, Ecological Framework' (1998) 4(3) *Violence Against Women* 262.

Hester M, 'Who Does What to Whom? Gender and Domestic Violence Perpetrators in English Police Records' (2013) 10(5) *European Journal of Criminology* 623.

Heywood I, Sammut D and Bradbury-Jones C, 'A Qualitative Exploration of "Thrivership" Among Women Who Have Experienced Domestic Violence and Abuse: Development of a New Model' (2019) 19 *British Medical Council Women's Health* 106.

Houston C, 'How Feminist Theory Became (Criminal) Law: Tracing the Path to Mandatory Criminal Intervention in Domestic Violence Cases' (2014) *Modern Law Review* 217.

Hoyle C, 'Feminism, Victimology and Domestic Violence' in Sandra Walklate (ed), *Handbook of Victims and Victimology* (Taylor and Frances 2012).

Hoyle C and Sanders A, 'Police Response to Domestic Violence: From Victim Choice to Victim Empowerment' (2000) 40(1) *British Journal of Criminology* 14.

Ishkanian A, 'Neoliberalism and Violence: The Big Society and the Changing Politics of Domestic Violence in England' (2014) 34(3) *Critical Social Policy* 333.

Johnson M, *A Typology of Domestic Violence: Intimate Terrorism, Violent Resistance and Situational Couple Violence* (Northeastern University Press 2008).

Kim M, 'Challenging the Pursuit of Criminalisation in an Era of Mass Incarceration: The Limitations of the Social Work Response to Domestic Violence in the USA' (2013) 43 *British Journal of Social Work* 1276.

Kimmel M, '"Gender Symmetry" in Domestic Violence: A Substantive and Methodological Review' (2002) *Violence Against Women* 1332.

Lewis R, 'Making Justice Work: Effective Legal Interventions for Domestic Violence' (2004) 44 *The British Journal of Criminology* 204.

Madden-Dempsey M, *Prosecuting Domestic Violence: A Philosophical Analysis* (Oxford University Press 2009).

Maguigan H, 'Wading into Professor Schneider's "Murky Middle Ground" Between Acceptance and Rejection of Criminal Justice Responses to Domestic Violence' (2002) 11 *American University Journal Gender Society Policy and Law* 427.

Mills L, 'Killing Her Softly: Intimate Abuse and the Violence of State Intervention' (1999) *Harvard Law Review* 550.

Naffine N, *Sexing the Subject (of Law)* (Oxford University Press 1995).

Natile S and Tapia S, 'Governance Feminism: An Introduction' (2018) 52(4) *Law and Society* 1106.

Nichols A, 'No-Drop Prosecution in Domestic Violence Cases: Survivor-Defined and Social Change Approaches to Victim Advocacy' (2014) 29(11) *Journal of Interpersonal Violence* 2114.

Norrie A, *Law and the Beautiful Soul* (Glasshouse 2005).

Reiner R, *Law and Order: An Honest Citizen's Guide to Crime Control* (Polity 2007).

Ribbens J and Edwards R, *Feminist Dilemmas in Qualitative Research: Public Knowledge and Private Lives* (Sage 1998).

Roulston K, 'Considering Quality in Qualitative Interviewing' (2010) *Qualitative Research* 199.

Saccuzzo D, 'How Should Police Respond to Domestic Violence: A Therapeutic Jurisprudence Analysis of Mandatory Arrest' (1998) 39 *Santa Clara Law Review* 765.

Schneider E, *Battered Women and Feminist Lawmaking* (Yale University Press 2000).

Smart C, *Feminism and the Power of the Law* (Routledge 1989).

———, 'Reflection' (2012) 20 *Feminist Legal Studies* 161.

Stark E, 'Mandatory Arrest of Batterers: A Reply to Its Critics' (1993) 36(5) *American Behavioral Scientist* 651.

Straus M, 'Measuring Intrafamily Conflict and Violence: The Conflict Tactics (CT) Scales' (1979) *Journal of Marriage and the Family* 75.

———, 'Yes, Physical Assaults by Women Partners: A Major Social Problem' in Mary Walsh (ed), *Women, Men and Gender: Ongoing Debates* (Yale University Press 1997).

Sunstein C, 'Social Norms and Social Roles' (1996) *Columbia Law Review* 903.

United Nations, '15 of the United Nations Special Rapporteur on Violence Against Women, Its Causes and Consequences: A Critical Review (1994–2009)' (2009) 27 available at http://www.ohchr.org/Documents/Issues/Women/15YearReviewofVAWMandate.pdf accessed 20 February 2020.

Walby S and Allen J, 'Domestic Violence, Sexual Assault and Stalking: Findings from the British Crime Survey' (Home Office 2004) vii.

Walker L, *The Battered Woman Syndrome* (4th edn, Springer 2016).

Watt D, 'On Becoming a Qualitative Researcher: The Value of Reflexivity' (2007) 12(1) *The Qualitative Report* 182.

Watts S, 'User Skills for Qualitative Analysis: Perspective, Interpretation and the Delivery of Impact' (2014) 11(1) *Qualitative Research in Psychology* 1.

Wexler D, 'Applying the Law Therapeutically' (1996) 5(3) *Applied and Preventive Psychology* 179.

Wills D, 'Domestic Violence: The Case for Aggressive Prosecution' (1997) *University California Los Angeles Women's Law Journal* 173.

Winick B, 'Applying the Law Therapeutically in Domestic Violence Cases' (2000) 69 *UMKC Law Review* 33.

Zedner L, *Criminal Justice* (2nd edn, Oxford University Press 2010).

2

Through the Lens of Feminism: State Responses to Domestic Abuse

Introduction

> Feminism, as a political and theoretical movement, is committed at its most fundamental level to highlighting the historical and contemporary sites of women's exclusion and/or subordination, to exploring the material, structural and ideological conditions that create and perpetuate this condition, and to making demands for their eradication.[1]

The purpose of this chapter is to set the subject addressed in the book—the emergence of 'tenacious domestic abuse prosecutions'—in the context of some key feminist frames and discourses. The first part of the chapter shines a light on significant moments of women's activism and feminist scholarship because, I argue, these have laid crucial foundations for the current prosecutorial approach. On the one hand, the legacy of past treatment of female victims of domestic abuse, which might be summarised as the criminal justice system's failure to effectively intervene, contextualises the current approach by pointing to its emergence as an attempt to right past wrongs. On the other, as second-wave feminists uncovered domestic abuse as widespread, gendered and largely ignored by the state, they also drew attention to a male perpetrator's belief in his right to coerce his partner as rooted in the legal, political and social history which condoned it. Feminists pointed to the historically

[1]Vanessa Munro, *Law and Politics at the Perimeter: Re-evaluating Key Debates in Feminist Theory* (Hart 2007) 11.

A. Porter, *Prosecuting Domestic Abuse in Neoliberal Times*, Palgrave Socio-Legal Studies,
https://doi.org/10.1007/978-3-030-61369-3_2

grounded patriarchal structures that produced systemic male dominance, power and control over women in both public and private arenas. I argue that 'tenacious prosecutions' reflect and instrumentalise such feminist analysis[2] because the state is able to claim that 'an effective criminal justice response to VAWG' targets 'deep rooted social norms, attitudes and behaviours that discriminate and limit women'[3] and that underpin domestic abuse.

The second and third parts of the chapter turn attention to two central second-wave feminist themes that offer potential insight into modern prosecutorial treatment of abused women; the public/private divide and the liberal legal subject.

Part One

(i) Domestic Abuse: Key Moments in Women's History

In the nineteenth century, law systematically restricted women's ability to resist men's privilege. Marriage was considered women's '*only* respectable career' yet marriage hugely limited women's legal status.[4] On marriage, a woman's property became her husband's[5] and she could neither enter into contracts, sue nor be sued. Moreover, a man's conjugal rights permitted him to forcibly 'chastise' his wife, to force her to live with him[6] and entitled him to sexual intercourse with her.[7] For women trapped in violent relationships, first-wave feminist campaigns that tackled women's limited access to divorce, to their property and to their children alleviated some of the restrictions on women's ability to leave.[8] More directly, Frances Power Cobbe's petition to

---

[2]Rebecca Dobash and Russell Dobash, *Violence Against Wives: A Case Against the Patriarchy* (Free Press New York 1979) was influential.

[3]Her Majesty's Government, 'Ending Violence Against Women and Girls: Strategy 2016–2020' (HMSO 2016) 9 available at https://www.gov.uk/government/uploads/system/uploads/attachment_data/file/505961/VAWG_Strategy_2016-2020.pdf accessed 10 May 2018.

[4]Rosemary Auchmuty, 'Marriage and Civil Partnership: Law's Role, Feminism's Response' in Maragret Davies and Vanessa Munro (eds), *The Ashgate Research Companion to Feminist Legal Theory* (Routledge 2013) 285.

[5]Unless they held property under a trust.

[6]Until the pivotal decision of R v Jackson [1891] 1 QB 671.

[7]Up until R v R [1991] 3 WLR 767; See Mary Turner, *The Women's Century* (The National Archives 2003) 5.

[8]Caroline Norton's work was notable in bringing about the Matrimonial Causes Act 1857. See Penelope Russell, 'The Matrimonial Cause Act 1857' in Rosemary Auchmuty and Erika Rackley (eds), *Women's Legal Landmarks: Celebrating 100 Years of Women and Law in the UK and Ireland* (Bloomsbury 2018) 65.

end 'wife torture' challenged law's apathy towards men's abusive behaviour.[9] The resulting Matrimonial Causes Act 1878 permitted women to leave their (convicted) violent husbands, to receive maintenance and have custody of their children up to the age of ten.

If the women's movement dwindled after the achievements of the suffragettes in 1918, some have suggested that the women of the 1970s had to 're-discover it'.[10] In 1971, a group of women, children and one cow (!), led a march in Chiswick, London, to protest about rising food costs and the proposed School Milk Bill which would take away free milk in schools.[11] Following the demonstration, the group were able to secure a building from the council and protestors came together to discuss other concerns and issues that affected their day-to-day lives. It became a place for women to share experiences and what unfolded was the revelation that many women suffered brutally at the hands of their husbands. As the issue of greatest concern, domestic violence became the sole focus of the group and the group became known as Women's Aid.[12]

Erin Pizzey established the first women's refuge for battered women in Chiswick that same year. This Women's Aid Centre was one example of the way the women's liberation movement began to take matters into their own hands in the 1970s, rather than appealing to politicians, institutions or demanding legislative change. The Chiswick centre's policy was to never turn away an abused woman and her family. The overcrowded conditions, however, only served to highlight the extent of male violence, and by 1976, the Chiswick centre had inspired an additional 90 centres in Britain alone.

Pizzey was vociferous about her cause. Her first book, *Scream Quietly or the Neighbours will Hear* highlighted the poor and inadequate support battered women received. She wrote of poor legal advice for women in crisis and poor police practice which treated domestic assault less seriously than assaults that took place in public. She noted that the law paid lip service to domestic assault and that there was a gap between 'what the law says and

---

[9]Frances Cobbe, 'Wife Torture in England' (1878) *Contemporary Review* 55; Catherine Euler, 'The Irons of Their Fetters have Eaten into Their Souls: Nineteenth Century Feminist Strategies to Get Our Bodies onto the Political Agenda' in Shani D'Cruze and Ivor Crewe (eds), *Everyday Violence in Britain 1850–1950: Gender and Class* (Pearson 2000) 199.

[10]Martin Pugh, *Women and the Women's Movement in Britain, 1914–1999* (Macmillan 2000) 316. Rosemary Auchmuty has suggested that though this period 'between the waves' might be described as 'fallow' it was not for want of women trying; in Auchmuty (n 4) 290.

[11]Caroline Charlton, 'The First Cow on Chiswick High Road' (1972) *Spare Rib* 24.

[12]Rebecca Dobash and Russell Dobash, 'Love, Honour and Obey: Institutional Ideologies and the Struggle for Battered Women' (1977) *Contemporary Crisis* 403, 403–404.

what the law will actually do'.[13] Pizzey noted the resistance of prosecutors to pursue abusers and, when criminal cases were brought, she reproached the common situation which found the abuser living back in the marital home awaiting trial. She also lamented the ineffectiveness of injunctions due to the absence of a power to arrest for breach.[14]

Britain's National Women's Aid Federation was an organisation entrenched in British socialist and radical feminist traditions and was responsible for the vast majority of refuges in the UK. At this time, feminists were not demanding penal solutions to domestic violence but were instead focused on providing permanent housing and social solutions to alleviate women's situations. Gottschalk contrasts this British emphasis to the approach taken by the 'battered women's movement' in the United States which expressly sought to hold the police to account for their failures to protect abused women.[15] She surmises that British feminists pursued alternative avenues for two reasons. The first was that Britain's welfare tradition was more developed.[16] The second had more to do with the British government keeping feminist groups at a distance[17] and, concomitantly, the Home Office's refusal to acknowledge failures in the criminal justice response to domestic violence. Accordingly, British feminist groups in the early 1970s concentrated their efforts by working outside of traditional state mechanisms to effect change.

However, the British government could not ignore the refuge movement for long. Through their persistent collective working and consciousness raising—in which they supported refuges to open in Europe and in the United States—the refuge movement generated extensive media coverage about domestic violence. Their work caused violence in the home to

[13]Erin Pizzey, *Scream Quietly or the Neighbours Will Hear* (Penguin 1974) 116.

[14]Pizzey later courted controversy by suggesting that many abused women were 'addicted to violence' and that men who recreated the violence of their childhoods derived a 'perverse kind of pleasure'. By simultaneously shifting blame onto the abused woman and excusing the actions of violent men, Pizzey was accused of perpetuating abusive relationships for women who blamed themselves and refused to leave. See Mary Turner, *The Women's Century* (The National Archives 2003) 147.

[15]See, e.g., Bruno v Codd 90 Misc.2d 1047 (1977) in which a victim was awarded substantial damages for police mishandling of her violent domestic situation.

[16]A UK government report commissioned in 1981, for example, cited housing as the primary obstacle for women wanting to escape abusive relationships in Val Binney, Gina Harkell and Judy Nixon in conjunction with Women's Aid Federation/Department for Environment, *Leaving Violent Men: A Study of Refuges and Housing for Battered Women* (King's English Book Printers 1981).

[17]Marie Gottschalk, *The Prison and the Gallows: The Politics of Mass Incarceration in America* (Cambridge University Press 2006) 136.

surface as a public issue[18] and prompted convening of a Select Committee on Violence in the Family in 1975. Representatives from Women's Aid, amongst other individuals and organisations, gave evidence describing domestic violence as a social problem and urged, first and foremost, that abused women needed welfare assistance. Throughout the gathering of evidence, the British government and Home Office continued to resist criticism of the criminal justice treatment of intimate partner violence. Evidence given by the Association of Chief Police Officers expressed the view that officers were doing their best given that,

> in the majority of cases the role of the police is a negative one. We are, after all, dealing with persons 'bound in marriage', and it is important for a host of reasons to maintain the unity of the spouses. Precipitate action by the police could aggravate the position to such an extent as to create a worse situation than the one they were summonsed to deal with. The 'lesser of two evils' principle is often a good guideline in these situations.[19]

It is clear therefore that domestic violence for the police was largely considered a private matter between husband and wife and only when obvious and serious infractions had occurred would it be necessary to remove the perpetrator through arrest.

Yet, despite the police downplaying the inadequacy of their response to domestic abuse, the Select Committee's report did suggest that police invocation of the law was unsatisfactory; 'If the Criminal Law of assault could be more uniformly applied to domestic assault there seems little doubt that it would give more protection to the battered wife'.[20]

The Domestic Violence and Matrimonial Proceedings Act 1976 followed. It offered stand-alone civil injunctions to protect a victim from her perpetrator; judges could exclude the perpetrator from the marital home and from coming within a specified distance of it and could also attach powers to arrest the perpetrator for breach. This represented demonstrable success for the refuge movement and prompted the movement to extend its ambitions to include not just welfare support, consciousness raising and education but also political lobbying to effect law reform.

---

[18]Jalna Hanmer, 'Violence to Women: From Private Sorrow to Public Issue' in Georgina Ashworth and Lucy Bonnerjea (eds), *The Invisible Decade: UK Women and the U.N. Decade for Women, 1976–1985* (Gower 1985) 145.

[19]House of Commons Select Committee, 'Report on Violence in the Family' (1975) 366.

[20]Ibid., xvi. The report made 28 recommendations, 11 of which related to law and law enforcement.

Following the Select Committee report and the welcome legislative development, there were improvements on the part of the police to exercise their discretion to effect arrest of the perpetrators of domestic abuse.[21] There was also a shift in police perception that complainants were 'wasting their time'.[22] Nonetheless, old habits persisted with police call-outs often ending with advice being given to the complainant or merely with the perpetrator being 'bound over to keep the peace'. There was still much work to be done in breaking down police assumptions that the full weight of the criminal law should not be used to handle 'disturbances', lest the family unit suffered.[23] Moreover prosecutors also continued to display indifference and inaction, treating these infractions of the criminal law as undeserving of a judicial response.[24]

In the 1980s, the status of abused women suffered a stalemate. On the one hand, campaigners in the 1970s had raised awareness of domestic violence not just as a private concern but also as a social concern. The government had responded by providing (limited) funding for research and services[25] and by passing legislation.[26] On the other hand, women in the 1980s experienced an ambivalent response from criminal justice agencies tasked with implementation of the law.[27] Hanmer describes a culture in the Home Office of victim-blaming and a refusal to accept the problem of intimate partner violence as gendered.[28] Women in the 1980s thus endured the effects of previous generations' sexism and the redress available to them through the criminal courts was still impeded by the belief in the inviolability of the family and the authority of the breadwinner,[29] even if that was at the expense of perpetuating the unhappy, intolerable and even violent

---

[21]Dobash and Dobash, *Violence Against Wives* (n 2) 210–211.

[22]Ibid., 210–211.

[23]Ibid., 210–211.

[24]Ibid., 218.

[25]Jalna Hanmer (n 18) 150.

[26]As well as the Matrimonial Proceedings Act 1976, the Select Committee had prompted passing of the Housing (Homeless) Persons Act 1977. It gave women with dependent children fleeing violence local authority priority housing status.

[27]Kathryn McCann, 'Battered Women and the Law: The Limits of Legislation' in Julia Brophy and Carol Smart (eds), *Women in Law: Explorations in Law, Family and Sexuality* (Routledge & Kegan Paul 1985) 71.

[28]Hanmer (n 18) 141–154. Indeed the 1984 national crime survey prompted the Home Office to conclude that what women required was 'fear reduction programmes'; Michael Maxfield, *Fear of Crime in England and Wales, Home Office Research Study No. 78* (HMSO 1984).

[29]Susan Atkins and Brenda Hoggett, *Women and the Law* (Basil Blackwell 1984) 159.

family.[30] The CPS was established in 1986 and the approach that was taken thereafter is examined in detail in Chapter 3.

As well as activism, second-wave feminism also involved more extensive academic analysis of the nature and causes of women's social disadvantage and men's violence. In 1977, sociologists Rebecca and Russell Dobash began their analysis of 'Violence Against Wives'.[31] They outlined the contribution of patriarchal structures, buttressed by hierarchical ideology, in the institutionalised subordination of one half of the population.[32] They argued that abused women's struggles were not only with their violent husbands but also with the social arrangements and ideologies that served to subordinate them. Extending Cobbe's claim that male authority in the family manifested as violence against wives, the Dobashes contended that domestic violence is also an expression of wider societal gender inequalities. The Dobashes declared that, 'the foundations of wife battering are written into the marriage contract',[33] referencing their belief that the historic legacy of a husband's right to castigate his wife[34] persisted in cultural norms.

The Dobashes argued that the family 'is the cornerstone of the patriarchal society' and a 'model upon which other social institutions are based'[35]; its moral order guides family members as they operate in society and in public. Having a male head of the household was society's 'sacred hierarchy' and the failure to challenge this meant that women's subordination was replicated and perpetuated beyond the family. The Dobashes perceived patriarchal attitudes to be at their most blatant at the point of law enforcement (or obvious lack of it).[36] Lenient sentences and ongoing police failures were indicative of the tiny inroads being made to confront men's coercive and violent treatment of their partners.[37] Legal responses, they suggested, merely offered 'cosmetic relief'[38] and did not systematically confront perpetrators nor the overall patriarchal system which contributed to men's violence. The state, they suggested, was resistant to intervening in domestic abuse because it had

[30]Kathryn McCann, 'Battered Women and the Law: The Limits of Legislation' in *Women in Law: Explorations in Law, Family and Sexuality* (Routledge & Kegan Paul 1985).

[31]Dobash and Dobash (n 2).

[32]Dobash and Dobash, 'Love Honour and Obey' (n 12) 403.

[33]Ibid., 403.

[34]See, e.g., Bradley v Wife (1663) ER 83 1157.

[35]Ibid., 408.

[36]Ibid., 410.

[37]Dobash and Dobash, 'Love Honour and Obey' (n 12) 406.

[38]Ibid., 406.

an interest in perpetuating the subordinate position of women for the benefit of the prevailing economic order which relied on women's role in social reproduction.

I have given a broad outline here of second-wave feminists' argument that violence against women is an expression of wider societal gender inequalities. In the next two parts of the chapter, I explore two particular aspects of feminist theorising of women's social subordination in more detail. Before examining feminist critique of the liberal subject, I show next that feminists exposed liberal society's categorisation of spheres of life as either 'public' or 'private'. Feminist scholars demonstrated how notions of the 'public' and the 'private' were woven into women's lives and into legal responses in multifarious ways that produced and re-enforced gendered roles and expectations.

Part Two

(i) The Public/Private Divide: A Prelude to Patriarchy

For Pateman, 'the dichotomy between the public and the private... is, ultimately, what the feminist movement is about'.[39] I interrogate the public/private divide in this part of the chapter because it has been described as a 'prelude' to understanding the production of the gender inequality[40] which underpins intimate partner violence. If law and legal reforms can be valuable means of addressing social problems and inequalities, then the way that liberalism traditionally imposes restrictions on law's reach into the so-called private sphere[41] is particularly problematic in the area of domestic abuse; the divide produces a tolerance of intimate partner abuse and a resistance to invoking the criminal law in respect of it. When the state seeks to maintain a sphere of 'privacy' (in line with liberal philosophy), this does not serve women in abusive relationships because it is used to justify a lack of state intervention.

Here, I explore feminists' critique of the supposed dichotomy between public and private life. I suggest that their critiques have been effective to the extent that contemporary criminal justice actors no longer recognise a

---

[39]Carole Pateman, 'Feminist Critiques of the Public/Private Dichotomy' in Stanley Benn and Gerald Gaus (eds), *Private and Public in Social Life* (Croom Helm 1993).

[40]Katherine O'Donovan, *Sexual Divisions in Law* (Weidenfeld and Nicolson 1985) 1 exposed how it contributes to the production of gender inequality both in society and in law.

[41]Ibid., 2.

divide. I present a re-engagement with the public/private divide here, not to endorse its rhetoric, but to show that its deconstruction has come at a cost for abused women. I want to suggest that there is still a place for an affirmative notion of 'privacy' in prosecutorial decision-making, all things being equal, because the concept is bound up with qualities integral to women's 'thrivership'.

The divide between what is said to be 'public' and that which is said to be 'private' evolved with the rise of capitalist production and wage labour between the sixteenth and eighteenth centuries. Up until as late as the seventeenth century, the basic unit of production had always been the household.[42] However, mercantilism and the factory system saw men, women and children go out to paid work. Whilst women's domestic labour in relation to child-bearing, caring and keeping the family home may have been revered by the Victorians,[43] it did not play a part in the wage economy and became increasingly devalued.[44] Women's domestic role became a role in an unrecognised economy and came to determine to what extent they could enter the marketplace and on what terms. Until second-wave feminists challenged this, many assumed that women's confinement to domestic life and the care role had always been 'natural and inevitable'.[45]

The Western intellectual tradition has not only emphasised a purported distinction between 'private' and 'public' spheres but it has placed more value and regard on the 'public' than on the 'private'. The superior status of the public sphere is evidenced by its affiliation with the rational, intellectual endeavour, the cultural and, undoubtedly, 'the masculine'. It includes the work place, the values of the market place and activities that are regulated by law. The private sphere by contrast is associated with non-rationality, personal relations, corporeality, the 'constellations of values associated with reproduction',[46] behaviour unregulated by law and 'the feminine'. Yet this purported dichotomy does not describe material reality, rather it is more 'a structure of consciousness'[47] that entrenches gendered delineations between men's and women's lives, and their respective value or worth. Olsen refers to

[42]Dobash and Dobash, *Violence Against Wives* (n 2) 50.

[43]See, by way of illustration, Coventry Patmore, *The Angel in the House* (4th edn, Macmillan 1866) first published in 1854.

[44]Hilaire Barnett, *Introduction to Feminist Jurisprudence* (Cavendish 1998) 129.

[45]Okin, *Justice, Gender and the Family* (Basic Books 1989) 125.

[46]Ibid., 14.

[47]Frances Olsen, 'The Family and the Market: A Study of Ideology and Legal Reform' (1983) 96(7) *Harvard Law Review* 1496, 1497.

the divide as a vision shared by society[48] that creates gendered expectations and pre-determines our opportunities along gendered lines.[49] In short, the ascendency of a so-called public sphere facilitates male advantage.

In the nineteenth century, the distinction also carried clear moral associations. Women were encouraged to be compliant, nurturing and dedicated to domesticity, providing a 'haven' for their husbands.[50] This moral project aligned with the ideas of traditional liberal political theorists who considered the existence of one's private realm to be central to the enjoyment of the autonomous self; the private sphere ought to be experienced as a sphere of freedom, buffering the private self (or family) from the pressures of the outside world[51] and escaping public scrutiny. In this liberal conception, the family is 'unproblematically private'[52] and the private life of home and family, it follows, became synonymous with the absence of regulation.[53]

Classical liberals defended the notion of a private sphere. Rousseau, for instance, reasoned that the family should be distinct from wider society and its systems of justice and regulation. The public sphere necessitates regulation because it is here that self-interest is pursued and because '[t]he legally regulated subject of the public realm [is]... a rationally instrumental being'.[54] This account of the subject of the public sphere does not apply to the familial subject, Rousseau argued, because of the family's unique foundation, love. Husbands, he argued, are guided by their hearts and can properly represent their wives' interests both in family and political life. Whilst the public sphere thus sees calculating, economic and rational self-interest, the private sphere gives way, supposedly, to altruism according to love.

In this liberal vision, women are simultaneously ruled in the home and denied participation in public politics, though without prejudice to their well-being because their husbands represent their best interests.[55] But the liberal assumption that generosity emanating from unconditional affection results in the fair sharing of the benefits and burdens of life ignores how

---

[48]Ibid., 1497.

[49]Okin, *Justice, Gender and the Family* (n 45).

[50]See, e.g., John Ruskin, *Sesame and Lillies* (Smith, Elder and Co 1864).

[51]Margaret Thornton, 'The Cartography of Public and Private' in Margaret Thornton (ed), *Public and Private: Feminist Legal Debates* (Oxford University Press 1995) 6.

[52]Ibid., 4.

[53]O'Donovan, *Sexual Divisions in Law* (n 40) 7.

[54]Jean-Jacques Rousseau, *A Discourse on Political Economy (translated from Oeuvres Completes)* (Plaiade 1959–1969) Volume 3, 241–242.

[55]Okin, *Justice, Gender and the Family* (n 45) 26–27.

freedoms enjoyed in the public sphere raise the status of the man both intellectually and materially. Second-wave feminists therefore drew attention to how the public and private divide elevates men's roles in the public sphere (socially, economically and politically) which further reinforces their superior status in the home. Crucially, they challenged the assumption that male supremacy in the home would be exercised benevolently; Okin, for example, argued that our 'personal life is not immune from the dynamic of power'.[56]

Such classical liberal reasoning about the private sphere is unlikely to meet with approbation today, least of all by those who actively seek gender equality. As far as intimate partner abuse is concerned, classical liberalism's ardent defence of the unregulated private sphere clearly risks concealing the harms that can occur in private. If the dynamics of family relationships are screened, power struggles, coercive abuse and physical violence go unnoticed and unchallenged. For that reason, that '"privacy" connotes insecurity, fear and oppression (often for women)' has been a 'constant refrain' of feminist critiques of the public/private distinction.[57] Second-wave feminists confronted the liberal 'myth of family bliss and security' and provided overwhelming evidence to the contrary.[58]

(ii) Confronting the Public/Private Divide: Patriarchy and Private Abuse

Feminists in the second wave challenged the essentialist construction of the public and private because, they argued, demarcation of the spheres perpetuated society's different treatment of men and women. They argued that the divide was an effect of and contributor towards 'patriarchy' in both its structural and ideological sense. Structurally, 'patriarchy' comprises the hierarchical organisation of social institutions and social relations that entrench the subordination, oppression and exploitation of women by men.[59] Patriarchy's 'wrongful structural inequality' thus 'systematically limits women's access

---

[56]Ibid., 128.

[57]Rosemary Hunter, 'Contesting the Dominant Paradigm: Feminist Critiques of Liberal Legalism' in Margaret Davies and Vanessa Munro (eds), *The Ashgate Companion to Feminist Legal Theory* (Ashgate 2013) 19.

[58]Dobash and Dobash, *Violence Against Wives* (n 2) 7.

[59]Sylvia Walby, *Theorizing Patriarchy* (Blackwell 1990) 20. See also Dobash and Dobash, *Violence Against Wives* (n 2) 43.

to options that are critical to the success of their lives'.[60] By virtue of their confinement (or perceived confinement) to the private sphere, women experienced restricted opportunities to challenge the social order and the institutions that subordinated them. This disadvantage was sustained not only by this inhibiting structural loop but also by cultural ideology that condoned the notional separation of spheres.[61]

Since second-wave feminists first invoked 'patriarchy' as a theoretical concept, the term has been widely criticised for its under-theorisation.[62] If 'patriarchy' is used too simplistically, it creates a 'false universalism' and eclipses the complexity of gender systems.[63] This criticism is perhaps most commonly levelled at radical feminists' use of the term. Yet, it has been the radical feminist appraisal of patriarchy and its link to domestic abuse that, I argue, has been harnessed by the state to justify stronger criminal justice interventions.[64]

For 'liberal' feminists, the harm of patriarchy lies in a failure to include women in pre-existing public institutions as equals. For 'difference' feminists, patriarchy's foundational operation lies in a conscious devaluing of women's unique offerings by giving precedence to men's ways of doing.[65] By contrast, for radical feminists '"difference" is the velvet glove on the iron fist of [male] domination',[66] meaning that, for radicals, patriarchy emerges as a system of male domination within which gender differences are constructed only to maintain and rationalise the power of men.

Building on this radical understanding, Dobash and Dobash firmly placed 'the foundation of wife beating' within women's subordination.[67] They grouped together what they considered an immutable progression from male dominance in public life and private life to female oppression in both spheres from which physical chastisement of women in the home is an inevitable consequence. Violence by men, they argued, is used as a way

---

[60]Michelle Madden-Dempsey, *Prosecuting Domestic Violence: A Philosophical Analysis* (Oxford University Press 2009) 139.

[61]Dobash and Dobash, *Violence Against Wives* (n 2) 43.

[62]Gwen Hunnicutt, 'Varieties of Patriarchy and Violence Against Women: Resurrecting "Patriarchy" as a Theoretical Tool' (2009) 15(5) *Violence Against Women* 553, 558–559.

[63]Ibid., 558–559.

[64]Claire Houston, 'How Feminist Theory Became (Criminal) Law: Tracing the Path to Mandatory Criminal Intervention in Domestic Violence Cases' (2014) *Michigan Journal of Gender and Law* 217.

[65]Carol Gilligan, *In a Different Voice: Psychological Theory and Women's Development* (Harvard University Press 1993).

[66]Catherine MacKinnon, *Toward a Feminist Theory of State* (Harvard University Press 1989) 219.

[67]Dobash and Dobash, *Violence Against Wives* (n 2) 45.

of securing and maintaining male dominance over women which is the key to the patriarchal social order.[68] For the Dobashes, 'coercive control', which they said is 'primarily purposeful behaviour',[69] both expresses the patriarchy and is a concerted effort to perpetuate it. Given, they said, that 'systems of power and authority are ultimately based on the use or threat of force',[70] the link between male dominance in society and violence against women is inevitable and endures because it is 'socially condoned'.[71]

Mirroring the Dobashes' explanation, for radical feminist Catharine MacKinnon, violence is also 'a paradigmatic symbol and strategy of patriarchy'.[72] For her, intimate partner violence cannot be reduced to individual explanations because it is a systemic invocation of men's position of power and privilege over women.[73] Writing about *sexual* violence against women, MacKinnon explains how the locus of privacy facilitates men's expression of the privilege: 'when women are segregated in private, one at a time, a law of privacy will tend to protect the right of men to be let alone to oppress [women] one at a time'.[74]

By contrast, post-modern feminists reject a single, universal foundation of women's experience of subordination or violence. So far as 'patriarchy' can be identified, post-modernists say that it should be recognised that power operates in a multiplicity of ways depending on context and perspective; for them, society and patriarchy are 'forever shifting, ambiguous and fluid'.[75] There is no one unified and collective experience of male supremacy and thus post-modernism develops a nuanced understanding of power, rejecting a straight correlation between power and domination.[76] For post-modernists, the radical feminist explanation minimises the 'complex ways in which

---

[68]Rebecca Dobash and Russell Dobash, *Rethinking Violence Against Women* (Sage 1998) 228.

[69]Dobash and Dobash, *Violence Against Wives* (n 2) 24.

[70]Rebecca and Russell Dobash, 'Research as Social Action: The Struggle for Battered Women' in Michelle Bograd and Kersti Yllo (eds), *Feminist Perspectives on Wife Abuse* (Sage 1990) 57. See also Kate Millet, *Sexual Politics* (Virago 1970) who similarly asserts that patriarchy relies on the use of force for its maintenance.

[71]Ibid., 24.

[72]Vanessa Munro paraphrases Catharine MacKinnon, *Feminism Unmodified* (Harvard University Press 1987) in Vanessa Munro, 'Violence Against Women, "Victimhood" and the (Neo)Liberal State' in Margaret Davies and Vanessa Munro (eds), *The Ashgate Research Companion to Feminist Legal Theory* (Ashgate 2013) 237.

[73]Munro, 'Violence Against Women, "Victimhood" and the (Neo)Liberal State' (n 72) 237.

[74]Catharine MacKinnon, 'Feminism, Marxism, Method, and the State: Toward Feminist Jurisprudence' (1983) *Signs* 635, 657.

[75]Hunnicutt, 'Varieties of Patriarchy and Violence Against Women' (n 62) 559.

[76]Munro, *Law and Politics at the Perimeter* (n 1).

violence is structured along axes other than gender'.[77] It is clear, I suggest, that intersectional discourses about how race, class and sexuality also create structural disadvantage are important as well.

Whilst feminists might understand 'patriarchy' in differing ways (some demonstrate a reluctance to use the term and some might even reject using the term altogether[78]), Davies has suggested that most Western feminists concede that feminism takes place within the 'horizon of patriarchy'.[79] Use of the term can, however, invoke images of static gendered hierarchies, and transcendent male power conspiracies and this can restrict the usefulness of the concept and essentialise women's experience. The radical depiction of structural patriarchy playing out in individual lives constructs women as passive victims whilst all men become the universal and undifferentiated oppressors. This is clearly an overly simplistic binary.[80] However, by drawing attention to the effect that structural inequality has in shaping our lives, radical feminists correctly require us to reconsider what we may have thought of as unconnected or personalised events that deny women's options and foster some men's violence. Considered collectively, Munro suggests that women's experiences 'reveal a net of restricting and reinforcing relations'[81] that will always form part of the context for violence committed against them.

Feminists campaigning to end violence against women challenged the public/private distinction because of its patriarchal construction and its contribution to gendered violence. They argued that a distinction between the two spheres should not be made and that domestic violence should be treated as a public concern. This necessarily required treating domestic violence as crime.

In the late 1970s, US attorneys Laurie Woods and Pauline Gee brought the respective suits of *Bruno*[82] and *Scott*,[83] in which they demanded legal protections for victims of domestic abuse through perpetrator arrest,

---

[77]Munro, 'Violence Against Women, "Victimhood" and the (Neo)Liberal State' (n 72) 238.

[78]Hunnicutt, 'Varieties of Patriarchy and Violence Against Women' (n 62) 553. Hunnicutt suggests that as the term was used persuasively and effectively by social activists, it received too little theoretical attention.

[79]Margaret Davies, *Asking the Law Question* (3rd edn, Thomson 2008) 264.

[80]Though see Joanne Conaghan's suggestion that radical feminism, which draws upon marxism 'never has entailed an assertion that all individual capitalists/men oppress all individual workers/women or that workers/women lack political agency' in Joanne Conaghan, 'Book Review: Vanessa Munro *Law and Politics at the Perimeter: Re-evaluating Key Debates in Feminist Theory*' (2009) *Feminist Legal Studies* 229, 230.

[81]Iris Young, *Inclusion and Democracy* (Oxford University Press 2002) 92.

[82]Bruno v Codd, 396 N.Y.S.2d 974 (N.Y. Sup Ct 1977).

[83]Scott v Hart, No. C-76-2395 (N.D. Cal. Oct 28, 1976).

prosecution and conviction. Woods explained that the cases were needed because 'every time a batterer [is] arrested, sexist beliefs [are] challenged'.[84] Both cases were settled when the police accepted that as far as arrests were concerned, 'domestic violence would be treated like any other behaviour' and, following (now controversial) empirical validation,[85] the US Department of Justice expressed that arrest was *the* preferred response to family violence, paving the way for pro-arrest and mandatory arrest policies across the United States.[86]

Houston explains that when, subsequently, prosecuting authorities in the United States widely adopted no-drop prosecutions,[87] they did so not only to challenge pervading sexist ideology that condoned men's use of domestic violence but also to confront those perpetrators who intimidated or coerced their victims into retracting. No-drop prosecutions were introduced as a way of overcoming a perpetrator's ongoing control of the victim; if a prosecution could be expected to continue, with or without the victim's support, there was no longer an incentive for him to manipulate her into withdrawing.

Both of these rationales justified a committed criminal justice response to domestic abuse in the United States and both rationales are evidenced in current CPS policy in England and Wales; on the one hand, the CPS recognises that victims may withdraw their support as a result of 'pressure from the perpetrator, the perpetrator's family or associates [or] fear of repercussions'.[88] On the other hand, the CPS violence against women strategy adopts the United Nations position, which urges prosecutorial pursuit to combat intimate partner abuse as a means of 'characteris[ing] the state as having values that lessen patriarchy'.[89]

If individual relationships are situated in and are reflective of broader social patriarchal structures (the 'patriarchal force'[90] thesis), domestic

---

[84]Houston, 'How Feminist Theory Became (Criminal) Law' (n 64) 257.

[85]Lawrence Sherman and Richard Berk, 'The Minneapolis Domestic Violence Experiment (Police Foundation)' 1984.

[86]Houston, 'How Feminist Theory Became (Criminal) Law' (n 64) 260.

[87]See the Introduction chapter for an explanation of this practice.

[88]Crown Prosecution Service, 'Domestic Abuse Guidelines for Prosecutors' (2014) available at https://www.cps.gov.uk/legal-guidance/domestic-abuse-guidelines-prosecutors accessed 19 November 2019.

[89]United Nations, '15 of the United Nations Special Rapporteur on Violence Against Women, Its Causes and Consequences: A Critical Review (1994–2009)' (2009) available at http://www.ohchr.org/Documents/Issues/Women/15YearReviewofVAWMandate.pdf cited in Crown Prosecution Service, 'Violence Against Women and Girls Report, 10th Edition, 2016–17' (2017) A1 available at https://www.cps.gov.uk/sites/default/files/documents/publications/cps-vawg-report-2017_0.pdf accessed 19 November 2019.

[90]Houston, 'How Feminist Theory Became (Criminal) Law' (n 64).

violence prosecution is, according to feminist jurisprudent Michelle Madden-Dempsey, ripe for feminist action. In targeting domestic violence that tends to sustain and perpetuate patriarchy (violence that bears hallmarks of stereo-typical gendered roles and expectations) prosecutors have the power to improve the moral character of the state, realise values that will reduce patriarchy and in turn reduce the incidence of domestic violence.[91] Referencing Madden-Dempsey's analysis, the UN Special Rapporteur on Violence Against Women, Yakin Ertürk, explains:

> [P]rosecutors working on cases of domestic violence have the potential and the obligation to change the prevailing balance of power [between men and women] by taking a strong stance to disempower patriarchal notions. Interventions at this level may have both consequential effects in that condemnations of patriarchy can lead to changes in socio-cultural norms, as well as intrinsic effects, in that prosecutors ... can be considered to be the 'mouthpieces' of society, and strong statements condemning violence against women made on behalf of society through the ... prosecutorial services will make that society less patriarchal.[92]

The assertion here is that the criminal law and public prosecutions can be an effective instrument to change societal norms because of their expressive effects. Kahan explains that simply by labelling conduct as 'illegal' one's 'moral appraisal' of the behaviour is impacted.[93] Kahan describes that if one's peers also denounce the behaviour, the influence on one's own moral view is significant.[94] Where the criminal law and its agents consistently condemn the contested behaviour, incrementally over time, the effect is 'a wave of condemnation' which will slowly begin to break the grip of the norm.[95] Ultimately, 'it might well initiate a process that culminates in the near eradication of the contested norm and the associated types of behaviour'.[96] This

---

[91]Madden-Dempsey, *Prosecuting Domestic Violence* (n 60).

[92]Yakin Erturk, 'Integration of the Human Rights of Women and the Gender Perspective: Violence Against Women: The Due Diligence Standards as a Tool for the Elimination of Violence Against Women' (2006) Report of the Special Rapporteur on Violence against Women, its Causes and Consequences, to the United Nations Commission on Human Rights, E/CN.4/2006/61 citing Michelle Madden Dempsey, 'What Counts as Domestic Violence—A Conceptual Analysis' (2006) 12 *William Mary Journal of Women and the Law* 301.

[93]Dan Kahan, 'Gentle Nudges vs. Hard Shoves: Solving the Sticky Norms Problem' (2000) *University of Chicago Law Review* 607, 613.

[94]Ibid., 614.

[95]Ibid., 609.

[96]Ibid., 609.

is the process that is relied upon by Madden-Dempsey and the UN Special Rapporteur when they assert that pursuing domestic violence prosecutions will render society less patriarchal.

Tenacious prosecutions, which are pursued regardless of expressed opposition from the victim, will have greater expressive value. Tenacious prosecutions are likely to receive more approval from a radical feminist perspective by virtue of their potential to challenge women's structural disadvantage. By contrast, post-modern feminists,[97] who recognise the myriad ways that 'patriarchy' operates on individual women depending on their unique experiences, are likely to prefer a presumption to prosecute, after which a 'survivor-defined',[98] 'empowerment'[99] or 'case-by-case' approach will be merited.[100]

For all feminists, however, violence ought not be reduced to an interpersonal level alone where victim or batterer psycho-pathological explanations are preferred.[101] Rather than being seen as taking place in a social vacuum, abuse between intimates should always be understood within broader institutional contexts and structural orders of power.[102] Whilst it may appear that violence is sparked by particular circumstances, for example, as a result of jealousy, financial stresses, failure to perform domestic chores, alcohol consumption or refusal of sex, in fact it is 'infused at every point with notions of female possibility and male power that are socially derived from a broad array of experiences in the community, economy and wider society'.[103] So long as gender inequality exists, it will always form a part of the context.

In this part of the chapter, I have outlined how feminist critique of the public/private dichotomy has highlighted the hierarchical and gendered

---

[97]In her article, Nichols describes these two approaches as either 'radical' or 'liberal', here I have preferred to distinguish between 'radical' v 'post-modern'. Andrea Nichols, 'No-Drop Prosecution in Domestic Violence Cases: Survivor-Defined and Social Change Approaches to Victim Advocacy' (2014) 29(11) *Journal of Interpersonal Violence* 2114.

[98]Ibid., 2116.

[99]Carolyn Hoyle and Andrew Sanders, 'Police Response to Domestic Violence: From Victim Choice to Victim Empowerment'(2000) 40 *British Journal of Criminology* 14.

[100]See Introduction chapter for a more detailed explanation about what 'survivor-defined' or 'tenacious prosecutions' mean.

[101]Prior to the women's movement prompting a 'structural turn', explanations about intimate partner abuse were often based on the exceptional mental health of victim/offender. See Houston, 'How Feminist Theory became (Criminal) Law' (n 64).

[102]See also Kersti Yllo, 'Political and Methodological Debates in Wife Abuse Research' in Michelle Bograd and Kersti Yllo (eds), *Feminist Perspectives on Wife Abuse* (Sage 1990).

[103]Evan Stark and Anne Flitcraft, *Women at Risk: Domestic Violence and Women's Health* (Sage 1996) 31.

binary order that the divide produces. The construction devalues women's labours and sustains a hierarchy whereby 'public' or so-called male labours are esteemed, ideologically and economically. Feminists have also called into question the coherence of the distinction as far as where the boundary between the two spheres lies.[104] Olsen argues that 'privacy' is merely a 'political, contestable designation'.[105] The two spheres are, in fact, implicated in each other';[106] personal lives reflect, and are embedded in, political decision-making and vice versa. State policies permeate family arrangements and, yet, without women's assignment to domestic labour, the pre-conditions for men's unencumbered participation in the public arena would not be met. The divide, then, is not only a function of patriarchy but also sustains it. Leaving the fabrication intact, therefore, would only be in the interests of the patriarchal status quo.

When subjected to analysis, the public/private distinction fails to be sustained. There is an obvious blending of the two spheres and O'Donovan maintains that '[t]he whole fabric of the personal life is imprinted with colours from elsewhere. Not to acknowledge this, and to pretend that the private is free, leads to a false analysis'.[107] Pateman also recognises that our personal lives are structured by public influence, 'by laws about rape and abortion, by the status of "wife", by policies on childcare and the allocation of welfare benefits and the sexual division of labor in the home and workplace'.[108]

For this reason, second-wave feminists have urged that problems designated 'personal' can only be solved through public means and political action. However, the consequence of critiquing the division in this way, according to Nicola Lacey, is that the 'solution' risks being framed in the very terms under critique.[109] In an attempt to do away with the dualism, in respect of domestic abuse, the 'solution' has been to map public sphere values onto private lives; specifically to have domestic abuse treated as a public concern and as if it were any other 'general' crime, as I explore now.

---

[104]Frances Olsen, 'Constitutional Law: Feminist Critiques of the Public/Private Distinction' (1993) 10 *Constitutional Commentary* 319–327.

[105]Frances Olsen, 'The Family and the Market: A Study of Ideology and Legal Reform' (1983) 96(7) *Harvard Law Review* 1496, 1497.

[106]Margot Young, 'Gender and Terrain: Feminists Theorize Citizenship' in Margaret Davies and Vanessa Munro (eds), *The Ashgate Research Companion to Feminist Legal Theory* (2013) 185.

[107]O'Donovan, *Sexual Divisions in Law* (n 40) 15.

[108]Carole Pateman, *The Disorder of Women: Democracy, Feminism and Political Theory* (Polity 1989) 118–140.

[109]Nicola Lacey, *Unspeakable Subjects: Feminist Essays in Legal and Social Theory* (Hart 1998) 83.

(iii) Treating Domestic Abuse as a Public Issue

In the area of domestic abuse, historically, as we have seen, the distinction was used to justify state inaction; privacy invoked immunity for male hegemonic practices, specifically violence in the home. It permitted what happened in the 'private sphere' to be considered wholly a concern between individuals, which there was no social responsibility to address.[110] What we see currently in criminal justice practice however is a reversal of approach, one that, however consciously, refuses to accede to classical liberal rhetoric about the value of privacy.

In Regina v C,[111] Lord Justice Moses in the Court of Appeal sums up the contemporary criminal justice approach. Here, a victim of domestic violence had made an emergency phone call to the police but did not wish, ultimately, to testify against the perpetrator. The Crown proceeded with the case to trial and subsequently appealed against the trial judge's decision to refuse to admit hearsay evidence of the complaint. The following passage is indicative of a system that is valiantly seeking to reverse the inadequate criminal justice approach of previous generations:

> To describe the particular partner, be it the woman (as it usually is) or a man as "the victim" conceals the truth of these cases, namely that the public are the victim. These cases are prosecuted not just in the interest of the particular person concerned who has been visited with violence, but in the interests of all of us. In that sense to describe it as "domestic violence" is an unfortunate term — it is violence, just as any other violence, and that is the concern of all of us.

The Court's understanding of 'private violence'[112] here goes further than suggesting that domestic violence is a public *concern*. It suggests that the public are the *victim*. It speaks to not only the 'particularity' of the offence vis-a-vis the victim, but also the crime's 'generality' vis-à-vis society.[113] It signals to those tasked with decision-making in such cases. It suggests that the 'public interest' is met through prosecution, irrespective of the views of the person who was subjected to the violence.

---

[110]Elizabeth Schneider, 'The Violence of Privacy' in Martha Fineman and Roxanne Myktiuk (eds), *The Public Nature of Private Violence: The Discovery of Domestic Abuse* (Routledge 1994) 43.

[111][2007] EWCA Crim 3463, para 13.

[112]Domestic violence is one form of 'private violence' in Fineman and Mykitiuk, *The Public Nature of Private Violence* (n 110).

[113]Elizabeth Schneider, *Battered Women and Feminist Lawmaking* (Yale University Press 2000) 65–73.

The judgement falls short of explaining *why* the public are the victim save to say that any violence is the concern of us all. The judges did not suggest that intimate partner abuse is a historic problem of sexism or a residue of male ownership of women. The judgement does not speak to women's subservient status in society, in the workplace or as carers. They do not propose their solution in a bid to tackle societal attitudinal norms or behaviours at a structural level. It falls short of asserting Madden-Dempsey's claim that committed prosecutions of violence against women will facilitate a less patriarchal state,[114] yet the dicta assists in effecting Madden-Dempsey's vision.

So, whilst the Court of Appeal does not attempt a diagnosis for the prevalence of male on female domestic violence, they do prescribe their preferred way forward: an interpretation of the rules of evidence to assist prosecutors in the future to pursue criminal convictions without victim support. The judgement expresses that 'the key to such cases [lies] in the published policy of the Crown Prosecution Service for prosecuting cases of domestic violence. Such cases are prosecuted not just in the interests of the particular person involved, but in the interests of the public as a whole'.[115] It supports feminists who have argued that domestic abuse should be treated as a public matter and, therefore, as crime.

Such a belief in the overriding public interest to prosecute domestic violence means that the state potentially falls into the trap that Lacey has cautioned against.[116] By mapping public sphere expectations and responses (criminal behaviour will be prosecuted) onto matters that take place between intimates in private, consequences follow. Firstly, there is a risk that private intimate partner coercion/patriarchy is simply replaced by public or state coercion/patriarchy.[117] The role of the state as protector can, paradoxically, render the state as oppressor. Secondly, when the state pursues a conviction irrespective of a victim's stated wishes, her personal experience and expressed wishes risk being erased as she becomes instrumentalised by the state. When the state is considered the victim, the *public* interest in prosecution trumps the victim's. When private violence is no longer insulated from society's

---

[114]Madden-Dempsey, *Prosecuting Domestic Violence* (n 60).

[115]R v C [2007] EWCA Crim 3463, para 13.

[116]Lacey, *Unspeakable Subjects* (n 109) 83.

[117]Coker warns about the potential for state action to simultaneously empower and disempower women: Donna Coker, 'Crime Control and Feminist Law Reform in Domestic Violence Law' (2001) *British Columbia Law Review* 801, 801. See also Linda Mills, 'Killing Her Softly: Intimate Abuse and the Violence of State Intervention' (1999) *Harvard Law Review* 550–613.

attention, should this mean the relinquishing of any notion of the value of private decision-making and privacy in people's lives?

The police and CPS radically altered their approach to the prosecution of domestic violence when they started to make pro-prosecution decisions in 2006.[118] This 'sameness of treatment' (of privately and publicly occurring violence) marked the seriousness with which law enforcement agencies would now be taking domestic violence and the equal treatment women could expect as victims before the criminal law. However, '[n]ow that it is generally accepted that domestic violence is wrong and against the law'[119] a more sophisticated analysis about how to prosecute violence between intimates, particularly when a victim expresses her wish for case discontinuance, is required. Decision-making that strives for the 'sameness of treatment' of privately and publicly occurring violence might be considered 'crude and non-discerning'.[120]

(iv) Retrieving the Affirmative Potential of Privacy

Whilst the concept of the private sphere has been overwhelmingly regarded as problematic for second-wave feminists as the facilitator of female oppression by allowing male domination in the home to pass with impunity, Boyd urges us to recognise an ideological division between the public and private as it can prove a useful concept for analysing evolving state action.[121] Schneider contends that simply ignoring the importance of privacy for battered women and opting for state intervention prevents the development of a 'more nuanced theory of where to draw the boundaries between public and private, and a theory of privacy that is empowering'.[122] Collapsing the public/private dichotomy into a single public realm is inadequate for survivors and overlooks their diverse needs and concerns. Whilst asserting the

---

[118]Jacqueline Sebire, 'The Policing of Intimate Partner Violence: Understanding Data and Managing Risk' (2015) Speaking at the Fighting Femicide Conference, Queen Mary University of London 6 November 2015.

[119]Home Office, 'Safety and Justice: The Government's Proposals on Domestic Violence' (HMSO 2003) 8.

[120]Fineman and Myktiuk, *The Public Nature of Private Violence* (n 110) 55.

[121]Susan Boyd, *Challenging the Public/Private Divide: Feminism, Law and Public Policy* (University of Toronto Press 1997) 4.

[122]Elizabeth Schneider, 'The Violence of Privacy' in Fineman and Myktiuk (eds), *The Public Nature of Private Violence* (n 110) 37.

'affirmative potential' in the concept of privacy,[123] feminists also try to assert its value without re-entrenching the false dichotomy between the purported public and private spheres.

As part of her consideration of feminist lawmaking for battered women, Schneider reminds us that feminism has not typically sought to defend 'privacy' because of its associations with individualism and its 'avoidance of a collective definition, systemic analysis and social responsibility'.[124] Nonetheless, she calls for us to consider that privacy can enable personal decision-making, opportunities for self-development, escape, autonomy, equality, liberty and bodily integrity.[125] Keenly aware that the concepts she valorises here speak to liberalism's individualistic registers and have, as such, received much feminist critique, Schneider nonetheless invites consideration of them because she asserts they are central to women's well-being. Okin similarly reflects on the opportunities privacy brings to develop intimate relationships, one's mental and creative capacities and the occasion to shed one's public 'role'.[126] In private, individuals have freedom to define themselves and choose how to live their lives, 'negotiating legitimately different views of the good life, freeing people from the constant burden of justifying their differences'.[127] Privacy thus affords individuals the capacity to realise their personal visions of a life worthy of a human being. So whilst the aspects of privacy being highlighted here connect to liberal notions of autonomous individuals, feminists simultaneously call for a 'symbolic "re-filling" of the contents of private freedom once the ideological load carried by liberalism's naturalizing constructions have been exposed'.[128] In other words, their respect for privacy does not demand commitment to a private *sphere* and all that the term entails.

Okin comments that liberalism's key contribution to gendered role assumptions has been its failure to perceive the family (the core of which is an intimate partnership, with or without children) as a political institution. Fineman, too, suggests re-thinking privacy to protect families'

---

[123]Ibid., 40. Lacey and Fineman also urge that privacy's value should be recognised and protected by the state and other powerful institutions in Lacey, *Unspeakable Subjects* (n 109) 82; Martha Fineman, *The Autonomy Myth* (The New Press 2004) 293.

[124]Elizabeth Schneider, 'The Violence of Privacy' (1990–1991) 23 *Connecticut Law Review* 973.

[125]Schneider, 'The Violence of Privacy' (n 122) 40.

[126]Susan Okin, 'Gender, the Public, and the Private' in Anne Phillips (ed), *Oxford Readings in Feminism: Feminism and Politics* (Oxford University Press 1998) 134.

[127]Jeffrey Rosen, *The Unwanted Gaze: The Destruction of Privacy in America* (Vintage Books 2001) 24.

[128]Pauline Johnson, 'Feminism and Public/Private Boundaries' in Harry Blatter, Pauline Johnson and Maria Markus (eds), *Modern Privacy: Shifting Boundaries, New Forms* (Palgrave Macmillan 2010) 41.

decision-making space, their 'authority to self-govern… [and their] right of self-definition'.[129] The private family entity Fineman envisages is simultaneously political; it is relational, integrated in society and is subsidised and supported by the state. Society's collective responsibility for its dependents and care-giving units should not, however, come at the expense of a correlative right of the state to control intimate decisions. For Fineman, recognising the special category of 'family' draws a line of privacy around the unit but 'privacy' here is 'an entity-based entitlement to self-government or autonomy' not a frame for 'separation, secrecy or seclusion'.[130] The line of 'privacy', Fineman notes, should never be used as a simple excuse to condone privately occurring abuses.

I am not proposing that we revert to the rhetoric of the public and private spheres. I simply want to draw attention to the value that privacy can have for victims and suggest that privacy is an aspect that, all other things being equal, prosecutors could bring into consideration. Privacy should not be synonymous with state inaction to the detriment of abused women, nor should a determination to treat privately occurring crime as any other publicly occurring crime mean mandatory arrest and prosecutions. Rather, prosecutors might consider the potential for acceding to a woman's 'decisional privacy' to permit and encourage her agency in her life.[131] In determining where to draw the boundaries of privacy, it might also be valuable to consider that the benefits for some women of privacy are that privacy (in the sense of freedom from regulation and state interference) is precisely what they want.

In addition to self-governance, a further attribute of privacy that I want to draw out is privacy's part in the 'creation of knowledge'.[132] Knowledge that is developed in the private sphere contrasts with 'public knowledge' which can be superficial, generalised and incomplete. Genuine knowledge of a person or relationship may only be ascertainable over the passage of time among a handful of close associates and a person's or situation's complexity may only be understood incrementally out of the gaze of public scrutiny.[133] Conceived in this way, information provided to prosecutors may only ever reveal partial truths about people and their relationships. Indeed,

[129]Martha Fineman, *The Autonomy Myth* (n 123) 303.

[130]Martha Fineman, 'What Place for Family Privacy?' (1999) 67 *George Washington Law Review* 1207.

[131]Schneider, *Battered Women and Feminist Lawmaking* (n 113) 89–90.

[132]Robert Post, 'Three Concepts of Privacy' (2001) 89(6) *Georgetown Law Journal* 2087, 2087.

[133]Rosen (n 127) 10.

'[a]ll public knowledge deals in stereotypes and generalizations, so that all individuals who become the subject of public knowledge risk misrepresentation'.[134] Those in the best position to possess 'true knowledge'[135] about a perpetrator and their relationship with the victim are likely to be those with insight into the complete picture.[136]

There is also a notable connection between privacy and dignity. Dignity refers to a state of being that is worthy of respect and is akin to decency. Dignity situates people within social relationships and communities and implies that individuals owe one another the social norms that allow self-worth.[137] Post suggests that certain professions are instrumentally organised and, for that reason, they can evade the social norms that exist in everyday interactions between people. When prosecutors consider survivors of domestic abuse simply as a means of providing the state the opportunity to express its abhorrence of domestic abuse, it is possible that prosecutors evade the norms of privacy as dignity as described by Post.

Finally, privacy might also be said to be a dimension of 'freedom'[138] as it permits individuals to carve out a space where they are permitted to define themselves.[139] The central tenet of liberal political theory is the idea that freedom means to be left alone, not interfered with, nor scrutinised.[140] This *negative* understanding of freedom as the absence of coercion or external constraints maintains the basis of freedom is to enjoy space which is 'not the law's business'.[141] I can therefore be said to be *negatively* free to the extent

---

[134]Post (n 132) 2090.

[135]Rosen (n 127) 8.

[136]Whilst I am clearly suggesting here that victims (or perhaps their support workers), as opposed to prosecutors, are likely to have this complete picture, discussion about when the victim may be so severely abused that she is no longer in a position to have objectivity about the perpetrator are considered more fully in Chapter 5. See Dennis Sacuzzo, 'How Should Police Respond to Domestic Violence: A Therapeutic Jurisprudence Analysis of Mandatory Arrest (1998) *Santa Clara Law Review* 765, 775 in which he identifies circumstances in which the victim may have become unable to voice her preferences.

[137]Post (n 132) 2092–2093.

[138]My appraisal of the value of freedom here clearly sits in contrast to the type of freedom and dignity that neoliberals envisage (see Chapter 3). For neoliberals, freedom and dignity are premised on the desirability of the rule of law, private property ownership and the competitive market. Polanyi criticises the neoliberal notion of freedom as likely 'degenerat[ing] into a mere advocacy of free enterprise' to the detriment of genuine freedoms enjoyable for all in Kari Polanyi, *The Great Transformation* (Beacon Press 1954).

[139]Rosen (n 127) 223.

[140]See, for example, Isaiah Berlin, 'Four Essays on Liberty' (Oxford University Press 2002).

[141]Wolfenden Committee, 'Report of the Committee of Homosexual Offences and Prostitution' (1957) cmd 247 HMSO.

that nobody interferes with my activities and choices. History has shown us, however, that this negative version of freedom has not assisted domestic violence victims and I do not propose, therefore, that it is a value to which prosecutors should adhere.

If *negative* freedom is the absence of regulation or, as Lacey puts it, 'being left in peace',[142] *positive freedom* acknowledges that there must be 'provision of certain positive goods and facilities'[143] by the state in order to enable freedom to be enjoyed. Feminists who prefer to think of freedom in this 'positive' way are aware that the state and its agents [in our example prosecutors] have the potential to both enhance the freedom privacy affords women and to threaten it.[144] To guard against the potential for the state to impact on freedom negatively, Nedelsky suggests we need to recognise that 'freedom' cannot exist without supporting relationships.[145] If the state wishes to enhance 'positive freedom', prosecutors could engage the question of how to foster supportive relationships (be they those with the perpetrator, the criminal justice system or elsewhere) for survivors in order to enable them to make free choices.[146]

From a feminist perspective, therefore, privacy could be re-drawn, not in terms of what the 'public sphere' ignores, but rather in terms of what a person has a right to exclude others from, or chooses to withdraw from public view.[147] Moreover, prosecutors might recognise that privately formed knowledge can represent the completest picture, and that respecting privacy is associated with respecting a person's dignity and positive freedom. Recognising the value of privacy in this way ought not, therefore, to be considered a 'wrong turn on the way to an answer'.[148]

When recognising the merits of privacy, I do not do so to re-entrench social or institutional divisions that perpetuate patriarchal structures by denying the private citizen or family political recognition. Rather, if the

---

[142]Lacey, *Unspeakable Subjects* (n 109) 77.

[143]Ibid., 77.

[144]Ibid., 77.

[145]Jennifer Nedelsky, *Law's Relations: A Relational Theory of Self, Autonomy and Law* (Oxford University Press 2011) 33.

[146]Ibid., 49. See Chapter 6 for a fuller discussion of how the theory of relational autonomy might guide prosecutors.

[147]Iris Marion Young, *Justice and the Politics of Difference* (Princeton University Press 1990) 120.

[148]Madden-Dempsey, *Prosecuting Domestic Violence* (n 60) 26 asserts that whilst the 'dichotomy generates neat analytic categories…[it is]…at the expense of obscuring the values that underlie the distinction' and that 'given the illegitimate use the distinction has been put in the context of domestic violence [creating a category of private in which some people are left free to exploit and abuse others with impunity] I believe the price we pay for its use is simply too high'.

decision whether or not to proceed with a domestic abuse case is in the balance, I simply wish to draw prosecutorial attention to the qualities of privacy and privately formed decision-making and the ways it might distinguish domestic abuse from other 'general crime'.

Part Three—The Legal Subject

(i) Criminal Law as a Blunt Instrument: The Legal Subject and Its Failure to Describe Abused Women's Subjectivities

In this final part of the chapter I outline feminist legal scholars' critique of the liberal legal person. Their critique offers further insight into how victims of domestic abuse were previously perceived and understood by criminal prosecutors and sheds light on why reluctant victims were frequently equated with non-credible witnesses, resulting in termination of the case. I also show how the liberal subject continues to be used as a 'standard' against which to assess abused women and motivates contemporary prosecutors to proceed in cases where a victim is no longer supportive.

Second-wave feminists' examination of the legal subject challenged law's claim to neutrality and genderlessness, and exposed law's inherent masculinity.[149] They showed that in seeking to treat everyone equally under the umbrella of the 'universal person', legal actors abstract individuals from social context.[150] In fact, the 'universal' qualities ascribed to the legal subject align with characteristics associated with the public actor; someone who acts with rationality, intelligence and self-sufficiency. This subject enters objectively into contracts, acts as the 'reasonable' man of tort law or as the unrestricted worker of employment law.[151] He is an impersonal individual who operates with emotional distance,[152] sovereign only to himself as a self-possessing logical creature. This masculine legal subject has evolved because 'privileged white men have populated law' and 'shaped it in their

[149]Rosemary Hunter, 'Contesting the Dominant Paradigm: Feminist Critiques of Liberal legalism' in Vanessa Munro and Margaret Davies, *The Ashgate Companion to Feminist Legal Theory* (Ashgate 2013) 13.

[150]Ngaire Naffine, *Law and the Sexes* (Allen and Unwin 1990).

[151]Hunter (n 149) 13.

[152]O'Donovan, *Sexual Divisions in Law* (n 40) 108–109.

own image'.[153] This subject's lineage can be traced to liberal philosophical understandings of the person.

Seeming to ignore difference, 'liberalism prefers to turn its face away from the diverse ways in which citizen identity is constructed'.[154] Liberals' universalistic approach tends to treat differences from the standard as 'anomalous or imaginary'.[155] As I have shown through my exploration of the characteristics of privacy, our identities, character and behaviours are at their most diverse, most pronounced and least constrained when they have been formed, expressed and iterated in the 'private' sphere. This is relevant for domestic abuse prosecutors because it serves as a reminder that there will be more than one way to understand domestic abuse victims and their intimate relationships (women's varied legal consciousness identified in Chapter 4 is illustrative).

The effect of recognising and privileging the 'paradigmatic legal person'[156] (or treating the 'masculine' as the norm) is the marginalisation of, inter alia, women.[157]

Ngaire Naffine has suggested that this analysis of the legal subject—in which it is alleged that men are the social and legal norm whilst women are excluded and exceptional—has started to look outdated. Modern legal personhood, she suggests, should be understood in a more multifaceted way than this simple critique of the liberal legal subject. However, of the 'cast of legal persons' that Naffine now identifies—rationalist, naturalist, legalist and religionist—the legal person that most resembles the liberal legal subject, 'the rationalist's person', 'has had the strongest purchase in criminal theory' and maintains a distinctively masculine bias.[158] For these reasons, as far as our problematic is concerned, second-wave legal feminism's early analysis of women's exclusion from the legal subject continues to resonate.

The paradigmatic 'rational' actor—or liberal legal subject—is at odds with those who do not reason in the way criminal law demands. Women, Naffine has observed, have not been able to develop a distinctively female

---

[153]Hunter (n 149) 13.

[154]Margaret Thornton, 'Embodying the Citizen' in Margaret Thornton (ed), *Public and Private: Feminist Legal Debates* (Oxford University Press 1995) 202.

[155]Ibid., 203.

[156]Ngaire Naffine, *Law's Meaning of Life* (Hart 2009) 66.

[157]Diane Polan, 'Towards a Theory of Law and Patriarchy' in David Kairy (ed), *The Politics of Law: A Progressive Critique* (Pantheon Book 1982) 95.

[158]Naffine identifies three further categories of legal person—naturalist, legalist and religionist—which she contends all maintain a masculine 'flavour'. See Ngaire Naffine, 'Women and the Cast of Legal Persons' in J Jones (ed), *Gender, Sexualities and the Law* (Routledge 2011) 15–25.

legal subjectivity because they are only recognised as women outside of the concept of the legal or public subject.[159] The 'private subject' has not generally been considered by law, Naffine notes, because, notionally, that is where the law does not encroach.[160] Nonetheless, she contends that the 'unofficial private subject of law' once again transpires to be sexed and male, denying women status even as private legal subjects[161]; 'in law the rational, knowing female subject …is an oxymoron'.[162] In essence then, the conventional understanding that women and men are equal before the law means that they are all treated as men, whilst female and other diverse subjects are dismissed.

Using domestic abuse by way of illustration, Naffine examines the legal response to abused women and, in so doing, spotlights the failures of law and legal actors. When abused women assert their right to remain with their abusive partner, Naffine suggests that 'the type of autonomy these women seek does not mesh well with the law's traditional view of the concept which is an all-or-nothing thing, developed in the public realm, where men are expected to relate to each other at a physical and emotional distance'.[163] When a woman withdraws her support for the prosecution of her abuser, in the eyes of the law and its agents, she fails to meet the expected or legitimate norm of acting 'reasonably'. By ignoring the many social, structural, physical and economic benefits of remaining with her '(not always) violent man',[164] or by discounting the many barrier-factors to leaving, a woman who retracts is attributed, at worst, antiquated notions of irrationality or, at least, the requirement to justify her decision. This necessitates an exploration of *her* pathology, not his.[165] In failing to meet the law's conception of its subject, women, not law became the object of criticism.

Instead of accepting that there may be many rational reasons and legitimate explanations for a woman's decision to withdraw her support for a criminal prosecution, law identifies the 'problem' as the woman's failure to understand what is in her and/or society's best interests. More than that, her

---

[159]Ngaire Naffine, 'Sexing the Subject (of Law)' in Margaret Thornton (ed), *Public and Private: Feminist Legal Debates* (Oxford University Press 1995) 20.

[160]Ibid., 21.

[161]Ibid., 21.

[162]Ibid., 21.

[163]Ibid., 31.

[164]Susan Boyd, *Challenging the Public/Private Divide: Feminism, Law and Public Policy* (University of Toronto Press 1997) 4.

[165]Naffine, 'Sexing the Subject (of Law)' (n 159) 33.

actions become diagnosed through 'battered women's syndrome', 'learned helplessness' or otherwise as 'vulnerability' due to her victimhood. Thus, her decision to stay becomes exceptional rather than natural; pathological rather than considered. Women's normal responses mean that women cannot be both distinctively women and, at the same time, legal subjects.[166] This analysis merits prosecutorial attention as failure to recognise the potential validity of the reasons behind the withdrawal of prosecutorial support risks elevating prosecutors into the position of asserting that they, not the woman herself, are best placed to know what is in her best interest.

Law's conception of the autonomous individual is someone who is free to leave any situation at will in accordance with their own choice. This clear division between the way the law conceives independence on the one hand and the way women live their lives is evidence of the legacy of women's relationship with the law as being 'other'. Thus, in reconceiving the 'legal subject'—as I do in Chapter 6—real women and their relational lives need to be recognised and legal rights, remedies and decision-making need to adequately reflect women's particularity.[167] Failure to do this will mean that, as legal 'others', women will not benefit from the law in the same way as men.

Naffine's work about perceptions of the legal subject speaks to the false dichotomy painted between women's victimisation and women's agency. Both concepts are too rigidly understood. On the one hand, there is great appeal in feminisms which promote women's agency and ability to effect change through individual will, choice and responsibility. However, the problem that arises is that those abused women who do not exit violent relationships are rendered 'victims by choice, despite the realities of gendered violence'.[168] Conversely, women activists have achieved recognition and change through spotlighting women's victimhood premised on gender subordination. Whilst being effective in calls for change, this has the unintended effect of fortifying the image of women as passive and fragile victims whilst at the same time failing to tackle the systemic nature of women's subordination.[169] 'Victimhood' is an effective rallying strategy because it piques sympathy and demands responsiveness. The danger of emphasising the helplessness or submissiveness of abused women though, is that, they are assumed to lack agency, so that any efforts they make to implement

[166]Ibid., 35.

[167]Ibid., 38.

[168]Schneider, *Battered Women and Feminist Lawmaking* (n 113) 76.

[169]Ibid., 74.

improved safety for themselves and their children by staying with their abusers, can be dismissed as 'pathological or incompetent',[170] whereas, the truth may be that incremental changes and gender-based obstacles are being negotiated. She may be doing this invisibly, possibly to mitigate separation assault, and she may be, for example, obtaining money, seeking support, acquiring information and building options.

By recognising the complex picture of women's resilience, we begin to appreciate that '[n]either concepts of agency or victimisation fully take account of women's experiences of oppression and resistance in relationships'.[171] At the same time, if the law and its agents only recognise two subject positions—agent (mirroring the masculine legal subject) or victim (reflecting the feminine exception in need of protection)—the law reproduces the false binary. Instead we might remind ourselves that agency (and legal personhood) is diverse, context specific and inconsistent. It will not always involve explicit opposition by the woman but behind the scenes she might be manoeuvring and mediating the dynamic. The 'all-or-nothing agency of liberal theory',[172] with its two polar options for domestic abuse victims; exit (exercising agency) or staying (indicating victimhood) simply do not reflect what might be going on for individual women. As I argue in Chapter 3, victim-centred discourse fortifies the two entrenched subject positions and underpins the contemporary commitment to pursuing prosecutions to protect 'vulnerable' victims. When the law relies on the polarising concept of the liberal legal subject, it is possible to see its limitations replicated in prosecutorial decision-making.

A more nuanced and context specific approach is also called for by Lewis and colleagues in assessing abused women's relationship with law and what they want law to achieve for them.[173] Calling for an end to the perception of domestic abuse victims as passive recipients of legal intervention they assert women as 'active agents, engaged in a complex process of active negotiation and strategic resistance'.[174] However, in Lewis' study they were also clear that women's agency frequently requires positive support from both their informal networks (friends, neighbours and family) and beyond (health services, social agencies, refuges, lawyers and counsellors). With the benefit of

---

[170] Martha Mahoney, 'Women's Lives, Violence and Agency' in Martha Fineman and Roxanne Mykitiuk (eds), *The Public Nature of Private Violence: The Discovery of Domestic Abuse* (Routledge 1994) 64.

[171] Ibid., 63.

[172] Schneider, *Battered Women and Feminist Lawmaking* (n 113) 85.

[173] Ruth Lewis et al., 'Protection, Prevention, Rehabilitation or Justice? Women's Use of the Law to Challenge Domestic Violence' (2000) 7(1–3) *International Review of Victimology* 179.

[174] Ibid., 179–180.

such networks, women may engage the law to fulfil objectives of protection, prevention, reform or justice. As such, legal intervention is unlikely to be sufficient on its own to end the violence[175] and women know this. However, invoking the law may allow women to reassert control in their relationship. By taking charge and using the law, women may gain leverage and a tool for managing conflict. Ford has therefore described law and criminal prosecutions as a 'power resource',[176] where a woman can use or threaten to use arrest and prosecutions by way of deterring their partner from further incidents.[177] Moreover, withdrawing support for the prosecution may be a way of seeking some sort of 'negotiated order' on her terms.[178]

Naffine highlighted how the law and its legal actors failed to understand the domestic abuse victim's commitment to her partner or the barriers to her leaving without questioning her rationality and reason. Modern domestic abuse prosecutorial policy offers a different emphasis; prosecutors are made aware that they should not have preconceptions about what a 'perfect victim' will look like.[179] Rather than dismissing a woman's decision to stay as irrational or questioning her credibility as a potential witness because of it, prosecutors are reminded that they 'need to understand the *vulnerability* of domestic abuse complainants'.[180]

A woman's decision to stay or withdraw her support for a prosecution has been re-framed by CPS policy to ensure that, instead of conceiving her as irrational, prosecutors recognise a woman's vulnerability. Indeed, the Guidance confirms that complainants may stay because they, 'will often not realise that they are in an abusive relationship'[181] and consequently her vulnerability extends to not knowing what is in her best (and safest) interests. Seeming to confirm this, a Chief Crown Prosecutor in Matthew Hall's 2009 work stated that women who withdraw their support may have 'very very low self-esteem. So that actually that individual might not be capable of making any major decisions about their lives because they're just totally undermined, feel pretty useless and downtrodden'.[182] In this way, though

[175]As Chapter 4 confirms.

[176]David Ford, 'Prosecution as a Victim Power Resource: A Note on Empowering Women in Violent Conjugal Relationships' (1991) *Law and Society Review* 313.

[177]William Goode, 'Force and Violence in the Family' (1971) *Journal of Marriage and the Family* 624.

[178]Ford (n 176) 320.

[179]Crown Prosecution Service, 'Domestic Abuse Guidelines for Prosecutors' (n 88).

[180]My emphasis. Ibid.

[181]Ibid.

[182]Matthew Hall, 'Prosecuting Domestic Violence: New Solutions to Old Problems' (2009) *International Review of Victimology* 255, 262.

the terminology may have altered and attempts at empathy have been made by the modern prosecutor, the effect is still the same. The woman's ability to form rational judgements in her own interest is potentially dismissed. Emphasising a woman's victimhood galvanises the prosecutor to prosecute; if she withdraws, she likely requires protection (through prosecution) because she has been manipulated or threatened into withdrawing; she may not know what is in her best interests due to learned helplessness or she may not have recognised that she has been experiencing coercive abuse because she has been gaslighted by her partner.

Bearing this in mind, we need to be move beyond monolithic understandings of victimhood by re-framing the legal subject bearing in mind her relationality and her potential to make decisions to facilitate her thrivership (as explored more fully in Chapter 6). Prosecutors working on an assumption that pursuing a case of domestic abuse is in the public interest—unless certain factors indicate otherwise—need to be aware of the potential of falling into the trap of thinking of the woman *only* as a victim. If an abused woman decides not to support a prosecution there should not be an automatic assumption that her decision has only been made due to her victimhood or inevitable vulnerability. She may well be practising active resilience. Such women are likely to be assessing how best to keep themselves and any children safe. They are likely to be assessing whether criminal prosecution will, amongst other things, anger the man further, assist her or support her in making the decision to leave, affect her children's relationship with their father, impose additional financial pressures or result in her partner being rehabilitated.[183] Prosecutors ought to be mindful that, at the point that she withdraws her support, the law may have been invoked to the extent that she required it for her own purposes.

(ii) Should Feminists Turn Away from Law? Criminal Law as a Site of Feminist Contestation

The legal subject needs to be reconceived not only to recognise 'women' but to recognise the diversity of women's lives. The ideal of the 'any personness'[184] of the legal subject is not sustainable. More than identifying the liberal subject to be a 'man of law'[185] or having 'a masculine flavour'[186] the

[183]Lewis et al. (n 173) 191.

[184]Naffine, *Law and the Sexes* (n 150) 148.

[185]Ibid., 148.

[186]Naffine 'Women and the Cast of Legal Persons' (n 158) 16.

above discussion exposes how women have historically been outsiders from the law and how law can be non-inclusive despite its purported objective to 'offer a universal, all embracing service'.[187]

If the law is flawed in this gendered way, should we not be pursuing Leigh Goodmark's call to de-criminalise domestic violence?[188] This book, at its heart, considers prosecutorial decision-making within the criminal justice system, seeking to assist those working within the existing legal order. By doing this, I am mindful of Smart's claim that 'in accepting law's terms to challenge law, feminism always concedes too much'.[189] Not only do I risk using the analytical parameters of patriarchal law to address (what is primarily) a feminist concern but I also accept a framework that is more and more being deployed by neoliberal agendas.[190] Neoliberalism's clear support of violence against women campaigning, as the following chapter confirms, strategically justifies 'punitive, carceral interventions that extend the surveillance and control to which citizens – including vulnerable women – are subject'.[191] The drawbacks of focusing on the prosecutorial response to domestic abuse can be summarised as threefold; firstly, the project risks leaving the law as it is (with women somehow being shoehorned into existing legal paradigms); secondly, in seeking to suggest improvements to prosecutorial praxis, it risks co-operating with potentially regressive neoliberal agendas; and thirdly, by default, it might also diminish state responsibility to provide and realise non-legal alternatives (housing, therapeutic and economic support) that women's best interests may also require.

Feminists have repeatedly made the mistake, according to Smart, of resorting to law. When we recognise the coincidence in history of the creation of both law and gendered divisions in society, she argues, we come to understand that law cannot resolve these societal structures of power.[192] The greatest latitude may come from *less* regulation so that alternative relationships and solutions can be developed.[193] Contrary to Madden-Dempsey's optimistic appraisal of the criminal law's potential for creating a just society

---

[187]Naffine, *Law and the Sexes* (n 150) 154.

[188]Leigh Goodmark, *De-criminalizing Domestic Violence: A Balanced Policy Approach to Gender Based Violence* (University of California Press 2018).

[189]Carol Smart, *Feminism and the Power of Law* (Routledge 1989) 5.

[190]Munro, 'Violence Against Women, "Victimhood" and the (Neo)Liberal State' (n 1) 242.

[191]Ibid., 192.

[192]Smart, *Feminism and the Power of Law* (n 189).

[193]Ibid., 84. See also Leigh Goodmark, *De-criminalizing Domestic Violence: A Balanced Policy Approach to Gender Based Violence* (University of California Press 2018).

through her vision of 'feminist' domestic abuse prosecutions, Smart is sceptical. Law, she cautions, does not hold the key to unlock patriarchy. Feminist jurisprudence only serves to maintain law's place in the hierarchy of solutions and outcomes. Smart argues that '[i]n constructing a new jurisprudence, feminists give a renewed legitimacy to the power of law to organise and regulate our lives'.[194] Perhaps it is better, she urges, to consider the value of law for feminism is simply as a rallying point for emergent accounts and visions. This project's engagement with the criminal law in the context of domestic abuse might therefore be an example of how Smart envisions law aiding feminists to think about their cause.

Yet, the law has the power to disqualify alternative discourse and resolutions outside of the law and can mislead us into thinking that only it holds the answer to alleviate women's oppression,[195] whereas non-legal alternatives may and ought to provide improved alternatives to legal solutions.[196] By relying on the pre-existing frames of law to achieve equality the solution becomes a need to change 'this' law or incorporate 'that' change, all the time trying to wrestle the solution into pre-existing procedures, language and emphases on adversarialism and 'winning' the case rather than seeking the truth or the most beneficial outcome.[197] Polan summarises thus, 'the whole structure of law, its hierarchal organisation, its combative adversarial format; and its undeviating bias in favour of rationality over all other values-defines it fundamentally as a patriarchal institution'.[198] On this account, small efforts to change the pre-existing legal order, such as this project, will be inadequate.

However, there is value in pursuing the aims of the book on the basis that women still need to be able to use the law, and as Hunter points out, often have no choice in being 'hauled' before it.[199] For abused women who call the police in an emergency situation, and then find themselves an indispensable part of the criminal justice machine, this is particularly so. Sandland,

[194]Ibid., 184.

[195]The danger of this perception is that it creates reactionary positivist alternatives as the only credible way to challenge it. See Carol Smart's critique of Catherine MacKinnon in Smart, *Feminism and the Power of Law* (n 189) 71.

[196]Deborah Epstein, 'Effective Intervention in Domestic Violence Cases: Rethinking the Roles of Prosecutors, Judges, and the Court System' (1999) 11 *Yale JL & Feminism* 3; See also Goodmark, *Decriminalizing Domestic Violence* (n 193) and Leigh Goodmark, *A Troubled Marriage: Domestic Violence and the Legal System* (New York University Press 2012).

[197]Naffine, *Law and the Sexes* (n 150).

[198]Polan (n 157) 301.

[199]Rosemary Hunter, 'The Power of Feminist Judgments?' (2012) 20 *Feminist Legal Studies* 143.

too, urges less pessimism about law's potential. He contends that reforms do not inevitably result in a simple reconfiguration of the maleness of the law and that real improvements have and can be shown to have been made since Smart wrote her groundbreaking work.[200] The feminist project can have impact on the law and the law, contrary to past accusations, has been receptive to feminist challenge.[201] Accordingly, calling for ameliorations to criminal justice responses and developing feminist theory to assist prosecutorial decision-making remain valid objectives.

Conclusion

Domestic abuse and the prosecutorial response should not be considered ahistorical, apolitical and nor should either be abstracted from social facts.[202] Rather, violence against women exists as part of the historical and social constructions that have permitted men's privilege over women. Social, cultural, legal and political relationships between men and women generated an ideology and moral order that has sanctioned men's use of violence against their female partners. Current government strategies and CPS policies to end violence against women, determinedly aim to dismantle such past tolerance of intimate partner abuse and strong prosecutions are intended to demonstrate contemporary societal condemnation of such abuse. If preceding criminal justice responses demonstrated a reticence to intervene in domestic violence and reflected 'institutional indifference',[203] current prosecutorial policy aims to denounce the past approach, to recognise domestic abuse as 'real crime' to be taken seriously and to make amends.

Feminists cited the public and private divide as a patriarchal construction that underpins gender inequality. The dichotomy also played a part in past state tolerance of domestic abuse and its failure to effectively criminalise what was considered a private matter. Second-wave feminists called on the state to regulate violence and abuse in the private sphere just as it would violence in the public sphere. Notwithstanding the considerable improvements for abused women of the police and prosecution presumption to

[200]Ralph Sandland, 'Between "Truth" and "Difference": Poststructuralism, Law and the Power of Feminism' (1995) 3(1) *Feminist Legal Studies* 3.

[201]Hunter, 'The Power of Feminist Judgments?' (n 199) 135.

[202]Dobash and Dobash refer to this as a 'context specific approach' in Dobash and Dobash, *Violence Against Wives* (n 2) 26.

[203]Dobash and Dobash, 'Love, Honour and Obey' (n 12) 410.

arrest and prosecute, I have suggested that simply mapping legal responses from publicly occurring violence onto privately occurring intimate partner abuse is inadequate. Without recognising the particular qualities of privately occurring crime, there is potential for intimate partner coercion simply to be replaced with state coercion and for the stated wishes of the victim to be overlooked in preference for what is perceived to be in the 'public interest'. I have proposed that prosecutors have regard for a woman's privacy to the extent that her private decision is based on a more complete picture than information held about her in the public sphere. Moreover, in respecting her privately made decision, prosecutors might respect her dignity and freedom.

Finally, in this chapter, I drew attention to the feminist critique of the invulnerable liberal legal subject as a means of describing women's lives. In responding to the critique, I argued that the CPS has brought the vulnerability and victimhood of abused women to the fore (as I further explore in Chapter3). The emergent binary construction of victim/agent fails sensitively to describe women as they navigate their abusive relationship. I outlined how the liberal subject is now used as a benchmark to assess how vulnerable a woman is and, as a result, how in need of state protection through prosecution she is. To sum up, I have reasoned that a more theoretically rich account of privacy, combined with a nuanced reanalysis of the legal subject (as explored further in Chapter 6), might properly form part of prosecutorial decision-making.

The next chapter considers how neoliberalism's turn to criminalisation has harnessed the demands of feminists outlined in this chapter to boost its own appeal and justify the criminal justice priority.

References

Ashworth G and Bonnerjea L, *The Invisible Decade: UK Women and the U.N. Decade for Women, 1976–1985* (Gower 1985).

Atkins and Brenda Hoggett, *Women and the Law* (Basil Blackwell 1984).

Auchmuty R and Rackley E, *Women's Legal Landmarks: Celebrating 100 Years of Women and Law in the UK and Ireland* (Bloomsbury 2018).

Barnett H, *Introduction to Feminist Jurisprudence* (Cavendish 1998).

Benn S and Gaus G, *Private and Public in Social Life* (Croom Helm 1993).

Berlin I, *Four Essays on Liberty* (Oxford University Press 2002).

Binney V, Harkell G and Nixon J in conjunction with Women's Aid Federation/ Department for Environment, *Leaving Violent Men: A Study of Refuges and Housing for Battered Women* (King's English Book Printers 1981).

Blatter H, Johnson P and Markus M, *Modern Privacy: Shifting Boundaries, New Forms* (Palgrave Macmillan 2010).

Bograd M and Yllo K, *Feminist Perspectives on Wife Abuse* (Sage 1990).

Boyd S, *Challenging the Public/Private Divide: Feminism, Law and Public Policy* (University of Toronto Press 1997).

Brophy J and Smart C, *Women in Law: Explorations in Law, Family and Sexuality* (Routledge & Kegan Paul 1985).

Charlton C, 'The First Cow on Chiswick High Road' (1972) *Spare Rib* 24.

Cobbe F, 'Wife Torture in England' (1878) *Contemporary Review* 55.

Coker D, 'Crime Control and Feminist Law Reform in Domestic Violence Law' (2001) *British Columbia Law Review* 801.

Conaghan J, 'Book Review: Vanessa Munro *Law and Politics at the Perimeter: Re-evaluating Key Debates in Feminist Theory*' (2009) *Feminist Legal Studies* 229.

Crown Prosecution Service, 'Domestic Abuse Guidelines for Prosecutors' (2014) available at https://www.cps.gov.uk/legal-guidance/domestic-abuse-guidelines-prosecutors accessed 19 November 2019.

Davies M, *Asking the Law Question* (3rd edn, Thomson 2008).

Davies M and Munro V, *The Ashgate Research Companion to Feminist Legal Theory* (Routledge 2013).

D'Cruze S and Crewe I, *Everyday Violence in Britain 1850–1950: Gender and Class* (Pearson 2000).

Dobash R and Dobash RE, 'Love, Honour and Obey: Institutional Ideologies and the Struggle for Battered Women' (1977) *Contemporary Crisis* 403.

———, *Rethinking Violence Against Women* (Sage 1998).

———, *Violence Against Wives: A Case Against the Patriarchy* (Free Press, New York 1979).

Erturk Y, 'Integration of the Human Rights of Women and the Gender Perspective: Violence Against Women: The Due Diligence Standards as a Tool for the Elimination of Violence Against Women' (2006) Report of the Special Rapporteur on Violence against Women, its Causes and Consequences, to the United Nations Commission on Human Rights, E/CN.4/2006/61.

Fineman M, *The Autonomy Myth* (The New Press 2004).

———, 'What Place for Family Privacy?' (1999) 67 *George Washington Law Review* 1207.

Fineman M and Myktiuk R, *The Public Nature of Private Violence: The Discovery of Domestic Abuse* (Routledge 1994).

Ford D, 'Prosecution as a Victim Power Resource: A Note on Empowering Women in Violent Conjugal Relationships' (1991) *Law and Society Review* 313.

Gilligan C, *In a Different Voice: Psychological Theory and Women's Development* (Harvard University Press 1993).

Goode W, 'Force and Violence in the Family' (1971) *Journal of Marriage and the Family* 624.

Goodmark L, *De-criminalizing Domestic Violence: A Balanced Policy Approach to Gender Based Violence* (University of California Press 2018).
Gottschalk M, *The Prison and the Gallows: The Politics of Mass Incarceration in America* (Cambridge University Press 2006).
Hall M, 'Prosecuting Domestic Violence: New Solutions to Old Problems' (2009) *International Review of Victimology* 255.
Home Office, 'Safety and Justice: The Government's Proposals on Domestic Violence' (HMSO 2003).
House of Commons Select Committee, 'Report on Violence in the Family' (HMSO 1975).
Houston C, 'How Feminist Theory Became (Criminal) Law: Tracing the Path to Mandatory Criminal Intervention in Domestic Violence Cases' (2014) 21 *Michigan Journal of Gender and Law* 217.
Hoyle C and Sanders A, 'Police Response to Domestic Violence: From Victim Choice to Victim Empowerment'(2000)' 40 *British Journal of Criminology* 14.
Hunnicutt G, 'Varieties of Patriarchy and Violence Against Women: Resurrecting "Patriarchy" as a Theoretical Tool' (2009) 15(5) *Violence Against Women* 553.
Hunter R, 'The Power of Feminist Judgments?' (2012) 20 *Feminist Legal Studies* 143.
Jones J, *Gender, Sexualities and the Law* (Routledge 2011).
Kahan D, 'Gentle Nudges vs. Hard Shoves: Solving the Sticky Norms Problem' (2000) *University of Chicago Law Review* 607.
Kairy D, *The Politics of Law: A Progressive Critique* (Pantheon Book 1982).
Lacey N, *Unspeakable Subjects: Feminist Essays in Legal and Social Theory* (Hart 1998).
Lewis et al, 'Protection, Prevention, Rehabilitation or Justice? Women's Use of the Law to Challenge Domestic Violence' (2000) 7(1–3) *International Review of Victimology* 179.
MacKinnon C, 'Feminism, Marxism, Method, and the State: Toward Feminist Jurisprudence' (1983) Signs 635.
———, *Toward a Feminist Theory of State* (Harvard University Press 1989).
Madden-Dempsey M, *Prosecuting Domestic Violence: A Philosophical Analysis* (Oxford University Press 2009).
Maxfield M, *Fear of Crime in England and Wales, Home Office Research Study No. 78* (HMSO 1984).
Millet K, *Sexual Politics* (Virago 1970).
Mills L, 'Killing Her Softly: Intimate Abuse and the Violence of State Intervention' (1999) *Harvard Law Review* 550.
Munro V, *Law and Politics at the Perimeter: Re-evaluating Key Debates in Feminist Theory* (Hart 2007).
Naffine N, *Law and the Sexes* (Allen and Unwin 1990).
———, *Law's Meaning of Life* (Hart 2009).

Nedelsky J, *Law's Relations: A Relational Theory of Self, Autonomy and Law* (Oxford University Press 2011).
O'Donovan K, *Sexual Divisions in Law* (Weidenfeld and Nicolson 1985).
Okin S, *Justice, Gender and the Family* (Basic Books 1989).
Olsen F, 'Constitutional Law: Feminist Critiques of the Public/Private Distinction (1993) 10 *Constitutional Commentary* 319–327.
———, 'The Family and the Market: A Study of Ideology and Legal Reform' (1983) 96(7) *Harvard Law Review* 1496.
Pateman C, *The Disorder of Women: Democracy, Feminism and Political Theory* (Polity 1989).
Patmore C, *The Angel in the House* (4th edn, Macmillan 1866).
Pizzey, *Scream Quietly or the Neighbours Will Hear* (Penguin 1974).
Post R, 'Three Concepts of Privacy' (2001) 89(6) *Georgetown Law Journal* 2087.
Pugh M, *Women and the Women's Movement in Britain, 1914–1999* (Macmillan 2000).
Rosen J, *The Unwanted Gaze: The Destruction of Privacy in America* (Vintage Books 2001).
Rousseau J, *A Discourse on Political Economy (translated from Oeuvres Completes)* (Plaiade 1959–1969) Volume 3.
Ruskin J, *Sesame and Lillies* (Smith, Elder and Co 1864).
Sacuzzo D, 'How Should Police Respond to Domestic Violence: A Therapeutic Jurisprudence Analysis of Mandatory Arrest' (1998) *Santa Clara Law Review* 765.
Sandland R, 'Between "Truth" and "Difference": Poststructuralism, Law and the Power of Feminism' (1995) 3(1) *Feminist Legal Studies* 3.
Schneider E, *Battered Women and Feminist Lawmaking* (Yale University Press 2000).
———, 'The Violence of Privacy' (1990–1991) 23 *Connecticut Law Review* 973.
Smart C, *Feminism and the Power of Law* (Routledge 1989).
Stark E and Flitcraft A, *Women at Risk: Domestic Violence and Women's Health* (Sage 1996).
Thornton M, *Public and Private: Feminist Legal Debates* (Oxford University Press 1995).
Turner M, *The Women's Century* (The National Archives 2003).
Walby S, *Theorizing Patriarchy* (Blackwell 1990).
Wolfenden Committee, 'Report of the Committee of Homosexual Offences and Prostitution' (1957) cmd 247 HMSO.
Young I, *Inclusion and Democracy* (Oxford University Press 2002).
———, *Justice and the Politics of Difference* (Princeton University Press 1990).

3

Neoliberalism, the CPS and Tenacious Domestic Abuse Prosecutions

Introduction

Neoliberal politics have permeated culture and society in Britain since at least the advent of Thatcherism.[1] In this chapter, I map and consider the part played by an era of neoliberalism on domestic abuse prosecutorial practices. I explore how neoliberalism has contributed to a strengthened state commitment to tackle domestic abuse through increased criminalisation. Neoliberal governments have embraced aspects of the feminist movement,[2] and this chapter therefore builds on and further contextualises the feminist discourses regarding domestic abuse examined in the preceding chapter. As increased criminal prosecutions publicly confront women's subordination in the private sphere, challenge sexist ideologies that tolerate abuse and promise women's protection, a criminal justice response has typically been demanded by many in the women's movement but usually only as part of a range of

[1]Emma Bell points to Alexander Rustow, the 1930s German economist, as the person who first identified and labelled those ideologically opposed to state interventionism in Emma Bell, *Criminal Justice and Neoliberalism* (Palgrave MacMillan 2011) 39. Whilst Jock Young suggests that policies associated with neoliberal politics emerged in the 1960s in Jock Young, 'Searching for a New Criminology of Everyday Life: A Review of "The Culture of Control" by David Garland' (2002) 43(1) *British Journal of Criminology* 228, 228.

[2]See, for example, Kristin Bumiller, *In an Abusive State: How Neoliberalism Appropriated the Feminist Movement Against Sexual Violence* (Duke University Press 2008); Nancy Fraser, 'Feminism, Capitalism, and the Cunning of History: An Introduction' (2012) FMSH-WP2012-17; and Vanessa Munro, 'Violence Against Women, "Victimhood" and the (Neo)Liberal State' in Vanessa Munro and Margaret Davies (eds), *Ashgate Research Companion to Feminist Legal Theory* (Ashgate 2013) 234.

A. Porter, *Prosecuting Domestic Abuse in Neoliberal Times*, Palgrave Socio-Legal Studies,
https://doi.org/10.1007/978-3-030-61369-3_3

community, education and welfare responses. A shared desire amongst feminists and neoliberal politicians for effective criminal responses to intimate partner abuse has resulted, I argue in this chapter, in a government preference for using criminal law at the expense of developing alternative and complementary solutions. I draw out some of the shortcomings of the neoliberal priority in this chapter.

The campaigning work of feminists was only one part in the transformation that has taken place within criminal justice in the last four decades. For, at the same time feminists were demanding strong state action in response to domestic violence, Britain experienced a rise in neoliberal political ideology and, concomitantly, powerful developments within the criminal justice and penal fields. Garland has rightly suggested, therefore, that 'the feminist revolution and the changing place of women were only one thread in a denser texture of social transformation'.[3] State techniques to control crime in the last 40 years have experienced a perceptible shift away from the prevailing twentieth-century norm of penal-welfarism and its associated correctional philosophy. As neoliberalism has risen to prominence, what also appears to have emerged is an 'intensification of punitiveness'[4] where offender rehabilitation is considered a failing ideal and its emphasis downgraded.[5] Wider than penal severity, the same period has seen an assertion of the criminal justice system as a vehicle to bring crime, order and people's sense of security under control. Both the 'punitive turn'[6] and the crime control imperative have resulted in, symbolically at least, an evolution from 'welfare state' to 'penal State'.[7]

Modern state treatment of domestic abuse, I argue, has become part of these overarching trends towards both tougher and preventive state responses to crime. Neoliberal ideology, together with its techniques of implementation, has embraced a women's movement that was focused on levering domestic abuse up the political agenda. The neoliberal state's response has been to move violence against women up the criminal justice agenda. The respective ambitions of the two movements, when combined, have effected a tenacious pursuit by prosecutors of abusers through the criminal courts.

---

[3]David Garland, 'Beyond the Culture of Control' (2004) *Critical Review of International Social and Political Philosophy* 160, 178.

[4]Bell (n 1) 119.

[5]David Garland, *The Culture of Control: Crime and Social Order in Contemporary Society* (Oxford University Press 2001) 8.

[6]Ibid., 142.

[7]Jonathan Simon, *Governing Through Crime: How the War on Crime Transformed American Democracy and Created a Culture of Fear* (Oxford University Press 2007) 6.

Part One

(i) Neoliberalism: Values, Strategies and Practices

Neoliberalism is, broadly, a philosophy that esteems economic rather than political freedom.[8] It is not, however, a singular economic strategy. It is a political economy and a theory or way of organising political and economic activity.[9] At the fore is a commitment to market fundamentalism, unhindered by regulation, to generate maximum prosperity.[10] Its governments strive for efficiency and value for money through free-market solutions. Neoliberalism thus champions the 'superiority of individualised, market-based competition over other modes of organisation'.[11] Its moral project, too, considers markets a 'necessary condition for freedom in other aspects of life'.[12]

The state's role in neoliberal theory is to favour the institutions that facilitate the free functioning of markets and free trade. Market competition is encouraged and the state aims to honour individual freedoms by facilitating choice between competing enterprises. With the primacy of the market at the fore, it is the market that comes to shape social and political decisions. The state becomes responsive to market demands; corporations are liberated whilst trade unions are curbed.[13] In addition to its preference for markets, the neoliberal state affects the conditions or frameworks within which people operate by favouring private individual property rights and the authority or rule of law.[14] Typically, neoliberalism is associated with stripping back the welfare state to enable reduced taxation and encourage individual betterment.

---

[8]Keith Tribe, 'Liberalism and Neoliberalism in Britain' in Philip Mirowski and Dieter Plehwe (eds), *The Road from Mont Pelerin: The Making of the Neoliberal Thought Collective* (Harvard University Press 2009) 68.

[9]John Campbell and Ove Pedersen, *The Rise of Neoliberalism and Institutional Analysis* (Princeton University Press 2001).

[10]Robert Reiner, 'Foreword' in Bell (n 1) ix.

[11]Stephanie Mudge, 'The State of the Art: What Is Neo-liberalism?' (2008) *Socio-Economic Review* 703, 706–707.

[12]Marion Fourcade and Kieran Healey, 'Moral Views of Market Society' (2007) 33 *Annual Review of Sociology* 285, 287.

[13]Susan George, 'A Short History of Neoliberalism' (1999) Conference in Economic Sovereignty in a Globalising World, Bangkok available at https://www.tni.org/en/article/short-history-neoliberalism accessed 20 April 2018.

[14]David Harvey, *A Brief History of Neoliberalism* (Oxford University Press 2005) 64.

However, it would be wrong to present neoliberalism as a coherent set of principles. Rather, neoliberalism ought to be considered multi-faceted and fragmented in its manifestations.[15] There may not, therefore, be a 'preconceived gospel'[16] of neoliberalism that one can neatly refer to; rather, there may be 'incongruous conclusions on specific questions in different locations'.[17] Neoliberalism in practice appears to have departed from any rigid dogmatic theory and its dilution or dismemberment comes as a result of its responsiveness to particular events which tend to add unique flavour or character to its practice dependent on context.[18] It is subject to adaptations that vary between regions and over time, rarely pausing long enough to be pinned down.[19] In particular, neoliberalism, it has been argued, has been shaped and defined at moments of economic crisis.[20] Nonetheless, key characteristics identify neoliberal thought and practice and it is possible to trace its manifestations into criminal justice practice. Bell suggests that dominant neoliberal characteristics have influenced, shaped and justified crime control priorities in Britain since around 1993.[21]

The crisis decade of the 1970s and its years of recession is now widely considered the 'major axis' after which the ideologies of the New Right and its associated theory, neoliberalism, were able to take hold.[22] However, the ideological seeds of neoliberalism were planted before its shoots were visible in political practice. The 'thought collective' or 'self-conscious communal project'[23] known as the Mont Pelerin Society, founded in 1947 by Friedrich Hayek and Milton Friedman, is widely attributed as marking the genesis of the philosophical and political ideas and ideals of neoliberalism.[24] Reagan

[15]Philip Mirowski, 'Defining Neoliberalism' in Mirowski and Plehe (n 8), 433.

[16]Nicholas Gane, 'Book Review: The Road from Mont Pelerin: The Making of the Neoliberal Thought Collective' (2012) 60(4) *The Sociological Review* 777, 778.

[17]Mirowski and Plehwe (n 8) 29–30.

[18]Harvey (n 14) 64.

[19]Ibid., 70; Pat O'Malley, 'Neoliberalism, Crime and Criminal Justice' (2016) 16(10) Sydney Law School Research Paper, 6 available at https://ssrn.com/abstract=2729627 accessed 17 May 2018.

[20]Jamie Peck, 'Zombie Neoliberalism and the Ambidextrous State' (2010) 14(1) *Theoretical Criminology* 104, 106 in which Peck describes neoliberalism as a 'creature of crisis'.

[21]Bell identifies the British 'punitive turn' from 1993 in Bell (n 1) 8.

[22]Young (n 1) 228.

[23]Philip Mirowski, 'Book Review: A Brief History of Neoliberalism' (2008) 24(1) *Economics and Philosophy* 111, 112.

[24]Mirowski and Plehwe (n 8) 5. Though see Nicolas Gane's article about the history of neoliberalism which urges us to consider neoliberal thought beginning as early as the 1920s with Ludwig Von Mises; Nicholas Gane, 'The Emergence of Neoliberalism: Thinking Through and Beyond Michel Foucault's Lectures on Biopolitics' (2014) 31(4) *Theory, Culture and Society* 3.

and Thatcher did not, therefore, originate the ideas of neoliberalism; rather they 'took what had hitherto been minority political, ideological and intellectual positions and made them mainstream'.[25]

Neoliberal doctrine opposes Keynesian state interventionist theory and centralised state planning. It considers state decision-making to be weakened by the potential for political bias whereas market signals provide the most accurate information. Yet, as I explore later in the context of neoliberal approaches to crime, at neoliberalism's heart is a 'fundamental paradox: as [state] power becomes less restrictive, less corporeal, it also becomes more intense, saturating the fields of actions and possible actions'.[26] So, whilst neoliberalism may emphasise a rolling back of the state, there is a simultaneous desire to build a strong state within which people may operate freely. Foucault talked about this new art of governance thus:

> It [government] must produce it [freedom], it must organise it... The new art of government therefore appears as the management of freedom... Liberalism must produce freedom, but this very act entails the establishment of limitations, controls, forms of coercion and obligations relying on threats etcetera.[27]

Read, too, describes that neoliberalism does not restrict behaviours directly, rather, it works on the conditions within which people operate.[28] Yet, in the field of crime control, neoliberalism has gone further than indirectly managing the conditions of being; in this area the so-called light touch state impacts much more directly. It would be wrong, therefore, to conceive neoliberalism as an ideology that definitively adheres to reducing state involvement in citizens' lives. Rather, it is committed to creating free spaces within which people can, in theory, profit.

Neoliberalism does not merely operate in the political and economic realm. More widely, it can also be conceived as 'the production of a particular conception of human nature, a particular form of subjectivity'.[29] Its presence can be felt in all aspects of the way we conduct ourselves and the way social and work life is performed, organised and managed. It has become the common hegemonic currency of our times which is presented in the absence

---

[25]Harvey (n 14) 62.

[26]Jason Read, 'A Genealogy of Homo-Economicus: Neoliberalism and the Production of Subjectivity' (2009) *Foucault Studies* 25, 29.

[27]Michel Foucault, *The Birth of Bio-Politics: Lectures at the College de France (1978–79)* translated by Graham Burchell (Palgrave MacMillan 2008) 63 cited in ibid., 29.

[28]Read (n 26) 29.

[29]Ibid., 26.

of alternative possibilities. Neoliberalism, Read argues, is thus not merely a transformation *in* ideology (from its classical liberal predecessor), it is a transformation *of* ideology that pervades everyday experiences and extends across social spaces.[30]

Next, I explore three core values that neoliberalism promotes and show how these ideals have fed into common consciousness. More particularly, I show how they underpin contemporary criminological understandings of crime and how the state should respond to transgressions. This has implications for state treatment of domestic abuse and helps explain why the primary state response to domestic abuse has been to respond to it as crime.

(ii) Neoliberal Valorisation of Freedom, Individualism and Responsibilisation

Neoliberal valorisations of freedom, individualism and responsibilisation can be contrasted with penology's post-war rehabilitative ideal which coincided with the birth of the welfare state. Bell argues that the state's belief in a 'criminal's' rehabilitative potential together with a commitment to welfarism in this period, is no coincidence. Rather, they are indicative of a state that had confidence in its ability to help and restore criminal offenders and a sense that it could also fix and remedy social disparities and misfortune.[31] If criminal offending was caused by such structural factors, addressing these, according to prevailing post-war logic, would reduce offending. The rehabilitative ideal is consistent with social democratic tenets of communitarianism, group membership and the conception of reciprocity between state and individual.[32] The Keynesian post-war British state gave way in the late 1970s and 1980s to a 'strongly articulated vision of a more individualistic society of self-reliant citizens'.[33]

Thatcher's incoming 1979 government made it plain that welfare provision would be reserved only for those who really needed it and that individuals had the responsibility to make a success of their lives because they had been afforded the market conditions to succeed.[34] This narrative saw the

---

[30]Ibid., 25.

[31]Bell (n 1) 65.

[32]Nicola Lacey, 'Punishment, (Neo)Liberalism and Social Democracy' in Jonathan Simon and Richard Sparks, *The Handbook of Punishment and Society* (Sage 2012) 260, 264.

[33]Ibid., 262.

[34]The Conservative Party, '1979 Conservative Party General Election Manifesto' http://www.conservativemanifesto.com/1979/1979-conservative-manifesto.shtml accessed 13 January 2018.

decline of state social support, particularly to those hitherto considered the most vulnerable. Neoliberalism became the antidote to state welfarism[35] and individual freedom and responsibility became the replacement strategies of rule. Neoliberals 'encourage people to see themselves as individualised and active subjects responsible for enhancing their own well- being.... We are all encouraged to "work on ourselves"'.[36] Earning becomes linked to pride, purpose, self-esteem and inclusion, whilst those who do not capitalise on opportunities, and who remain financially dependent on the state, lack identity, stability, commitment and purpose.[37] Welfare recipients, Rose argues, become a breed of 'failing quasicitizen' because they have failed to take advantage of market freedoms and have failed to take individual responsibility for self-advancement.[38]

The idea that hard work will reap rewards is, I argue, an example of 'common sense' rhetoric typical of neoliberal politics.[39] Viewed this way, responsibilisation is rendered the essential, even natural way for social order to be arranged.[40] Neoliberalism has become the new ideological hegemony because its political leadership has an ability to construct 'subject positions' that make sense to people across the social spectrum.[41] Governmental discourse about responsibility is deployed not simply as rhetoric (which suggests a superficial dissemination of ideas) but more as a 'system of meaning' that shapes and comes to constitute people's practices and identities.[42] This more profound shift in belief systems, it has been argued—and as I argue with respect to the impact of neoliberalism on feminist violence against women discourse—is to the detriment of critical engagement with issues and obfuscation of the systemic roots of people's day-to-day problems.[43] The next section looks at how this neoliberal ideology manifests in neoliberal criminology.

[35]Bell (n 1) 140.

[36]Wendy Larner, 'Neo-liberalism: Policy, Ideology and Governmentality' (2000) 63(1) *Studies in Political Economy* 5, 13.

[37]Nikolas Rose, 'Community, Citizenship and the Third Way' (2000) 43(9) *American Behavioral Scientist* 1395, 1407.

[38]Ibid., 1407.

[39]Harvey (n 14) 39.

[40]Ibid., 41.

[41]Stuart Hall, 'The Toad in the Garden: Thatcherism Among the Theorists' in Carey Nelson and Lawrence Grossberg (eds), *Marxism and the Interpretation of Culture* (Macmillan Education 1988).

[42]Larner (n 36) 12.

[43]Harvey (n 14) 39.

(iii) Neoliberalism and Increased Criminalisation

Neoliberalism, and the associated decline of social democracy, has frequently been linked by scholars to the punitive turn.[44] Indeed, there might now be considered a body of work constituting the 'neoliberalism-as-penality thesis'.[45] Before I critique and draw into question this straightforward cause and effect paradigm, I want to outline the various ways in which the connection between neoliberalism and the punitive turn has been made.

The first link between neoliberalism and increased penality flows from the value placed by neoliberals on freedom, individualism and responsibility. For those who do not proactively seek self-improvement and who do not exercise their freedom responsibly and instead commit crime, the same trumpeted tenets can be used against them to justify prosecutions and tough carceral and community penalties. For, when all citizens are given equal freedom to access resources for personal growth, any commission of crime becomes understood as an individual 'choice' to commit crime from a range of opportunities.[46]

This idea of a rationally thinking criminal who *chooses* to violate the law was articulated by James Wilson in 1975 and became defining in neoliberal criminology.[47] If criminals operate strategically to make some gain or profit (rather than being understood as acting from drivers of under-privilege), they must equally bear the consequences of their choice to operate illegally and face the costs. This 'volitional theory'[48] of the cause of criminal activity as personal choice has had huge policy ramifications; penal severity has increased so that individuals are deterred (or conform).[49] It also sets an expectation that those who commit crime should expect prosecution so that justice can be done. In this way, O'Malley identifies that offenders, rather than victims, are required to pay for crime with the result being that victims reappear as the 'wronged party' and achieving justice for them becomes the central concern as I explore in this chapter in more detail below.[50]

---

44 O'Malley, 'Neoliberalism, Crime and Criminal Justice' (n 19).

45 Lacey, 'Punishment, (Neo)Liberalism and Social Democracy' (n 32) 260.

46 Pat O'Malley, 'Risk and Responsibility' in Andrew Barry, Thomas Osborne and Nikolas Rose (eds), *Foucault and Political Reason. Liberalism, Neo-liberalism and Political Rationalities* (University College London Press 1996) 197–198.

47 James Wilson, *Thinking About Crime* (Basic Books 1975); Michael Feeley, 'Crime, Social Order and the Rise of Neo-conservative Politics' (2003) 7(1) *Theoretical Criminology* 111.

48 Ibid., 112.

49 Ibid., 112.

50 Pat O'Malley, *Risk, Uncertainty and Government* (Glasshouse 2004) 126.

Nonetheless, the punitive turn cannot be attributed solely to neoliberal ideals about freedom, responsibilisation, individual choice and their coherence with the volitional theory of crime. Wacquant highlights another way in which tough state responses to crime are, he argues, intrinsic to neoliberalism. Neoliberalism sees inequality as the driver of ambition and contends that reductions in state social support can therefore be motivational.[51] With a rolling back of the welfare state and a reduction in economic regulation comes social insecurity and inequality; some individuals and groups can get left behind. Harvey has concluded that 'one of the few serious options for the poor' becomes redistribution through the commission of crime.[52] Wacquant suggests that this emergence of a failing or even criminal class means that the neoliberal movement can also be blamed for incubating and cultivating marginalising attitudes. Those who do not aspire or those who do not succeed come to be considered, what Garland terms, 'the other', the socially excluded or the poor and undeserving underclass who deserve to pay for their criminal activity.[53] Under the volitional theory of crime, those who turn to crime have no one but themselves to blame and do not require *understanding* for the purposes of rehabilitation but *managing* for the purposes of preventing future commission of crime. For these 'precariat'[54] groups or 'dangerous populations',[55] warehousing in prisons is the most expeditious way of controlling 'them' and protecting 'us'.[56] Wacquant concludes that harsh penal policies are therefore in fact wholly consistent with, indeed intrinsic to, neoliberal ideology.

Neoliberalism might also be said to be part of the punitive turn to the extent that its values, strategies and practices contributed to the change in social conditions which destabilised the public's moral compass. The effects of neoliberal market fundamentalism saw a shift in society's traditional hierarchies, organisation, authorities and associated norms. Privatisation, de-regulated finance and reduced labour costs were de-stabilising for a population used to 'solidaristic solutions' such as the welfare state and trade union

---

[51]Nikolas Rose, 'Community, Citizenship and the Third Way' (n 37).

[52]Harvey (n 14) 48.

[53]Garland, *The Culture of Control* (n 5) xii.

[54]John Lea and Simon Hallsworth, 'Bringing the State Back In: Understanding Neoliberal Security' in Peter Squires and John Lea (eds), *Criminalisation and Advanced Marginality: Critically Exploring the Work of Loïc Wacquant* (Policy Press 2013) 20.

[55]Malcolm Feeley and Jonathan Simon, 'The New Penology: Notes on the Emerging Strategy of Corrections and its Implications' (1992) 30(4) *Criminology* 449, 466.

[56]Loic Wacquant, *Punishing the Poor: The Neoliberal Government of Insecurity* (Duke University Press 2009) 292.

influence.[57] Prompted by a population who felt a need for principled re-anchoring, a strong neo-Conservative call for a reassertion of moral disciplines and structures emerged.[58] Social anxiety that values were waning and that modern life was unpredictable, precarious and even dangerous saw governments offer up criminal justice and penal responses as 'expressive justice' and a means of social ordering.[59]

Tougher and increased law and order responses accord with the neoliberal promotion of the authority of the state. Harvey considers the idea of the strong authoritative state to be a contradiction of the neoliberal enterprise which he suggests should be affiliated with the 'light touch', non-interventionist, laissez-faire state. But Mirowski has suggested that to conceive neoliberalism as paradoxical in this way is not to appreciate that neoliberalism's market society 'must be constructed, and will not come about "naturally" in the absence of concerted political effort and organisation'.[60] The state therefore depends on its ability to express authority because it must provide the conditions for individual freedom.[61]

Bernard Harcourt similarly describes the 'illusion of free markets'.[62] Unregulated spaces or free markets do not in fact exist at all,[63] rather such apparently 'free spaces' require 'an intricate regulatory mechanism to make that space possible'.[64] If neoliberal governance has slammed the competence of the socialist 'bloated state' in providing efficient housing, government jobs and welfare programmes then it seems, ironically, to suggest the state enjoys competence (and corresponding legitimacy) in one area; the sphere of policing and criminal justice. In this way, but perhaps for different reasons to Wacquant, Harcourt also persuasively suggests that a state with strong policing, criminalisation and incarceration powers is integral to neoliberalism.

The link between neoliberalism and tough crime responses may not be, however, as irrefutable as Wacquant and Harcourt present. For example,

---

[57]Garland, *The Culture of Control* (n 5) 99.

[58]Ibid., 98–102.

[59]Malcolm Feeley, 'Crime, Social Order and the Rise of Neo-conservative Politics' (2003) *Theoretical Criminology* 111. The 'turn' may also have been due, in part, to a neo-Conservative rejection of the 'permissive era' that had preceded; see Garland, *The Culture of Control* (n 5) 97.

[60]Philip Mirowski, 'Book Review: A Brief History of Neoliberalism' (n 23) 113.

[61]Jason Read, 'A Genealogy of Homo-Economicus' (n 26) 25.

[62]Bernard Harcourt, *The Illusion of Free Markets* (Harvard University Press 2011).

[63]Harcourt illustrates this point with reference to the myriad of regulation at the Chicago Board of Trade in ibid.

[64]Ibid., 11.

Feeley evidences that the penal turn in the United States pre-dates the actual rise in crime witnessed in the latter part of the 1980s. This challenges Wacquant's assertion that the punitive turn came on the back of a rise in crime committed by an emergent underclass. In Britain, Bell confirms that 'the turn' did not emerge until around 1993 despite Thatcher's premiership commencing in 1979, suggesting that being tough on law and order is not ideologically integral to the neoliberal project. In fact, the early years of Thatcherism saw increased rates of diversions away from court, particularly for juvenile offenders, which is more consistent with Thatcher's priority of shrinking the state. Bell's distinctly British appraisal thus calls into question Wacquant's 'incautious'[65] American hypothesis.[66] Moreover, in Britain, social spending has continued to grow and the state continues to intervene in the economic field.[67] Thus, in contrast to Wacquant, Bell asserts that the link between neoliberalism and a crime control imperative in the UK appears to be 'indirect' and less consequential.[68]

Lacey more roundly critiques the force of Wacquant's rhetoric or what she terms the 'neoliberalism-as-penality thesis', refusing to accept Wacquant's neat notion of an overarching, monolithic 'neo-liberal penal state'.[69] On the one hand, Lacey notes that neoliberalism manifests differently across geographies and histories,[70] perhaps only ever existing in hybrid form (if a unified form can be identified without resorting to abstraction at its highest level[71]). On the other hand, 'increased penalty' varies between countries, not least between American states.[72] In rejecting a causal linkage between neoliberalism and increased penality, Lacey also notes that the demonisation of lower socio-economic groups and contrasting expressions of 'respectable fears' are nothing new.[73] Referring to Wacquant's 'abstract version of conspiracy theory', Lacey argues the 'neoliberalism-as-penality thesis' fails to examine

---

[65]Lacey, 'Punishment, (Neo)Liberalism and Social Democracy' (n 32) 261.

[66]Albeit Wacquant purports to argue with respect not just to the US experience but to 'western countries' more broadly.

[67]Bell (n 1) 6.

[68]Ibid., 7.

[69]Ibid., 261.

[70]O'Malley, 'Neoliberalism, Crime and Criminal Justice' (n 19).

[71]Ibid., 5–11.

[72]Take for example the example of the death penalty, available in some American states and not in others indicating, according to Lacey, that such policies are less to do with neoliberalism and perhaps more to do with institutional variances at a more local level.

[73]Nicola Lacey, 'Differentiating Among Penal States' (2010) 61(4) *British Journal of Sociology* 778, 783–784.

how 'hyperincarceration' has been effected by state institutions *in practice*.[74] Thus, Lacey contends that on an explanatory level neoliberalism-as-penality suffers 'institutional deficit and conceptual vagueness'.[75]

In practice and specifically in Britain, Lacey is right to question any overly expedient analysis that ties neoliberal ideology with the crime control imperative. In respect of domestic violence for instance, the first Home Office circulars that encouraged pro-arrest practices were not until 1986 and 1990.[76] Furthermore, the rhetoric of the 2010–2015 coalition and subsequent Conservative governments appeared to support 'a rehabilitation transformation'[77] which saw diversions away from courts[78] and a stabilisation of the prison population.[79] This suggests something other than neoliberal *ideology* is at play.

In the 1990s, neoliberalism *in practice* played a part in the 'penal turn' as neo-Conservatives and New Labour promoted traditional values, triggered by rising moral panics.[80] The New Labour government is particularly associated with a proliferation of criminal legislation that tied in with rhetoric about responsibilisation. More recently, efforts to reduce prison numbers by the coalition and Conservative governments are clearly a pragmatic response to the impact of 'austerity'.[81] Furthermore, during the tenure of the coalition, despite rhetoric to the contrary, in practice 'there were few exceptions [in outcomes] to the general drift towards punitiveness and managerialism'.[82] Consequently, Bell is persuasive when she suggests that criminal justice reflects less neoliberal '*ideology*' (as far as this thought collective might be said to constitute a singular system) and more neoliberalism *in practice*. This analysis appears to support Peck's contention that neoliberalism comprises 'opportunistic searches…ameliorative firefighting, trial-and-error

[74]Ibid., 783.

[75]Lacey, 'Punishment, (Neo)Liberalism and Social Democracy' (n 32) 260.

[76]Home Office, 'Violence Against Women' (Home Office Circular 1986) 1986/69; Home Office, 'Domestic Violence' (Home Office Circular 1990) 1990/60.

[77]Members of Parliament Kenneth Clarke and Chris Grayling are quoted to this end in David Skinns, *Coalition Government Penal Policy 2010–2015* (Palgrave Macmillan 2016) 1.

[78]Legal Aid and Sentencing of Offenders Act 2012, s135 saw the introduction of the youth caution and, youth conditional cautions. The reprimand and final warning scheme consequently came to an end and youths may now be diverted away from court in excess of two times.

[79]Georgina Sturge, 'UK Prison Population Statistics' (House of Commons Library 2018) 5.

[80]Increased criminalisation of juveniles is widely attributed to public concerns about 'problem youth' following the James Bulger killing in 1993. The Labour party's criminal responses to public perceptions of 'anti-social behaviour' are also well documented.

[81]For a full definition of 'austerity', see this chapter. Put succinctly, austerity is an economic imperative that reduces government public spending.

[82]David Skinns, *Coalition Government Penal Policy 2010–2015* (Palgrave Macmillan 2016) 207.

governance, devolved experimentation, and the pragmatic embrace of "what works"'.[83]

In this section, I have drawn out the aspects of neoliberal ideology that support and justify a crime control imperative.[84] Yet I have argued that Wacquant's assertion that the new punitiveness is *integral* to neoliberal *ideology* overlooks that neoliberalism lacks coherent comprehensive ideology; neoliberal governments often adapt and shift to appease their people and often react to populist demands. Neoliberalism is perhaps more a set of practices expressed in its political operation and punitiveness only becomes a part of that when it is adopted (or not) by different governments in different ways to meet different objectives.

Part Two

(i) The Political Independence of the Crown Prosecution Service?

It is of fundamental constitutional importance that the CPS is independent. CPS lawyers must act fairly and impartially to deliver justice for victims, witnesses, defendants and the public. Yet, the CPS is not an island and it must be responsive, reactive and accommodating of various influential external demands; from the police, to public opinion and treasury budgets. In this section, I outline how three neoliberal techniques—managerialism, victim-centred discourse and risk assessments—permeate the CPS and thereby show that the CPS is not impervious to either direct or indirect influence from pervading neoliberal governmentality, discourses and techniques.

The CPS was formed in 1986 following the recommendation by the Royal Commission on Criminal Procedure 1981 (The Phillips Report).[85] The proposal came on the back of centuries of 'notoriously ramshackle'[86] police prosecutions that were piecemeal in approach and undirected and non-uniform across geographies. The motivation for recommending a single prosecution authority was to unify standards of decision-making across

---

[83]Jamie Peck, 'Zombie Neoliberalism and the Ambidextrous State' (n 20) 106.

[84]The 'volitional' theory of crime, the need for deterrent sentencing and committed prosecutions are indicative here.

[85]Royal Commission on Criminal Procedure 1981 (Cmnd 8092) and its supplement The Investigation and Prosecution of Criminal Offences in England and Wales: The Law and Procedure (Cmnd 8092-1).

[86]Francis Bennion, 'The New Prosecution Arrangements' (1986) *Criminal Law Review* 3, 3.

regions and to reduce the numbers of weak cases that were resulting in high numbers of judge directed acquittals. The report announced that, whilst offenders needed to be brought to justice, the rights of the accused must be respected and secured. This followed criticism levied at police prosecutions that had seen errors and miscarriages of justice throughout the 1970s.[87]

The Phillips Report recognised that the functions of investigation and the decision to prosecute should be made separate because, once invested in the investigation stage, officers 'could not be relied on to make a fair decision whether to prosecute'.[88] Balance needed to be restored and the purpose of the subsequent Police and Criminal Evidence Act 1984 was to provide a framework for the fair exercise of police powers; it aimed to deliver standardised practice and make suspects aware of their rights. In fact, PACE proved controversial because the Act *extended* a number of police powers in relation to searches, arrests and the treatment of detainees in police custody. It was for that reason also, that an independent prosecuting authority may have been required to counter-balance the public perception that powers were tipping too far in favour of the police.[89] PACE came into force the same year as the CPS was established (1986) and the CPS's initial insistence that they were to be considered *entirely* independent of the police speaks to the widespread public concern.[90]

Initially at least, the CPS' high regard for its own objectivity and independence carried the risk that the service was isolated from police, victims and the public. Sanders pejoratively likens the CPS to a fortress at this time.[91] However, the CPS has the responsibility of implementing the 'prosecutive power of the state'[92] and it would be misleading to suggest that the CPS operates in isolation, unaffected by police, courts or executive action.[93] Rather, the CPS is embedded within the various agencies and institutions of the criminal justice system and at the very least 'there has to be a measure of co-ordination between the various limbs of the criminal justice system'.[94]

---

[87]JUSTICE: Criminal Justice Committee, 'The Prosecution Process in England and Wales: Report By' (1970) *Criminal Law Review* 668.

[88]Crown Prosecution Service, 'History' available at https://www.cps.gov.uk/about/history.html accessed 13 March 2018.

[89]Andrew Sanders, 'The CPS—30 Years On' (2016) *Criminal Law Review* 82, 84.

[90]David Rose, *In the Name of the Law: The Collapse of Criminal Justice* (Vintage 1996).

[91]Sanders (n 89) 84.

[92]Francis Bennion, 'The New Prosecution Arrangements' (1986) *Criminal Law Review* 3, 3.

[93]Roger Daw, 'A Response' (1994) *Criminal Law Review* 904, 909.

[94]Ibid., 909.

Good co-ordination should not, however, imply some loss of proper independence cautions the 1994 Director of Public Prosecutions (DPP).[95]

Despite the independence a prosecutor enjoys with regard to individual casework decisions, the CPS as an institution is answerable to government in various ways. Whilst the head of the CPS, the DPP,[96] 'operates independently'[97] this is qualified as she or he does so 'under the superintendence of the Attorney General who is accountable to Parliament for the work of the CPS'.[98] For example, the DPP has responsibility to appoint and remunerate staff but this is with the approval of the Treasury as to numbers and budget and the CPS' budget has been heavily reduced during the recent times of austerity. Indeed, from the 2009–2010 budget of £672 million per annum, the funds fell by £185 million to £487 million in 2015 which required the service to restructure and streamline its ways of working.[99] The DPP is also required to provide an annual report to the Attorney General every April which includes a summary of the discharge of his functions in the preceding year and any other matters that the Attorney General may specify. This report is laid before parliament for scrutiny. In this way, and through the Justice Select Committee, parliament has the opportunity to comment upon and make suggestions about the work of the CPS.[100]

CPS independence will also be directly affected by legal changes such as the introduction of statutory charging,[101] the availability of the conditional

[95]Ibid., 909.

[96]The role of DPP has existed since 1880 and was formalised in 1986.

[97]Crown Prosecution Service, 'Facts About the CPS' available at http://www.cps.gov.uk/about/facts.html accessed 21 March 2018.

[98]Crown Prosecution Service, 'Casework Quality Standards' (2014) available at www.cps.gov.uk/publications/docs/cqs_oct_2014.pdf accessed 9 March 2018.

[99]Hansard Online, 'Crown Prosecution Service: Funding' (Hansard Online 2017) Volume 619. The impact of these cuts on prosecutorial working practice is discussed by way of empirical insight in Chapter 4.

[100]See, for example, Justice Committee 'The Work of the Crown Prosecution Service' (2015) available at http://www.parliament.uk/business/committees/committees-a-z/commons-select/justice-committee/news-parliament-20151/crown-prosecution-service-evidence/ accessed 4 April 2018.

[101]Statutory charging was introduced by part 4 of the Criminal Justice Act 2003 (which amended s37 of PACE, inserting s37A into the Act). The CPS currently charge only 28% of cases; these are cases that are deemed 'more serious and complex' and include domestic abuse. The police charge all other offences; see Crown Prosecution Service, 'About Charging' available at https://www.cps.gov.uk/about/charging.html accessed 14 December 2018.

caution[102] or the criminalisation of coercive and controlling behaviour.[103] Moreover, government priorities are mirrored in CPS policies; the CPS Violence Against Women and Girls' (VAWG) strategy, for example, is drafted to meet the aims of the cross-government VAWG strategy. The CPS is also responsive and receptive to developments in public opinion. Not to be so would risk the CPS losing legitimacy in the eyes of the public it serves. To ignore evolving societal norms and expectations about which behaviours ought and which ought not to be prosecuted would expose the CPS to criticism that might, ultimately, undermine the authority of the criminal law.[104] For those reasons, Sir David Calvert-Smith, former DPP, first opened up a working relationship between the CPS and the academic community to assist with keeping the CPS abreast of public expectations.[105] The Justice Committee, too, hears the views of academics about the impacts of CPS practice and makes recommendations accordingly. Moreover, the CPS openly invites public consultation when they formulate prosecution policy.[106] For example, with respect to the prosecution of domestic violence cases, the CPS published a draft policy and invited commentary from interested parties.[107] It is in this way that activist groups such as Women's Aid, Refuge, the Fawcett Society and feminist legal scholars contributed to the development of the Domestic Abuse Guidance for Prosecutors.

Perhaps surprisingly, however, my contention that the CPS is not an island here has little to do with the 'public interest' test contained within the Code for Crown Prosecutors (The Code). For, whilst the requirement that prosecutors consider the 'public interest' might conjure images of

[102]Conditional cautions were introduced by PACE 1984, s37A and were brought into force following the Criminal Justice Act 2003. However, their use in domestic abuse cases is almost entirely restricted as '[i]t is unlikely that domestic abuse in intimate (whether current or previous) partner cases would ever be appropriate for Conditional Caution'. Any consideration of the use of conditional caution in domestic abuse cases will require referral to the Head Quarters Violence Against Women Strategy Manager in London. In practice this requirement inhibits their use. See Crown Prosecution Service, 'Conditional Caution Guidance' available at www.cps.gov.uk/publications/directors_guidance/adult_conditional_cautions.html#a01 accessed 21 March 2018.

[103]S76 Serious Crime Act 2015.

[104]The CPS considered over 5000 responses from the public when determining their assisted suicide policy in 2010. Crown Prosecution Service, 'Assisted Suicide' available at https://www.cps.gov.uk/publication/assisted-suicide accessed 4 June 2018.

[105]Andrew Ashworth, 'Developments in the Public Prosecutors Office in England and Wales' (2000) 8(3) *European Journal of Crime, Criminal Law and Criminal Justice* 257, 261.

[106]Crown Prosecution Service, 'Consultations' available at www.cps.gsi.gov.uk/consultations/ accessed 21 March 2018.

[107]Crown Prosecution Service, 'Consultation: The Prosecution of Domestic Violence Cases' (2014) available at http://www.cps.gov.uk/consultations/dv_consultation_14.pdf accessed 4 April 2018.

prosecutors reflecting upon public opinion and societal norms, the public interest test in fact remains largely constrained to matters dealing with the gravity of the offence and any of its aggravating or mitigating features. The 8th and current edition of The Code, published in 2018, indicates that where there is sufficient evidence, prosecution is ordinarily merited 'unless there are public interest factors against tending to outweigh those tending to favour'.[108] The Code outlines the factors that prosecutors must weigh up in the 'public interest'; the seriousness of the offence and the harm caused to the victim; whether the offence was premeditated or demonstrates a pattern of behaviour; whether the offender was in a position of trust or the victim was otherwise vulnerable; and the proportionality of bringing a prosecution bearing in mind the cost of prosecution versus the likely penalty to the suspect. These factors are largely concerned with the gravity or severity of the offending behaviour in context and the defendant's antecedent offending. They do not invite the prosecutor to consider whether a criminal justice response best meets the needs of the public or society as a whole.

Whilst government or public opinion should not dictate decisions in particular cases, CPS policies and ways of working are, nonetheless, influenced and swayed by the various external factors outlined here. The CPS understands that public confidence in the service it provides is critical to its legitimacy; Alison Saunders (former DPP) suggested that the CPS encourages scrutiny of its work and aspires to transparency of working to improve public understanding of their priorities and role.[109] The CPS's accountability, through the Attorney General, to parliament and The Treasury, means that it comes under pressure to deliver its service effectively and efficiently. I explore now how principles of managerialism, a technique I argue of neoliberalism, have become expected and adopted within the service.

(ii) New Public Managerialism and CPS Targets

If the neoliberal state regulates all domains by the market and disseminates economic principles in all aspects of life, then economic ideologies also

[108] Crown Prosecution Service, 'The Code for Prosecutors' (CPS 2018) available at https://www.cps.gov.uk/sites/default/files/documents/publications/Code-for-Crown-Prosecutors-October-2018.pdf accessed 21 March 2018.

[109] DPP Alison Saunders speaking before the Justice Committee. See Justice Committee, 'The Work of the Crown Prosecution Service' available at http://www.parliament.uk/business/committees/committees-a-z/commons-select/justice-committee/news-parliament-20151/crown-prosecution-service-evidence/ accessed 4 April 2017.

permeate state institutions even where monetary profit is not considered the end goal. Through the rise of neoliberal governance, political and business idiolects converge and shape everyday conduct. If neoliberalism is an 'art of governance'[110] then, in the public sector, the tenets of New Public Managerialism (NPM) are its masterpiece and the CPS is its quintessence. The next chapter (Chapter 4) draws out how the strategies of managerialism that I identify here contribute to the CPS working practice of tenacious domestic abuse prosecutions, often in unanticipated ways.

As neoliberal theory champions privatisation, the public sector, considered inherently inefficient, is targeted for reduction.[111] In dogmatic neoliberal doctrine, competition is considered a virtue and its results are not considered negative. However, as Bell has noted, neoliberal theory rarely corresponds exactly to neoliberalism as it is actually practised; at its most doctrinaire, neoliberalism would advance the 'privatisation of all state functions'.[112] But the CPS has not been privatised, for example by the contracting out of prosecution services to private firms. Instead, in the absence of other organisations competing for its core business, what has emerged is a way of working in line with the precepts of managerialism.[113] NPM, introduced to the English and Welsh criminal justice system since at least the mid-1990s,[114] was heralded as a means of achieving a 'post-bureaucratic criminal justice'[115] because it demands public sector modernisation and expects productivity, value for money and the delivery of core quality standards.[116] Within this framework the CPS is effectively encouraged to compete with itself for improved conviction rates, victim satisfaction, efficiency and meeting reduced budgetary targets year on year. In this way, the principles of competition can be seen to operate within the four walls of the CPS.

---

[110]Michel Foucault in Michel Senellart (ed), *The Birth of Biopolitics: Lectures at the College de France, 1978–79* (Picador 2004) 131.

[111]Susan George, 'A Short History of Neoliberalism' (1999) Conference in Economic Sovereignty in a Globalising World, Bangkok available at https://www.tni.org/en/article/short-history-neoliberalism accessed 20 April 2018.

[112]Bell (n 1) 140.

[113]For a comprehensive account of New Public Managerialism see, for example, Gerry Stoker (ed), *The New Management of British Local Governance* (Macmillan 1999).

[114]Eugene McLaughlin, John Muncie and Gordon Hughes, 'The Permanent Revolution: New Labour, New Public Management and the Modernization of Criminal Justice' (2001) *Criminal Justice* 301, 301.

[115]Ibid., 301.

[116]The CPS implemented 'Core Quality Standards' in December 2009 (renamed 'Casework Quality Standards' in 2014). Crown Prosecution Service, 'Casework Quality Standards' available at https://www.cps.gov.uk/publications/casework_quality_standards/index.html accessed 31 March 2018.

Managerialism is not simply a 'modern management method' but an ideology or 'all-pervasive creature'[117] that uses the generic tools of management to 'establish itself systematically in organisations'.[118] Managerialism can have the consequence of depriving employees of decision-making discretion (as my interviews with prosecutors in Chapter 4 explore).[119] In part this de-skilling or downgrading of the skilled worker's role may have something to do with the expansion of management personnel who are tasked with overseeing operations.[120] But it may also be to do with the introduction of systems and standardised ways of working to attain its 'performance goals' or 'organisational objectives' (such synonyms conceal the organisation's profit motives or, in the case of the CPS, its money saving interests).[121] Moreover, as Managerialism, unlike neoliberalism, lacks political or democratic ambition it may feel oppressive to work under. Nonetheless, it strives for legitimacy through its quest for productivity.[122]

The introduction of NPM has not, I argue here, seen a diminishing government presence in the day to day operations of the CPS. That might have been expected, given that managerialism itself imposes the most streamlined ways of working to achieve policy aims. A 'stepping back' of government from the business of prosecuting might be more consistent with neoliberal free market priorities that have imposed market discipline and solutions on the CPS.[123] However, the presence of an interventionist government is felt at the CPS through government target setting both in budgetary terms and performance monitoring. These operational goals, based on government evidence or 'what-works' agendas, are set against policy objectives (e.g. the elimination of violence against women and girls).[124] Once again we see the apparent contradictions of neoliberal ideology which advocates the

---

[117]Garland, *The Culture of Control* (n 5) 18.

[118]Thomas Kilkauer, 'What Is Managerialism?' (2015) *Critical Sociology* 1103, 1106.

[119]Ibid., 1106.

[120]In the CPS Crown Prosecutors and Senior Crown Prosecutors fall into teams managed by District Crown Prosecutors overseen by Assistant Chief Crown Prosecutors managed by Chief Crown Prosecutors (CCP) who are accountable to the DPP. Area Business Managers also assist the CCPs. It is notable that managerialism is characterised by unrelenting organisational restructuring in its quest for streamlined working; the CPS has seen countless reconfigurations of its management structures and ways of working.

[121]Kilkauer (n 118) 1106.

[122]Ibid., 1109.

[123]Bell (n 1) 141.

[124]Ibid., 177. As already mentioned, the DPP and the service her organisation delivers is scrutinised by the Justice Committee and Parliament (the latter directly through the Attorney General).

free market on the one hand and neoliberalism in practice which promotes the strong state on the other.[125] Also visible is the shift from 'government' (and its associations with monolithic, transcendental rule[126]) to the art of 'governance' in collaboration with state actors, in this instance, criminal prosecutors.

From the outset, one of the triggers for establishing the CPS was 'the need for the efficient and economical use of resources'.[127] Thus, the Prosecution of Offences Act 1985 set the expectation that the CPS would make financial savings.[128] Conservatives at the time were simultaneously wedded to the idea that sheer numbers of police officers, prosecutions and punitive sentencing would have long term deterrent effect.[129] Flowing from this premise, coupled with a drive for economy and efficiency, it is easy to draw parallels between the way managerialism has operated in the criminal justice system since that time and Packer's Crime Control Model.[130] The Crime Control Model, according to Packer, aims to repress crime through efficiency in achieving large numbers of convictions; speed and finality are prized. By operating a conveyor belt system of justice where cases are dealt with in an efficient, routinised and even stereotyped way, the obstacles to conviction, Packer observes, are diminished. Following an initial screening process, a 'presumption of guilt' allows the Crime Control Model to proceed with high volume and, Packer comments, '[t]he model that will operate successfully on these presuppositions must be an administrative almost managerial model'.[131]

In the area of domestic abuse, CPS targets and achievements are recorded annually in the Violence Against Women and Girls Crime Report.[132] The report assesses CPS 'performance' by retrieving statistical data from CPS case

[125]Andrew Gamble, *Free Economy and the Strong State* (Macmillan Education 1988).

[126]Lisa Downing, *The Cambridge Introduction to Michel Foucault* (Cambridge University Press 2008) 18.

[127]Royal Commission on Criminal Procedure 1981 (Cmnd 8092).

[128]The Prosecution of Offences Act 1985.

[129]McLaughlin, Muncie and Hughes (n 114) 302.

[130]Herbert Packer, 'Two Models of the Criminal Process' (1964) *University of Pennsylvania Law Review* 1, 9.

[131]Ibid., 11.

[132]Crown Prosecution Service, 'Violence Against Women and Girls Crime Report: 2018–2019' (2019) available at https://www.cps.gov.uk/sites/default/files/documents/publications/cps-vawg-report-2019.pdf accessed 3 March 2020.

management systems.[133] The report reveals that in 2019 the percentage of prosecution outcomes that resulted in conviction (guilty plea or following trial) was the highest ever recorded at 76.5%.[134] This continues the steady increase in domestic abuse conviction rates witnessed over the recent past. In 2014–2015 the percentage of domestic abuse cases dropped by the CPS post-charge was 19.3%, in 2018–2019 there was a lower proportion of cases dropped; 17.5%. The report clearly demonstrates that the CPS is committed to improving and driving up conviction rates in domestic abuse cases (it's policy objective) and considers its advances in this regard commendable.

A Domestic Abuse 'Deep Dive' exercise illustrates the commitment. Carried out in 2015, the exercise analysed six courts which had achieved the highest conviction rates. The aim of the process was to identify 'best practice components' (or the 'what works' approach) that might then be rolled out to other courts. From this, it is clear that the CPS equates 'success' in these cases with convictions. Evident in the report is the importance placed on managerial measurements of performance through statistical goals and targets. There is no equivalent statistical information available in relation to victim satisfaction or the number of victims of domestic abuse who were kept safe following their contact with the CPS. This directly speaks to the reservations some feminists have about the women's movement's alignment with the neoliberal state-run criminal justice system; what becomes prioritised are criminal justice goals and not the best interests or safety of women, despite the rise to prominence of victim-centred discourse. The next section explores how the recent focus on prioritising the victim simply translates into obtaining 'justice' through convictions on their behalf.

(iii) The Victim-Centred Priority

The CPS prosecutes in the public interest and confirms that it 'does not act for victims or the families of victims in the same way solicitors act for their clients. [Prosecutors] act on behalf of the public and not just in the interests of any particular individual'.[135] Thus, together with its stated aims

---

133 The CPS uses 'Compass Management Software' or CMS which records/flags information such as whether the case is a domestic abuse case, the gender of the victim and perpetrator, the ethnicity of parties and the outcome of the case. The data depends upon the accuracy of data input by CPS staff.

134 The statistics also reveal that 82.5% of victims were female.

135 Crown Prosecution Service, 'Decision to Charge' available at www.cps.gov.uk/victims_witnesses/reporting_a_crime/decision_to_charge.html accessed 7 April 2017.

of independence and fairness, the CPS brings and presents the police case before the criminal court whenever the evidential and public interest tests are met. The state is then traditionally understood to conduct criminal prosecutions on behalf of the community; the state's and prosecutor's interests are considered synonymous with the victim's as, ultimately, the state's correctional policies will serve public, offender and victim.[136]

In the past, however, the approach attracted criticism as it was perceived that, once the wheels of justice had started rolling, the criminal justice system often marginalised victims[137] and treated them as incidental and secondary to the greater pursuit of achieving justice through conviction and sentencing of the offender. The criminal process was charged with lavishing on defendants the right of the presumption of innocence, procedural due process safeguards and the assessment of their needs for rehabilitation, whilst the alleged victim's interests appeared relegated and subsumed by the greater good.[138]

Aiming to redress the balance, and in line with neoliberal notions that criminals should receive their 'just desserts', New Labour's political promises vowed to put victims 'at the heart' of the criminal justice system and made parallel calls to 're-balance the system in favour of the victim'.[139] Since the late 1990s, the question of who properly 'owns' any particular crime[140] may have, technically, remained unchanged as far as the Crown Prosecution Service is concerned but there can be no doubt that the status of the victim has been considerably elevated within the service and the wider justice system. Victims are no longer a 'bit part player'; they are now 'central actors'.[141]

Several CPS policies exemplify the shift. Most significantly, the 'No Witness, No Justice' project recognised that by improving support offered to victims and witnesses the 'justice gap' could be narrowed and public

[136]Matt Matravers, 'The Victim, the State, and Civil Society' in Anthony Bottom and Julian Roberts (eds), *Hearing the Victim: Adversarial Justice, Crime Victims and the State* (Willan 2010) 1.

[137]Carolyn Hoyle, 'Victim's, The Criminal Process and Restorative Justice' in Rodney Morgan, Robert Reiner and Mike Maguire (eds), *The Oxford Handbook of Criminology* (7th edn, Oxford University Press 2007) 407.

[138]Garland, *The Culture of Control* (n 5) 121.

[139]The Queen's Speech (2006) full text available at http://news.bbc.co.uk/1/hi/uk_politics/6150274.stm accessed 10 April 2017. This 'rebalancing' was a recurring mantra throughout New Labour policy documentation see Michael Tonry, '"Rebalancing the Criminal Justice System in Favour of the Victim": The Costly Consequences of Populist Rhetoric' in Anthony Bottom and Julian Roberts (eds), *Hearing the Victim: Adversarial Justice, Crime Victims and the State* (Willan 2010) 72.

[140]I borrow this framing of the issue from Matravers (n 136) 1.

[141]John Spencer, 'The Victim and the Prosecutor' in Anthony Bottom and Julian Roberts (eds), *Hearing the Victim: Adversarial Justice, Crime Victims and the State* (Willan 2010) 141.

confidence restored.[142] Consequently, dedicated Witness Care Units in police stations became tasked with keeping victims updated with progress in the case and discussing their needs such as the availability of special measures when giving evidence at court. Likewise, the Prosecutor's Pledge[143] makes clear what victims can expect from the CPS.[144] Prosecutors should now take into account the impact on the victim when making charging decisions, seek the view of the victim when considering the acceptability of pleas, communicate withdrawn or altered charges, protect victim identity in court where appropriate[145] and explain court procedures and processes in accordance with Speaking To Witnesses At Court (STWAC) guidance.[146] The Victims' Right to Review Scheme[147] also assists victims to challenge CPS decisions and, since its inception in 2013, provides further evidence of a transformation in the dynamic between the CPS and victim.

In practical terms, Hall notes that provision for victims at court is now well considered. He observed appropriately designated waiting rooms, clear and obvious reception desks, signage and a designated witness service at court all present in the courts he attended.[148] Taken together such developments illustrate significant improvements in awareness about victimhood and victims' needs. These measures do not realign the role of the CPS in adversarial proceedings—the state still conducts a public prosecution—but they do signal an adjustment in victims' participatory rights and lend merit and legitimacy to criminal justice because it aims to dispense proper treatment of victims.[149] Changes to the status of the victim are not just evidenced in CPS policies or the physical conditions provided to victims

[142]Avail Consulting, 'NWNJ Pilot Evaluation Final Report: Crown Prosecution Service and ACPO' (2004) 6.

[143]Introduced in October 2005, Crown Prosecution Service, 'The Prosecutors 10 Point Pledge to Victims' (CPS 2005) available at www.cps.gov.uk/news/articles/prosecutor_pledge211005/ accessed 7 April 2017.

[144]Though John Spencer contends that the Prosecutors' Pledges are high on rubric but distinctly lacking redress for victims should the CPS be non-compliant in Spencer (n 141) 151.

[145]Crown Prosecution Service, 'Victims and Witnesses: Care and Treatment' available at https://www.cps.gov.uk/legal-guidance/victims-and-witnesses-care-and-treatment accessed 19 December 2019.

[146]Speaking to Witnesses at Court (STWAC) guidance can be found at Crown Prosecution Service, 'Speaking to Witnesses at Court' available at https://www.cps.gov.uk/legal-guidance/speaking-witnesses-court accessed 19 December 2019.

[147]Crown Prosecution Service, 'Victims' Right to Review Scheme' available at http://www.cps.gov.uk/victims_witnesses/victims_right_to_review/index.html accessed 21 April 2017.

[148]Matthew Hall, *Victims of Crime: Policy and Practice in Criminal Justice* (Willan 2009).

[149]Anthony Bottoms and Julian Roberts, 'Preface' in Anthony Bottom and Julian Roberts (eds), *Hearing the Victim: Adversarial Justice, Crime Victims and the State* (Willan 2010) xix.

at court; statute now similarly reflects the priority. Examples include the Domestic Violence, Crime and Victims Act 2004 which made both common assault and breach of a non-molestation order arrestable offences. This, combined with a police presumption to arrest in instances of domestic violence,[150] gave police clear powers to 'step in' and act on behalf of the victim of domestic abuse. The Act also made available restraining orders for victims, even on acquittal. Prior to that, the availability of special measures for prosecution witnesses at court (but not for defendants) became commonplace[151] whilst the Criminal Justice Act 2003 saw the provision of indeterminate sentencing[152] and the duty of the adjudicator to consider compensation at sentence.[153] The Legal Aid, Sentencing and Punishment of Offenders Act 2011, may have reduced the criteria for a remand into custody by requiring a 'real prospect' of the defendant receiving a custodial sentence, but it specifically preserved protection for victims of domestic abuse. As 'associated persons',[154] where fear or physical/mental injury is likely to result from a remand on bail, the prosecutor need not evidence a real prospect of a custodial sentence.

This reflects an awareness of victim needs, even prior to a finding of guilt against the defendant. Finally, though not imposed through statutory mechanism, victim personal statements, detailing the impact of the crime on the victim, are now widely referred to at sentencing hearings. This means that the harm caused to victims can be reflected at sentence[155] and may go further in meeting victims' expressive needs.[156]

However, it has been argued that not everything that has been achieved for victims has been borne of legitimate concern for them. The introduction of the Domestic Violence Protection Order for example, on the face of it,

[150]Home Office, 'Justice for All—A White Paper on the Criminal Justice System' (2002) Cm 5563, para 8.7

[151]Youth Justice and Criminal Evidence Act 1999, s23–30.

[152]Criminal Justice Act 2003, s225 (which was subsequently abolished by LASPO 2011, s122–128. However, I suggest this was a response to concerns about prison overcrowding and its associated costs as opposed to a diminishing of concern about victims).

[153]Legal Aid, Sentencing and Punishment of Offenders Act 2011, s63.

[154]As defined by Family Law Act 1996, s62; spouses or former spouses, civil partners, cohabitants, intimate partners or relatives.

[155]Victim Personal Statements were first announced in the Victim's Charter 1996 and were introduced in October 2001 in 'Practice Direction—Crime Victim Personal Statements' (2001) 4 All ER 640: III 28.

[156]Carolyn Hoyle and Lucia Zedner, 'Victims, Victimization and Criminal Justice' in Mike Maguire, Rod Morgan and Robert Reiner (eds), *The Oxford Handbook of Criminology* (4th edn, Oxford University Press 2007) 461–495.

affords the police additional opportunity to protect the victim from having contact with the perpetrator. However, these orders merely substitute for the use of the suspect being released on bail from police custody with conditions attached not to contact the victim. Following the Police and Crime Act 2017, where the investigation is ongoing, the suspect is simply 'released under investigation' from the police station which affords the police no power to impose conditions unless they apply separately to the magistrates courts for the same.

Ostensible 'victim-centred' approaches might also have been implemented because they often meet managerialist targets; when victims are 'on board' with prosecutions, there is greater efficiency within the system and conviction rates improve. The No Witness, No Justice Pilot Evaluation report confirms this.[157] Managerialism complete with its performance focus aligns with 'meeting the needs' of victims during the course of proceedings because victim compliance secures efficient productivity in the system and the need for fewer adjournments.

The delivery of victim-centred policies has attracted further criticism from those who perceive the focus on victim rights to be 'by-products of other agendas'.[158] A less benevolent explanation about the emergence of the victim as a central figure in criminal justice is that it has been in the 'service of severity'[159] or has served 'as an all-purpose justification for measures of penal repression'.[160] In the UK, victim personal statements cannot express a sentencing preference, but the detailing of the impact of the offence on the victim, arguably, legitimates a 'just deserts'[161] approach to sentencing. It seems that 'rebalancing the criminal justice system in favour of the victim' has been delivered through responding in a more authoritarian manner to offending behaviour.

Just as, as I argue below, neoliberal governments have enveloped the violence against women movement, neoliberalism has been similarly attracted to the victim-rights movement. As a movement advocating individual rights, neoliberals have been able to use victim rights discourse to deliver and advance the criminal justice priority with managerial efficiency. The ease with which neoliberalism adopted victim-centred practices can also

[157]Avail Consulting, 'No Witness, No Justice (NWNJ) Pilot Evaluation Final Report: Crown Prosecution Service and ACPO' (2004) available at www.cps.gov.uk/publications/docs/NWNJ_pilot_evaluation_report_291004.pdf accessed 10 April 2017.

[158]Hall (n 148) 44–88.

[159]Matravers (n 136) 3.

[160]Garland, *The Culture of Control* (n 5) 143.

[161]The perpetrator receives his 'comeuppance' or punishment, in contrast to a rehabilitative response.

be understood when we recall the 'volitional theory' of criminal offending. Neoliberal criminology draws out the contrast between the law-abiding majority and the deviant few who wilfully choose to offend. It emphasises the separation between the 'decent' versus the 'bad' and with it constructs the public at large as the 'metaphorical victim'.[162] Prioritisation of the victim, as we saw in the case of R v C[163] in Chapter 2, thus becomes an expression of a rebalancing in favour of society.

(iv) Actuarialism and Risk-Based Discourse

The neoliberal concern about obtaining justice for victims and concern for efficient public administration has resulted in the use of the criminal law and its sanctions as a means of controlling *future* risks to *future* victims and the law-abiding public.[164] The neoliberal New Right has therefore advocated a perspective of (administrative) criminology that is grounded upon goals of *preventing* crimes and victimisation before they happen. Under neoliberal governments, controlling crime has become dependent on using predictive techniques and actuarialism (the calculation of risk).[165] Offenders are conceived as prone to a collection of potentially harmful behaviours and are assigned a category of risk whilst future victims are assessed in terms of their level of vulnerability to that potential harm. For this reason, the same period that has been associated with the 'punitive turn' has also been associated with a 'preventive turn'.[166]

In practical terms, to assess the risk of discontinuing a case, prosecutors must make enquiries with the police (who should be in contact with other agencies tasked with supporting the complainant) before making a decision.[167] Most commonly, risk assessments will be provided to the CPS from the police in the Domestic Abuse Stalking and Harassment (DASH) form. The form is a risk identification checklist and questionnaire that police

[162]Bell (n 1) 96.

[163]R v C [2007] EWCA Crim, 3463.

[164]Jonathan Simon, *Governing Through Crime* (n 7).

[165]For example, this assessment is made by the charging prosecutor, the sentencing authority or by the parole board. See Pat O'Malley, *Crime and Risk* (Sage 2010) 1.

[166]Adam Crawford and Karen Evans, 'Crime Prevention and Community Safety' in Alison Leibling, Shadd Maruna and Lesley McAra (eds), *Oxford Handbook of Criminology* (6th edn, Oxford University Press).

[167]Police may liaise with Multi-Agency Risk Assessment Conferences (MARACs), Mult- Agency Public Protection Arrangements (MAPPAs) or Multi-Agency Safeguarding Hubs (MASH), General Practitioners or Schools.

should routinely conduct with complainants and which concludes with an assessment of whether the victim is at 'standard', 'medium' or 'high' risk of future harm.[168] Questions require simple 'yes' or 'no' answers and follow-up probing questions require further details for 'yes' answers. The police should refer to their intelligence databases before being satisfied that they have completed the form to the appropriate standard. Those completing the form should not merely add up the number of risk factors to assess the level of risk (by way of guidance 14 or more ticks indicates 'high' risk), rather they should apply professional judgement to assess the type of risk(s) in context; a small number of more serious factors might nonetheless result in the victim being deemed at 'high' risk.

The DASH form itself quite rightly explains that it cannot predict future risk and that 'there is no existing accurate procedure to calculate or foresee which cases will result in homicide or further assault and harm'.[169] In truth, there may never be a perfect tool to assess risk and a victim's risk is liable to change over the course of criminal proceedings, rendering the form outdated despite professionals being urged to assess risk on an ongoing 'dynamic' basis. Risk is inescapable and unlikely ever to be eliminated, yet such a risk assessment tool can give the impression that someone is not at risk. The form also implies that standardised and considered assessments are taking place and the very presence of this type of actuarial science generates a confidence in subsequent decision-making due to it being based on apparent rationality and consistency.[170] The potential consequence of risk assessment tools might be that individual prosecutors simply defer to the form and fail to make adequate and context specific enquiries with victim support workers.

The CPS Domestic Abuse Guidelines indicate that DASH questionnaires 'inform victim management decisions where necessary'.[171] What is lacking from the Guidelines is a breakdown of *how* the prosecutor should be guided by the risk assessment when a woman withdraws her support for the prosecution. CPS Domestic Abuse Guidelines acknowledge that some complainants will be at 'particularly heightened risk' following a report to police,

---

[168]Domestic Abuse, Stalking and Harassment and Honour Based Violence (DASH 2009) Risk Identification and Assessment and Management Model, available at http://www.dashriskchecklist.co.uk/wp-content/uploads/2016/09/DASH-2009.pdf accessed 12 April 2018.

[169]See ibid.

[170]China Scherz, 'Protecting Children, Preserving Families: Moral Conflict and Actuarial Science in a Problem of Contemporary Governance' (2011) *Polat-Political and Legal Anthropology Review* 33.

[171]Crown Prosecution Service, 'Domestic Abuse Guidelines for Prosecutors' (2014) available at https://www.cps.gov.uk/legal-guidance/domestic-abuse-guidelines-prosecutors accessed 9 February 2018.

once a charging decision is confirmed or when the case is concluded.[172] The Guidelines simply suggest that when a woman is no longer supportive, her 'risk' is relevant when coming to the pivotal decision whether to prosecute or not. But 'risk' might play out in opposing ways here and the Guidelines appear to leave the question of how to weigh up the part 'risk' will play in the decision to individual prosecutors to assess, as long as, it would seem, they have been mindful of it. Given the uncertainty, it is possible that prosecutors will be minded to pursue a prosecution because, assuming one has faith in the criminal justice system, such a course appears to demonstrate that the prosecutor has been 'pro-active' in preventing future risk. As I describe in Chapter 5, however, pursuing a case might actually have the unintended effect of exacerbating a woman's risk of future harm.

This preceding section of the chapter considered how neoliberal ideology and ways of working emerge in the CPS via three neoliberal priorities or practices; managerialism, victim-centrality and actuarialism. I want to consider next the neoliberal state's alliance with feminist groups and note how the union has promoted and been used to justify the criminal justice system as the primary means of addressing domestic abuse.

Part Three

(i) Neoliberalism's Strategic Alliance with Feminist Groups: Implications for State Treatment of Domestic Abuse

In 1986 the Thatcher government issued the first Home Office circular on violence against women and in 1990, the first on domestic violence.[173] These were released despite neither the issue of violence against women nor domestic violence being included in the 1983 or 1987 Conservative manifestos. The 1983 manifesto did, however, headline 'Responsibility and the Family' and the need to return more choice to individuals and their families as a way of increasing personal freedom. Such declarations prompted Jill

---

[172]Ibid.

[173]The Domestic Violence circular 1990 urged the police to develop force policies to protect victims; to treat domestic violence as seriously as other forms of violence; to use powers of arrest in circumstances of domestic violence; the circular reiterated the dangers of conciliation between the victim and the offender; and put forward the consideration to the police of pursuing a case, even if the victim had withdrawn her support.

Radford and Elizabeth Stanko to suggest that the two circulars were drafted not in response to the demands of violence against women campaigners, per se, but rather as a means to shore up traditional moral values and the central institution of the heterosexual family.[174] Agreeing that the Conservative government was less motivated by the campaigns to end violence against women, Sandra Walklate and others in 1993 expressed the view that improvements in police responses to domestic violence were being made as part of increased recognition that victims of crime were the consumers of criminal justice services as I described above.[175]

Nonetheless, throughout the 1980s and 1990s, violence against women campaigners were working to raise the profile of domestic violence in the UK by campaigning, educating the public and lobbying for changes in government policy and legislation. But despite the increased public awareness, Thatcher's government in the 1980s reduced refuge funding as part of a neoliberal rolling back of the welfare state. It was perhaps in light of this reduction in funding that feminists' attention in Britain shifted towards criminal justice responses in the mid-1980s.[176] Sandra Horley became the Chief Executive of Refuge in 1983 and her efforts in this regard marshalled the Metropolitan police to issue a Force Order to take domestic violence seriously in 1987.[177]

In 1992 the Home Affairs Select Committee on Domestic Violence heard from a number of interested groups and individuals including; social workers, non-governmental organisation support workers, the police and legal professionals. In her evidence, Sandra Horley commended to the committee action taken in Canada where publicity campaigns had led to greater public awareness about domestic violence.[178] Yet in spite of the Committee praising the work Refuge was doing at this time, the charity suffered financial crisis in 1992. Horley took the initiative to ask Diana Princess of Wales to provide

[174]Jill Radford et al., 'Violence Against Women and Children: The Contradictions of Crime Control Policy Under Patriarchy' in Kevin Stenson (ed), *The New Politics of Crime Control* (Sage 1991).

[175]Sandra Walklate et al., 'Responding to Women as "Consumers" of a Police Service: The UK Experience 1980–1990' in Louise Shelley and Jozsef Vugh (eds), *Social Changes, Crime and the Police* (Psychology Press 1995).

[176]Marie Gottschalk, *The Prison and the Gallows: The Politics of Incarceration in America* (Cambridge University Press 2006) 155.

[177]Felicity Kaganas, 'The First Women's Refuge' in Rosemary Auchmuty and Erika Rackley (eds), *Women's Legal Landmarks: Celebrating the History of Women and Law in the UK and Ireland* (Bloomsbury 2019) 304.

[178]House of Commons Debate 21 July (Hansard 1993) Vol 229 368–403.

funds and to visit refuges which successfully raised the profile of the charity, its cause and the need for its continued financing.[179]

Joan Ruddick, Labour MP for Lewisham, spoke at the parliamentary debate concerning the 1992–93 Home Affairs Committee Report on Domestic Violence. She commented that the prevailing climate of public concern about the level of crime and the increase in violent crime was opportune for those seeking action against domestic violence. Though domestic violence was not a new crime, campaigners had successfully brought it to public attention and, Ruddick explained, 'the difference now is that women are increasingly less prepared to tolerate violence and more prepared to report it to the police and other agencies'.[180]

The 1993 report made 42 recommendations for improving the way domestic violence was being handled in society.[181] The Committee recommended that policy be developed at an inter-ministerial national level and that, at a local level, multi-agency co-ordination was required to implement policy and to provide services. The report urged government to provide refuge services and housing and to educate the public about the unacceptability of the behaviour. In the area of criminal law the report recommended the expansion of specialist domestic violence police units and the dissemination of best practice to all agents of the justice system.[182] Following the Select Committee recommendations, the CPS published their domestic violence strategy. Chairman of the Select Committee, Conservative MP Sir Ivan Lawrence, reported at the debate that the Home Office and the Lord Chancellor's Department 'have taken on board many of our recommendations, particularly in respect of proposals for the police, Crown Prosecution Service, court procedure and the support and protection of witnesses and victims'.[183]

In 1999 the New Labour Home Office and Women's Unit of the Cabinet Office produced the government strategy for tackling and preventing violence against women: 'Living without Fear: An Integrated Approach to Tackling Violence against Women'.[184] The executive summary described

[179]Noreen Taylor, 'Exclusive: Di Pays Secret Visit to Battered Wives' Refuge' (1992) *Daily Mail*.

[180]House of Commons Debate 21 July (1993, Hansard) Vol 229 368, 392.

[181]The Third Report from the Home Affairs Committee of Session 1992–93 on Domestic Violence (1993) House of Commons Paper No. 245-I.

[182]The report was also particularly concerned with making improvements to the law of provocation so that abused women might benefit from this partial defence to murder.

[183]House of Commons Debate 21 July (1993, Hansard) Vol 229 368, 370.

[184]'Living Without Fear: An Integrated Approach to Tackling Violence Against Women' (Home Office and the Women's Unit of the Cabinet Office 1999).

that the government would be 'adding value and supporting' locally driven and non-governmental multi-agency initiatives but did not itself assume a leading role in this regard. Rather, the government—perhaps as a result of their election promises to be tough on crime—framed their chief role as being in the implementation of criminal justice measures and crime reduction.[185] The same observation of policy implementation was subsequently made in 2008 in the sixth Home Affairs Select Committee Report on Domestic Violence; criminal justice responses were still being given disproportionate precedence at the expense of effective prevention and early intervention and the context of domestic abuse as violence against women was being side-lined.[186]

A strong criminal justice response, at once protectionist and interventionist, might signal that feminism has successfully engaged the state to adopt their frames of analysis as far as violence against women is concerned. Committed prosecutorial condemnation of domestic abuse, as Chapter 2 explored, has the effect of denouncing the behaviour and inducing a 'norm cascade'[187] which can in turn reconstitute the state as less patriarchal.[188] However, contrary to this optimistic appraisal of 'feminist prosecutions', the expansion of criminal justice in line with neoliberal crime control agendas may not represent progress from all, including social democratic, feminist perspectives.

Neoliberal governments have openly worked with women's groups to develop their policy direction to tackle domestic abuse. To do so at once bolsters their public credentials (we are taking domestic abuse seriously and are victim-centred!) yet it also has the effect of diminishing feminists as adversaries by silencing what were their hitherto discordant demands (including feminist critiques of economic and political asymmetry which were inherent in the feminist movement). The pragmatic union typifies neoliberal governments' tactical manoeuvring; by consulting with its opposition it garners itself legitimacy which in turn supports its bid to retain its elected authority. It simultaneously permits the pushing of its own criminal justice agenda in preference to tackling gender inequality more holistically.

---

[185]Anna Matczak, Eleni Hatzidimitriadou and Jane Lindsay, 'Review of Domestic Violence Policies in England and Wales' (2011) Kingston University and St George's, University of London.

[186]Select Committee on Home Affairs, 'Sixth Report: Broad-Ranging Inquiry into Domestic Violence' (2008) available at https://publications.parliament.uk/pa/cm200708/cmselect/cmhaff/263/26305.htm accessed 12 March 2020.

[187]Cass Sunstein, 'Social Norms and Social Roles' (1996) *Columbia Law Review* 903, 909.

[188]Michelle Madden-Dempsey, *Prosecuting Domestic Violence: A Philosophical Analysis* (Oxford University Press 2009) 165.

Neoliberal governments have been 'particularly hospitable'[189] to those feminists who engage the state on its own terms and recognise the criminal law for its emblematic role and indicator of collective standards.[190] For some feminists leaving the law 'undefended' would only allow men to impress patriarchal norms without challenge. Engaging in government consultations means that legal and political opportunities can be exploited by devising and pursuing pragmatic reforming solutions. Yet when women's groups understandably engage in government consultation processes, the danger is that feminists appear to endorse the government approach which prioritises criminal responses, subject only to 'tweaks'. Whilst few feminists would deny that the criminal justice system provides essential recourse for abused women, many would argue that this should not come at the expense of community support for women (and men) and preventative education.

Criminal law alone is unlikely to upend conventional societal arrangements and ideological norms.[191] Indeed, the greatest opportunities might actually arise from a move away from the law towards less regulation[192] or even decriminalisation.[193] Snider recognises that by moving away from law we make space and possibility for 'creating alternative models, of envisaging different ways of seeing to counter the dead weight of hegemony, for acceptance of the status quo rests heavily on notions that it constitutes the necessary and inevitable ordering of the world'.[194]

If the underlying goal of the women's movement has been social change to end domestic abuse, then in seeking law reforms and criminal justice responsiveness, the women's movement may have suffered more than unintended corollaries of joining forces with the state which could be considered 'just collateral damage in the gender war'.[195] The individualised framing of the criminal law (particularly bearing in mind the neoliberal 'volitional' criminology) detracts from violence against women as a gender equality

---

[189]Ibid., 341.

[190]Clare McGlynn and Vanessa Munro, *Re-thinking Rape Law: International and Comparative Perspectives* (Routledge 2010) Introduction.

[191]See, for example, Smart, *Feminism and the Power of Law* (n 189).

[192]Smart, *Feminism and the Power of Law* (n 189).

[193]Leigh Goodmark, *Decriminalizing Domestic Violence: A Balanced Policy Approach to Intimate Partner Violence* (University of California Press 2018).

[194]Laureen Snider, 'Toward Safer Societies: Punishment, Masculinities and Violence Against Women' (1998) *British Journal of Criminology* 1, 27.

[195]Bumiller (n 2) 15.

issue.[196] Moreover, Bumiller is right when she asserts that the 'mainstreaming' of the movement has resulted in an allegiance with a neoliberal pursuit of social control.[197] Conceived as crime, violence against women appears reconstructed as a consequence of failed responsibilisation and, consequently, potential for future reform to address ongoing gender inequity is diminished. Even in the shadow of neoliberal government rhetoric which recognises violence against women as a systemic manifestation,[198] if the tendency is towards criminalisation, then the effect is towards de-contextualisation and individualisation.[199]

The neoliberal volitional theory of crime sees the integration of domestic abuse into the routine business of crime control, complete with its professional language, rational categorisations and managerial tendencies. Gruber sums up the position thus: 'rather than the criminal justice system adopting a feminist agenda, feminist reformers essentially adopted the criminal justice system's agenda'.[200] With criminal justice used as a primary framework to meet women's safety needs, if concepts like patriarchy or sexual domination are ever considered they are only in so as far as they are applicable to a highly rational conception of diagnosis or social control.[201]

Annette Ballinger concurs. In her recommendations for the 2011 incoming coalition government, she accused the preceding New Labour government's VAWG strategy of having 'undermined the gendered nature of domestic violence... redefining [it] as gender-neutral'.[202] She asserts this is because by tackling the gendered violence problem as crime, what becomes prioritised are police targets and criminal justice goals, not women's safety (as Chapter 4 evidences). Pro-arrest initiatives and pro-prosecution emphases are pursued by criminal justice actors as the end in themselves and VAWG becomes one piece of a broader government programme to reduce crime and bring perpetrators to account. A criminal justice approach to

[196] Lise Gottell, 'Canadian Sexual Assault Law: Neoliberalism and the Erosion of Feminist Inspired Law Reforms' in Clare McGlynn and Vanessa Munro (eds), *Re-thinking Rape Law: International and Comparative Perspectives* (Routledge 2010) 209–223.

[197] Ibid., 15.

[198] See, for example, Crown Prosecution Service, 'Violence Against Women and Girls Report 2015–2016' (2016) 3 available at http://www.cps.gov.uk/publications/docs/cps_vawg_report_2016.pdf accessed 19 May 2018.

[199] Gottell, 'Canadian Sexual Assault Law' (n 196).

[200] Aya Gruber, 'A "Neo-Feminist" Assessment of Rape and Domestic Violence Reform Law' (2012) *Gender, Race and Justice* 583, 589.

[201] Bumiller (n 2) 13.

[202] Annette Ballinger, 'Lessons for the Coalition' (2011) *Criminal Justice Matters* 16, 17.

VAWG also fails women because it detracts from proper funding for refuges or rape crisis centres which have been shown to support women who may not call on the criminal justice system at all.[203]

Furthermore, neoliberal strategies focused on assisting victims of abuse have tended to emphasise *individual* explanations of the occurrence rather than looking for more comprehensive understandings that might counteract broader forms of discrimination in women's lives. In short, by understanding crime as the choice of individual actors, the heteropatriarchal social order is left unchallenged.[204] Through reactive criminal responses, once victims make themselves known, rather than proactive preventative strategies before victimisation has occurred, there has been an emphatic failure to confront male power and its associated violence.[205]

Conclusion

The examination of 'neoliberalism' presented here describes more than just the economic and political climate in which the CPS operates. Neoliberalism is a far-reaching ideology, framework or way of thinking that has social, cultural and intellectual qualities which saturate day to day decision-making in all areas of life. Tenets of 'freedom', 'individualism' and 'responsibilisation' have been used in the service of increased criminalisation to manage and control transgressive behaviours. Neoliberalism's new criminology rejects social democratic theories of criminality and unambiguously presents crime as a rational choice made by responsible actors. The tenacious prosecutions of domestic abuse offenders must be considered in light not only of this neoliberal criminology, but also in light of techniques of neoliberalism—for example managerialism, the centrality of the victim and the use of risk assessments.

Neoliberal governments strategically navigate for retention of power, pandering to public demands for 'expressive justice', even if the resulting criminal justice expansion is at the expense of the neoliberal ambition to roll back the state. Neoliberal governments appear, paradoxically, ready

[203]Ibid., 16.

[204]Ibid., 17.

[205]Maggie Wykes and Kirsty Welsh, *Violence, Gender and Justice* (Sage 2009); Bumiller (n 2) has argued that any stall in the progress of the social reform the women's movement seeks can be attributed to the neoliberal 'appropriation' of the feminist movement.

to heavily regulate spaces to ensure the conditions for freedom are created with the expectation that benefitting individuals will ultimately self-regulate. The expectation that those who commit domestic abuse should face criminal conviction speaks to this crime control imperative.

To facilitate their retention of power, neoliberal governments do not wed themselves to theoretical or ideological orthodoxy. Affiliating with activist groups such as VAWG or victim-rights groups is, for neoliberals, strategically advantageous; the theory justifies the action and garners them legitimacy. As Harvey has pointed out, '[a]ny political movement that holds individual freedoms to be sacrosanct is vulnerable to incorporation into the neoliberal fold'.[206]

Whilst the affiliation clearly meets the demands of feminists for improved criminal justice responses, the union carries certain disadvantages for feminists; any remaining discordant demands become less urgent once the state is seen to be acting on women's behalf. Moreover, if feminists still seek and aspire to society's wholesale restructuring to break down gender inequality, allegiance with the neoliberal penal state will fall short and genuine transformative ameliorations outside of the law and order paradigm are lost at the expense of the symbolic and partial gains effected through criminalisation.[207] The consequence of the criminal justice response is the silencing of feminist explanations about the causes of domestic abuse and of feminist demands for strategies that have 'potential to transcend criminalisation and nurture transformative, counter-hegemonic change'.[208]

The next chapter offers empirical analysis of how techniques of neoliberalism, and particularly managerialism, manifest and perform as a 'tactical organisation of society'[209] vis-a-vis everyday 'working practice' at the CPS.

References

Ashworth A, 'Developments in the Public Prosecutors Office in England and Wales' (2000) 8(3) *European Journal of Crime, Criminal Law and Criminal Justice* 257.

Auchmuty R and Rackley E, *Women's Legal Landmarks: Celebrating the History of Women and Law in the UK and Ireland* (Bloomsbury 2019).

---

[206] Harvey (n 14) 41.

[207] Snider (n 194) 28.

[208] Ibid., 28.

[209] Downing (n 126) 18.

Avail Consulting, 'NWNJ Pilot Evaluation Final Report: Crown Prosecution Service and ACPO' (2004) 6.

Ballinger A, 'Lessons for the Coalition' (2011) *Criminal Justice Matters* 16.

Barry A, Osborne T and Rose N, *Foucault and Political Reason. Liberalism, Neo-liberalism and Political Rationalities* (University College London Press 1996).

Bell E, *Criminal Justice and Neoliberalism* (Palgrave MacMillan 2011).

Bennion F, 'The New Prosecution Arrangements' (1986) *Criminal Law Review* 3.

Bottom A and Roberts J, *Hearing the Victim: Adversarial Justice, Crime Victims and the State* (Willan 2010).

Bumiller K, *In an Abusive State: How Neoliberalism Appropriated the Feminist Movement Against Sexual Violence* (Duke University Press 2008).

Campbell J and Pedersen O, *The Rise of Neoliberalism and Institutional Analysis* (Princeton University Press 2001).

Conservative Party, '1979 Conservative Party General Election Manifesto' (1979) available at http://www.conservativemanifesto.com/1979/1979-conservative-manifesto.shtml accessed 13 January 2018.

Crown Prosecution Service, 'About Charging' available at https://www.cps.gov.uk/about/charging.html accessed 14 December 2018.

———, 'Casework Quality Standards' (2014) available at www.cps.gov.uk/publications/docs/cqs_oct_2014.pdf accessed 9 March 2018.

———, 'Conditional Caution Guidance' available at www.cps.gov.uk/publications/directors_guidance/adult_conditional_cautions.html#a01 accessed 21 March 2018.

———, 'Domestic Abuse Guidelines for Prosecutors' (2014) available at https://www.cps.gov.uk/legal-guidance/domestic-abuse-guidelines-prosecutors accessed 9 February 2018.

———, 'The Code for Prosecutors' (CPS 2018) available at https://www.cps.gov.uk/sites/default/files/documents/publications/Code-for-Crown-Prosecutors-October-2018.pdf accessed 21 March 2018.

———, 'Violence Against Women and Girls Crime Report: 2018–2019' (2019) available at https://www.cps.gov.uk/sites/default/files/documents/publications/cps-vawg-report-2019.pdf accessed 3 March 2020.

———, 'Violence Against Women and Girls Report 2015–2016' (2016) 3 available at http://www.cps.gov.uk/publications/docs/cps_vawg_report_2016.pdf accessed 19 May 2018.

Daw R, 'A Response' (1994) *Criminal Law Review* 904.

Downing L, *The Cambridge Introduction to Michel Foucault* (Cambridge University Press 2008).

Feeley M, 'Crime, Social Order and the Rise of Neo-conservative Politics' (2003) *Theoretical Criminology* 111.

Feeley M and Simon J, 'The New Penology: Notes on the Emerging Strategy of Corrections and Its Implications' (1992) 30(4) *Criminology* 449.

Fourcade M and Healey K, 'Moral Views of Market Society' (2007) 33 *Annual Review of Sociology* 285.
Fraser N, 'Feminism, Capitalism, and the Cunning of History: An Introduction' (2012) FMSH-WP2012-17.
Gamble A, *Free Economy and the Strong State* (Macmillan Education 1988).
Gane N, 'Book Review: The Road from Mont Pelerin: The Making of the Neoliberal Thought Collective' (2012) 60(4) *The Sociological Review* 777.
———, 'The Emergence of Neoliberalism: Thinking Through and Beyond Michel Foucault's Lectures on Biopolitics' (2014) 31(4) *Theory, Culture and Society* 3.
Garland D, 'Beyond the Culture of Control' (2004) *Critical Review of International Social and Political Philosophy* 160.
———, *The Culture of Control: Crime and Social Order in Contemporary Society* (Oxford University Press 2001).
George S, 'A Short History of Neoliberalism' (1999) Conference in Economic Sovereignty in a Globalising World, Bangkok available at https://www.tni.org/en/article/short-history-neoliberalism accessed 20 April 2018.
Gottschalk M, *The Prison and the Gallows: The Politics of Incarceration in America* (Cambridge University Press 2006).
Gruber A, 'A "Neo-feminist" Assessment of Rape and Domestic Violence Reform Law' (2012) *Gender, Race and Justice* 583.
Hall M, *Victims of Crime: Policy and Practice in Criminal Justice* (Willan 2009).
Hansard Online, 'Crown Prosecution Service: Funding' (Hansard Online 2017) Volume 619.
Harcourt B, *The Illusion of Free Markets* (Harvard University Press 2011).
Harvey D, *A Brief History of Neoliberalism* (Oxford University Press 2005).
Home Office, 'Domestic Violence' (Home Office Circular 1990) 1990/60.
———, 'Justice for All—A White Paper on the Criminal Justice System' (2002) Cm 5563.
———, 'Violence Against Women' (Home Office Circular 1986) 1986/69.
House of Commons Debate 21 July (Hansard 1993) Vol 229 368.
Justice Committee, 'The Work of the Crown Prosecution Service' (2015) available at http://www.parliament.uk/business/committees/committees-a-z/commons-select/justice-committee/news-parliament-20151/crown-prosecution-service-evidence/ accessed 4 April 2018.
JUSTICE: Criminal Justice Committee, 'The Prosecution Process in England and Wales: Report By' (1970) *Criminal Law Review* 668.
Kilkauer T, 'What Is Managerialism?' (2015) *Critical Sociology* 1103.
Lacey N, 'Differentiating Among Penal States' (2010) 61(4) *British Journal of Sociology* 778.
Larner W, 'Neo-liberalism: Policy, Ideology and Governmentality' (2000) 63(1) *Studies in Political Economy* 5.
Leibling A, Maruna S and McAra L, *Oxford Handbook of Criminology* (6th edn, Oxford University Press).

Madden-Dempsey M, *Prosecuting Domestic Violence: A Philosophical Analysis* (Oxford University Press 2009).
Maguire M, Morgan R and Reiner R, *The Oxford Handbook of Criminology* (4th edn, Oxford University Press 2007).
Matczak A, Hatzidimitriadou E and Lindsay J, 'Review of Domestic Violence Policies in England and Wales' (2011) Kingston University and St George's, University of London.
McGlynn C and Munro V, *Re-thinking Rape Law: International and Comparative Perspectives* (Routledge 2010).
McLaughlin E, Muncie J and Hughes G, 'The Permanent Revolution: New Labour, New Public Management and the Modernization of Criminal Justice' (2001) *Criminal Justice* 301.
Mirowski P, 'Book Review: A Brief History of Neoliberalism' (2008) 24(1) *Economics and Philosophy* 111.
Mirowski P and Plehwe D, *The Road from Mont Pelerin: The Making of the Neoliberal Thought Collective* (Harvard University Press 2009).
Mudge S, 'The State of the Art: What Is Neo-liberalism?' (2008) *Socio-Economic Review* 703.
Munro V and Davies M, *Ashgate Research Companion to Feminist Legal Theory* (Ashgate 2013).
Nelson C and Grossberg L, *Marxism and the Interpretation of Culture* (Macmillan Education 1988).
O'Malley P, *Crime and Risk* (Sage 2010).
———, 'Neoliberalism, Crime and Criminal Justice' (2016) 16(10) Sydney Law School Research Paper, 6 available at https://ssrn.com/abstract=2729627 accessed 17 May 2018.
———, *Risk, Uncertainty and Government* (Glasshouse 2004).
Packer H, 'Two Models of the Criminal Process' (1964) *University of Pennsylvania Law Review* 1.
Peck J, 'Zombie Neoliberalism and the Ambidextrous State' (2010) 14(1) *Theoretical Criminology* 104.
Radford J et al, 'Violence Against Women and Children: The Contradictions of Crime Control Policy Under Patriarchy' in Kevin Stenson (ed), *The New Politics of Crime Control* (Sage 1991).
Read J, 'A Genealogy of Homo-Economicus: Neoliberalism and the Production of Subjectivity' (2009) *Foucault Studies* 25.
Reiner R and Maguire M, *The Oxford Handbook of Criminology* (7th edn, Oxford University Press 2007).
Rose D, *In the Name of the Law: The Collapse of Criminal Justice* (Vintage 1996).
Rose N, 'Community, Citizenship and the Third Way' (2000) 43(9) *American Behavioral Scientist* 1395.
Sanders A, 'The CPS—30 Years On' (2016) *Criminal Law Review* 82.

Scherz, 'Protecting Children, Preserving Families: Moral Conflict and Actuarial Science in a Problem of Contemporary Governance' (2011) *Polat-Political and Legal Anthropology Review* 33.

Senellart M, *The Birth of Biopolitics: Lectures at the College de France, 1978–79* (Picador 2004).

Shelley L and Vugh J, *Social Changes, Crime and the Police* (Psychology Press 1995).

Simon J, *Governing Through Crime: How the War on Crime Transformed American Democracy and Created a Culture of Fear* (Oxford University Press 2007).

Simon J and Sparks R, *The Handbook of Punishment and Society* (Sage 2012).

Skinns D, *Coalition Government Penal Policy 2010–2015* (Palgrave Macmillan 2016).

Snider L, 'Toward Safer Societies: Punishment, Masculinities and Violence Against Women' (1998) *British Journal of Criminology* 1.

Squires P and Lea J, *Criminalisation and Advanced Marginality: Critically Exploring the Work of Loïc Wacquant* (Policy Press 2013).

Stoker G, *The New Management of British Local Governance* (Macmillan 1999).

Sturge G, 'UK Prison Population Statistics' (House of Commons Library 2018).

Sunstein C, 'Social Norms and Social Roles' (1996) *Columbia Law Review* 903.

Taylor N, 'Exclusive: Di Pays Secret Visit to Battered Wives' Refuge' (1992) *Daily Mail.*

Wacquant L, *Punishing the Poor: The Neoliberal Government of Insecurity* (Duke University Press 2009).

Wilson J, *Thinking About Crime* (Basic Books 1975).

Wykes M and Welsh K, *Violence, Gender & Justice* (Sage 2009).

Young J, 'Searching for a New Criminology of Everyday Life: A Review of "The Culture of Control" by David Garland' (2002) 43(1) *British Journal of Criminology* 228.

4

Domestic Abuse, Managerialism and Crown Prosecution Service 'Working Practice'

This fourth chapter turns attention to the handling of intimate partner abuse cases by Crown Prosecutors in their daily working lives. Part One of the chapter briefly traces past prosecutorial approaches in relation to victim retraction, noting that from CPS' inception in 1986, prosecutors invariably assented to victim withdrawal. The first CPS domestic abuse policy came in 1993 but it merely paid lip-service to a CPS commitment to pursuing domestic violence cases.[1] The key shift towards the current climate of 'tenacious prosecutions' only took place between 2005 and 2008 with the advent of revised policy and mandated training.

Part Two of the chapter illustrates, through qualitative research with a sample of nine prosecutors in the South of England, how neoliberal political idiolects and managerial business stratagems have now converged to shape prosecutorial 'working practice'. Recall from Chapter 3 that successive neoliberal governments have promoted economic ideologies in state institutions, even where monetary profit is not considered the end goal, and that the principles and practices of managerialism have been evident in the English and Welsh criminal justice system since at least the mid-1990s.[2] This chapter highlights how techniques of managerialism in the CPS promote increased standardisation in working practices through the development of policies and guidance; how modernisation, efficiency and financial prudence have

[1]Antonia Cretney and Gwynn Davis. 'Prosecuting Domestic Assault: Victims Failing Courts, or Courts Failing Victims?' (1997) *The Howard Journal of Crime and Justice* 146, 147.

[2]Eugene McLaughlin, John Muncie and Gordon Hughes, 'The Permanent Revolution: New Labour, New Public Management and the Modernization of Criminal Justice' (2001) *Criminal Justice* 301, 301.

A. Porter, *Prosecuting Domestic Abuse in Neoliberal Times*, Palgrave Socio-Legal Studies,
https://doi.org/10.1007/978-3-030-61369-3_4

become prized; and how target setting, performance monitoring and managerial accountability can have the effect of curbing the discretionary decision-making of Crown Prosecutors.[3]

I illustrate that New Public Managerialism in the CPS now frames prosecutorial practice in terms of administrative outcomes and organisational objectives, particularly in the CPS through the expectation of increased conviction rates. The tendency towards 'tenacious prosecutions' can therefore be attributed, at least in part, to features of New Public Managerialism; I draw out the unexpected and often clandestine ways that this happens. The primary research also reveals that, in the CPS, managerialism's dominant ideology obscures the gendered nature of intimate partner abuse and leads to insufficient consideration of women's diverse needs.

Part One—Tracing CPS Approaches to Domestic Abuse

(i) 'Working Practice' Prior to 2008: Automatic Drop

The CPS issued their first domestic violence policy statement in 1993. It pledged to prosecute all evidentially viable cases in the public interest in a bid to address wider concerns that the criminal justice system was failing to do enough to protect abused women in the private sphere.[4] It also followed specific criticism of the CPS that too few domestic violence cases were being charged, too many cases were having charge levels reduced and discontinuance rates were too high.[5] The CPS was only therefore delivering 'modest achievement' in such cases.[6] Yet, despite police services simultaneously introducing pro-arrest policies in 1993,[7] the CPS policy statement resulted in insignificant shifts in working practices. Consequently, in 2005 the CPS published a policy restatement and, alongside it, mandated domestic

[3]John Raine and Michael Willson, 'Beyond Managerialism in Criminal Justice' (1997) 1(3) *The Howard Journal of Crime and Justice* 80–95. See also Chapter 3 for a detailed appraisal of managerialism.

[4]House of Commons Report from the Select Committee on Violence in Marriage, 1975; Marie Gottschalk, *The Prison and the Gallows: The Politics of Incarceration in America* (Cambridge University Press 2006).

[5]Mandy Burton, *Legal Responses to Domestic Violence* (Routledge Cavendish 2008) 93; Cretney and Davis (n 1) 147–148

[6]Cretney and Davis (n 1) 147.

[7]Carolyn Hoyle and Andrew Sanders, 'Police Response to Domestic Violence: From Victim Choice to Victim Empowerment' (2000) 40(1) *British Journal of Criminology* 14, 17.

violence training for all prosecutors. CPS training was delivered nationally between 2005 and 2008 and definitively signalled domestic violence as an augmented priority within the organisation.[8]

Prosecutors in my study who had been with the service for sufficiently long duration recalled the approach of prosecuting domestic violence prior to the 2008 sea-change. Their sense was that domestic violence had never previously been differentiated from other sorts of crime; 'It certainly wasn't flagged... They weren't called domestic violence... Sometimes you would get a conviction and sometimes you wouldn't. They weren't kind of given specialist treatment [or] looked at specifically as quite a serious statistic'.[9] These prosecutors recognised that the past CPS approach had encouraged the accused to 'play the system'. There was an expectation that defendants would be advised to make 'no comment' during the police station interview and then wait to see if the complainant attended court to give evidence against him: 'The culture was very much, let's wait and see if she turns up and if she doesn't turn up, it will be binned. So, if you were defending, your client wouldn't really say anything until you had gone to him [on the day of trial] and said, 'She's here'... But mostly she wouldn't ever be there'.[10] This prosecutor did not expressly comment on the extent to which the approach of lawyers prior to 2008 incited perpetrators to intimidate the victim into retracting their complaint. Clearly, however, if defence lawyers were giving defendants advice that the prosecution would likely drop the case if the victim was unsupportive, the risk that defendants would then pressurise the victim into submission must have been understood.

The 1993 CPS 'Statement of Prosecution Policy' in relation to domestic violence[11] indicated that victim withdrawal *should* prompt the obtaining of a retraction statement outlining her reasons and whether she had been put under any pressure not to proceed with the criminal prosecution. The policy at that time also suggested that prosecutors *ought* to consider alternative evidence and ways of proceeding with the case, absent the victim's support. However, Cretney and Davis' 1997 empirical research exposed the fact that despite the policy, prosecutors frequently failed to obtain victim retraction statements or to explore pursuing the case with an unsupportive complainant, for example through summons or relying on other corroborative

[8]Matthew Hall, *Victims of Crime: Policy and Practice in Criminal Justice* (Willan 2009) 143–149.

[9]Prosecutor 6.

[10]Prosecutor 8.

[11]Crown Prosecution Service, 'A Statement of Prosecution Policy: Domestic Violence' (CPS Policy Group 1993).

evidence.[12] Rather, prosecutors would typically terminate proceedings on victim withdrawal, justifying their decision on evidential grounds; because a hostile witness was unlikely to provide a realistic prospect of conviction.[13] What ran parallel to the evidential sufficiency test, according to Hoyle, was a prosecutor's 'working rule' that equated 'non-cooperative' witnesses with 'unwinnable' cases.[14]

In addition to citing evidential justifications, prosecutors in the past were persuaded to discontinue cases for, what Burton calls, 'humanitarian reasons' which might see prosecutors justifying their decision under the second stage of the prosecutors' code; the 'public interest' test (where the views of the victim can be taken into account). Such reasons included not wanting to compel an unwilling witness against her stated wishes (complete with explanations of not wanting to deny a woman's autonomy or control[15]) and also of not wishing to exacerbate further violence[16] (by providing the perpetrator with a reason for vengeful action). Hoyle added that the 'working rule' seemed to be genuinely motivated by prosecutors not wishing to disempower a victim by ignoring her wishes because it might discourage her from seeking future criminal justice support (lest her wishes be ignored again).[17] Prosecutors were also mindful that criminal proceedings might damage the parties' attempts at reconciliation. Burton suggests that prosecutors were not concerned with keeping abusive families together, but rather failed to see how prosecution helped the situation where partners were reconciling.[18] These rationalisations, in conjunction with prosecutors' assessment of the likely 'paltry sentence' and perceived benefit for a reluctant victim, seemed to weigh against prosecution. Taken together, Louise Ellison recounted in 2002 that complainant retraction in the context of prosecuting domestic violence appeared to have 'an almost singular effect; namely, discontinuance'.[19]

---

[12]Cretney and Davis (n 1) 146–157.

[13]Ibid., 146–157.

[14]Carolyn Hoyle, *Negotiating Domestic Violence: Police, Criminal Justice and Victims* (Clarendon Press 1998) 168.

[15]Ibid., 170.

[16]Cretney and Davis (n 1) 146–157.

[17]Hoyle, *Negotiating Domestic Violence* (n 14) 170.

[18]Burton (n 2) 100.

[19]Louise Ellison, 'Prosecuting Domestic Violence Without Victim Participation' (2002) 65(6) *The Modern Law Review* 834, 834.

This 'working rule' or informal 'automatic drop'[20] policy therefore seems, ostensibly, to be based on the victim's request.[21] Prior to the mandated 2008 training, the individual wishes of the victim frequently surpassed any of the other 'public interest' tests irrespective of whether criminal prosecution could be said to have symbolic power or deterrent effect.[22] Burton notes that the informal 'automatic-drop' practice was possible due to the extensive discretion afforded to prosecutors when weighing up public interest factors. Fionda and Ashworth agreed that the Code offered a paucity of guidance on the matter of how to resolve the conflict between victim and public interest.[23]

As well as frequently acceding to the victim's request to discontinue proceedings, the practice of 'criming down' (or reducing the level of charge of) domestic abuse offences was also prevalent prior to 2008.[24] 'Criming down' prevailed amongst prosecution and defence lawyers once a matter was before the court and also amongst the police. As far as the police were concerned, the practice meant that they frequently failed to arrest the perpetrator at all or that they would arrest an offender for a 'breach of the peace' (which does not result in a conviction but a bind-over—or promise in court—to keep the peace). Arrest might also have resulted in a police caution or a prosecution for the non-imprisonable offence of being drunk and disorderly. When the police took no further action in a case, Edwards reports that the police would often recommend that a woman take out a private prosecution for common assault instead.[25]

Prosecutor 8 explained that, if a matter did come before the criminal court, '[t]here was a lot of dealing behind the scenes... If you would accept that he smashed up her phone, isn't that good enough? It was very much brushing it under the carpet, how can we just deal with this without actually acknowledging how serious it is that somebody is being violent or controlling or whatever with their partner'.[26] Prosecutor 8 did not suggest that this was being done in any 'untoward' way, rather she explained that the

[20]Lisa Goodman and Deborah Epstein, *Listening to Battered Women: A Survivor Centered Approach to Advocacy, Mental Health and Justice* (American Psychological Association 2008) 73.

[21]Crown Prosecution Service, 'Code for Crown Prosecutors' (HMSO 1992) para 6.4.

[22]Hoyle, *Negotiating Domestic Violence* (n 14) 174–175 and Cretney and Davis (n 1) 146.

[23]Julia Fionda and Andrew Ashworth, 'The New Code for Crown Prosecutors: Part 1: Prosecution, Accountability and the Public Interest' (1994) *Criminal Law Review* 894, 902.

[24]Hoyle, *Negotiating Domestic Violence* (n 14) 151.

[25]Susan Edwards, *Policing Domestic Violence: Women, the Law and the State* (Sage 1989).

[26]Prosecutor 8.

focus and priority for prosecutors at court was the 'legitimate' pursuit of saving the public purse the expense of a contested hearing. She also commented that the aim was to 'save people from having to go through with it, so to speak'. Here, she was presumably referring to the ordeal of the victim (and witnesses) having to testify against an intimate partner in a courtroom. But one wonders to what extent she may also have been inadvertently referring to lawyers seeking to short circuit contested hearings for their own benefit; of avoiding the need to stay longer than necessary and the more arduous chore of conducting contested proceedings in court?

(ii) 'Working Practice' in 2008–2009: Summons and Convict

In 2005, the CPS re-launched its Policy for Prosecuting Cases of Domestic Violence,[27] together with its Good Practice Guidance.[28] The Guidance outlined how the service was going to be taking 'a more sophisticated approach to prosecuting hate crimes such as domestic violence'.[29] The new strategy was based on insights gained from a two-year project in which Specialist Domestic Violence Courts in Croydon and Caerphilly were monitored for 'improvements'. 'Improvements' here referred to outcomes which demonstrated that the offender was being brought to justice; increased convictions, reductions in discontinuances, reductions in victim retraction and the increased reporting and prosecutions of cases.[30] The financial implications of successful prosecutions (and the belief that convictions reduce recidivism)

[27]Crown Prosecution Service, 'Policy for Prosecuting Cases of Domestic Violence: 2005' (n 5).

[28]In Crown Prosecution Service, 'Domestic Violence: Good Practice Guidance' (2005) available at http://webarchive.nationalarchives.gov.uk, http://www.crimereduction.homeoffice.gov.uk/domesticviolence/domesticviolence51.pdf accessed 31 August 2017, '[t]he revised Domestic Violence Guidance to CPS staff provides advice on how to proceed if victims withdraw, including the use of evidence other than the victim's, when and if summonses may be required and which factors should be considered, advice on warrants and reasons to discontinue. In this Circular, police and prosecutors will be reminded of the need for effective gathering of evidence such as photographs of injuries, 999 tapes, CCTV evidence and statements from other witnesses both to strengthen the case and to enable a case to progress, even if victims withdraw their support for the prosecution'.

[29]Attorney General quoted in the foreword of Crown Prosecution Service, 'CPS Domestic Violence: Good Practice Guidance Summary' (2005) available at https://www.cps.gov.uk/publications/docs/dv_protocol_goodpractice_summary.pdf accessed 31 August 2017.

[30]The new approach tied in with the broader CPS 'No Witness, No Justice' project. In 2005, the NWNJ scheme introduced 165 witness care units focused on supporting victims and witnesses through the trial process; the aim was to reduce the rate of cracked and ineffective trials through improved witness attendance at court; enable more witnesses to give their best evidence; and increase victim and witness satisfaction.

were forefronted. The Good Practice Guidance also promoted gathering evidence and building the case absent the victim, ensuring appropriate bail conditions and information exchange between professional agencies. Witness summonses were to be considered but only after full consideration of the 'safety issues'. The guidance suggested that a successful conviction is a successful outcome for the victim, save only where her safety would have been compromised by pursuing the case.

The following account of the 2005–2008 training that ran parallel to the publication of the CPS policy and guidance has been compiled from my recollection, having undertaken the training myself, together with information contained in the CPS training evaluation report.[31] The training stressed that violence between intimate partners was a crime that must be afforded high priority by criminal justice agents. It imparted practical and 'consistent'[32] ways to take a proactive approach. Prosecutors were educated about the dynamics of abusive relationships and about how perpetrators often manipulated the system to maintain control over their partner and to effect their preferred outcome. The objective of the training was to shift any permissive attitudes amongst prosecutors. In practical terms, prosecutors were invited to be robust with defence requests to 'crime down' (reduce the level of charge) or to vary bail conditions. They were encouraged to liaise with Independent Domestic Violence Advocates (IDVAs) or the Officer in the Case (OIC) before agreeing to any alterations. Trainers used case studies to illustrate and model the new approach and, in practical terms, prosecutors were encouraged to apply to admit bad character evidence for like previous convictions, to apply for special measures to assist witnesses giving testimony, to use res gestae evidence where possible, to make use of victim personal statements at sentencing and to apply for witness summonses where appropriate. Attaining convictions where possible and delivering 'high quality service to victims'[33] was paramount.

The impact of the training programme and new policy was clear; domestic abuse conviction rates rose from 55% in 2005 to 70.7% in 2008; discontinuance rates fell from 37 to 22.9%; and the use of bind-overs fell from

[31]Crown Prosecution Service, 'Evaluation of the National Domestic Violence Training Programme 2005–2008' available at https://www.cps.gov.uk/publications/equality/evaluation_of_national_domestic_violence_training_programme.html accessed 29 June 2018. The training was coordinated across the police and the CPS and was designed and delivered in person by a number of regional trainers. The national strategy was made available afterwards through the staff intranet and each participant received a copy of the training on CD Rom for future reference.

[32]Ibid.

[33]Ibid.

18.2 to 5.3% in the same period.[34] The statistics illustrate the extent of the re-education in the service, from 'automatic drop' to 'tenacious pursuit'.[35]

The CPS conducted its own qualitative research with focus groups in 2008[36] to examine the cultural impact of the new approach. The professionals interviewed attested to the seriousness with which domestic violence was now being treated by the CPS. Prosecutors were described as determined to achieve successful outcomes yet showing sympathy for victims and the way perpetrators might interfere with witnesses to terminate the case. One prosecutor interviewed in 2008 summarised that, 'The defence now know we don't just drop DV cases because the victim doesn't wish to give evidence'.[37]

In 2009, sociologist Matthew Hall examined the treatment of domestic violence cases in courts in the North of England and surmised that the new approach rendered domestic violence 'one on its own'.[38] The 'general thrust', according to one Magistrates' Court District Judge in Hall's study, was that the CPS 'prosecute every case'.[39] At the time of Hall's work, new Association of Chief Police Officers Guidance[40] also urged officers to build cases with as much supporting and corroborative evidence as possible.[41] This *should* have led to a rise in the number of 'victimless prosecutions' in line with recommendations urged by Louise Ellison in 2002.[42] However, the drive to prosecute whenever possible appears to have been achieved, at least according to Hall, through the summonsing of unsupportive victims.

One area Chief Crown Prosecutor confirmed that summons would be the 'proper' way to proceed, in accordance with the new policy, when a woman

[34]All statistics taken from ibid.

[35]Whilst I have cited the CPS training programme as pivotal in impacting DA prosecutorial decision-making, other factors may also have contributed; IDVA support, the introduction of witness care units, parallel police commitment to the crime, the establishment of Specialist Domestic Violence Courts in 2006 and community safety partnership support for victims. The judiciary also recognised the public interest in prosecuting domestic abuse, see, e.g., R v C [2007] EWCA Crim 3463.

[36]The groups comprised prosecutors and domestic violence professional partners.

[37]Crown Prosecution Service, 'Evaluation of the National Domestic Violence Training Programme 2005–2008' (n 31).

[38]Hall (n 8) 143.

[39]Ibid., 144.

[40]National Policing Improvement Agency on behalf of Association of Chief Police Officers, 'Guidance on Investigating Domestic Abuse' (2008) available at http://library.college.police.uk/docs/npia/Domestic_Abuse_2008.pdf accessed 24 August 2017.

[41]In the event that a complainant withdrew her support, prosecutors ought to have been able to exploit res gestae 999 calls, medical evidence of her injuries, third-party witness testimony, recent complaint and/or confession evidence to pursue the case against him.

[42]Ellison (n 19) 834.

withdrew her statement.[43] The summons should be backed up, he explained, with the promise of a witness warrant for non-attendance. In practice, the 'threat' to issue a warrant was rarely acted on but its potential use had the effect of inducing guilty pleas. The Chief Crown Prosecutor explained that the imperative to prosecute and in turn to summons arose because of the particular vulnerability of victims due to their ongoing abuse. Victims, he explained, often have low self-esteem such that it impacts their ability to make decisions effectively because they may no longer be able to see their situation objectively.[44] The new approach thus marked a shift in the way that prosecutors made and justified decisions and was based on an understanding that the public interest would almost always expect determined prosecution in the service of the vulnerable victim.

(iii) 'Working Practice' in 2017: Ingrained Habits and Routine Reliance on Summons

Of the sample of nine prosecutors I interviewed in 2017, three prosecutors with sufficiently long tenure supported Hall's findings; that the 2005 policy and guidelines had indeed encouraged pursuance of prosecutions, safety considerations permitting, and that in practice this had translated into, 'Just push it and push it as far as it will go',[45] meaning that after 2008 unsupportive victims were invariably being *required* by prosecutors to come to court to testify by means of summons.

Eleven years later, the prosecutors I interviewed expressed some reservations about the advantages summons offered. Prosecutors were now, largely, aware of the complexity pertaining to the decision to prosecute absent a supportive complainant. Prosecutor 2 understood the matter to be finely balanced and the factors he cited as relevant in deciding how to proceed were typical of those expressed by most prosecutors interviewed. The factors he weighed up fell into two broad categories. The first had to do with the seriousness of the offence; whether children were present, the extent of the injury and whether the defendant had like previous convictions. These are features of the offence that traditionally aggravate the sentence and are therefore aspects that are more likely to justify and require punishment and condemnation through prosecution if present. The second category had more to

[43]Chief Crown Prosecutor in Hall (n 8) 144.

[44]Chief Crown Prosecutor in ibid.

[45]Prosecutor 1.

do with the assessment of risk; whether there was a history of violence and whether parties were likely to reconcile. Where both aspects were present, prosecutors were more likely to consider that the case merited ongoing prosecution due to the potential future risk to the victim. In these circumstances, prosecution carries the advantages of imposing bail conditions prohibiting the defendant from contacting the victim and of potentially imposing a sentence that would serve to protect the victim from future harm.

Prosecutor 2's weighing up of these factors reflected the factors most prosecutors indicated they took into account. They treated the woman's retraction as a trigger for considering the merits of ongoing prosecution but the retraction itself appeared, at least in the absence of any prosecutor stating it expressly, not to act as a factor to be weighed into the mix. It seems that a woman's voice was being heard only to the extent that it prompted review of the case, not to the extent that acceding to what she wanted might also have been considered to have empowering value or to have been the right thing to do given her unique understanding of the power dynamic between her and her abuser.

Whilst most prosecutors professed to employing this more detailed analysis of the advantages and disadvantages of summonsing the reluctant witness, 6 out of 9 prosecutors perceived that significant numbers in the service still obtained a summons as a matter of routine. Prosecutor 4 summed up the position; 'If she's unequivocally saying she doesn't want to attend, then I think the CPS do tend to summons'. This suggests that even though prosecutors may be engaging with the possibility of not summonsing, they are reluctant to discontinue cases and frequently summons in any event. Prosecutor 2 expressed concern that habitual use of summons, in essence a 'no-drop' approach, was being favoured by colleagues simply because it is 'the easy way to do it… "Let's issue a summons!" without maybe thinking about it as much as they should'.

Three prosecutors, all women, however articulated more awareness of the victim's voice or preference and how facilitating empowering outcomes might be dependent upon a respectful consideration of her preference. Victim retraction was considered 'the hardest thing for us. Because at what point do you intervene and potentially overrule someone's wishes? It's a difficult balance'.[46] Showing awareness of the potential for secondary victimisation and the fallibility of the criminal justice system more generally, another of the three prosecutors suggested that instead of forcing victims through the 'trauma' of the court process,

[46]Prosecutor 7.

> if that can be avoided and a positive outcome achieved where the victim is safe and leads a... positive, healthy, happy life then surely that is the better thing to do? Decisions really have to be made on a case by case basis and these kind of blanket policies, I don't think are appropriate in domestic violence cases.[47]

This prosecutor considered whether a non-conviction restraining order in combination with a police referral to domestic abuse support agencies would be sufficient to protect the unsupportive victim, whilst affording the opportunity to adhere to her wishes. However, despite themselves demonstrating awareness of occasions when prosecution may not be preferable, prosecutors 5 and 7 expressed concern that the managers with whom they had to consult and ultimately defer—see below—regularly chose to summons victims and to treat them as hostile witnesses at trial if necessary.

Three of the nine prosecutors however indicated that the tendency to rely on summons is diminishing. This readjustment appears to have been prompted by recent ongoing e-learning training in 2016–2017 which, according to prosecutors, highlighted the potential problems with the use of summonsing and promoted preference for evidence-led (or victimless) prosecutions where the victim is no longer supportive. This was delivered in four mandatory online modules and required prosecutors to work through case studies.[48]

Prosecutor 1 outlined the practice prior to the training,

> I certainly think that 12 months ago, most prosecutors would have been, their first reaction to a withdrawal would have been to appoint a witness summons. It kind of takes the decision out of their hands. They don't need to worry. Just send the summons.

But he went on to identify that since the recent training about victimless prosecutions, 'I do think there has been a change and it's not so trigger happy'. Prosecutor 9, a domestic abuse 'champion',[49] agreed that, 'at the moment, there is a tendency to not necessarily summons. To look at cases as individual cases. Decide whether or not there is any merit in summonsing'.

The third prosecutor who did not identify the routine use of summons was relatively new to the service having worked there for just over a year. She

---

[47]Prosecutor 5.

[48]Prosecutor 2.

[49]As a domestic abuse champion, this prosecutor had enjoyed attending joint meetings with police, courts and IDVAs. These meetings were forums where best practice was disseminated and poor practice considered. They no longer take place according to Prosecutor 9.

herself observed and practised tenacious domestic abuse prosecutions but she was the only prosecutor not to identify that routine summonsing had been practised previously or still did occur. She suggested that the practice is 'not encouraged. It's very much seen as the last resort'.[50] The latest training, undertaken by recently recruited Prosecutor 8, might provide an explanation for why she was the only prosecutor not to identify that there is or ever was a practice of routine summonsing and suggests that there is sensitive and positive change afoot in the service in terms of practising a 'victim-informed' approach.

Despite CPS policy and guidance that clearly advocates the use of summons 'as a last resort' eight out of nine prosecutors in the sample indicated that between 2008 and 2017 the practice was cultivated. Since the 2016 and 2017 training, three prosecutors identified that they were being encouraged to draw back from applying for summonses. Nonetheless, most prosecutors in 2017 still identified a usual 'working practice' akin to 'no-drop' prosecutions, at least in their 'soft form'. The next section examines how neoliberal priorities and managerial pressures may have contributed to the tendency to issue a summons (despite CPS guidance that cautions against its use) and to pursue the case.

Part Two—New Public Managerial Techniques and Prosecutorial Decision-Making

(i) Policy Objectives: Taking Domestic Abuse 'Seriously'

Recall how a preferred technique of managerialism is the deployment of organisational objectives to establish preferred and consistent modes of working. In the area of intimate partner abuse, CPS guidelines immediately establish the culture; 'domestic abuse offences are regarded as particularly serious'.[51] More precisely, as part of the broader government violence against women strategy, the CPS aims 'to bring more perpetrators to justice as well as further protect victims of [domestic] abuse'.[52]

---

[50]Prosecutor 8.

[51]Crown Prosecution Service, 'Domestic Abuse Guidelines for Prosecutors' (2014) available at http://www.cps.gov.uk/legal/d_to_g/domestic_abuse_guidelines_for_prosecutors/ accessed 24 January 2020.

[52]Crown Prosecution Service, 'Violence Against Women and Girls Report, 2016–17' (2017) available at http://www.cps.gov.uk/publications/docs/cps-vawg-report-2017.pdf accessed 16 October 2018.

There is no doubt that prosecutors in my sample thought about domestic abuse cases as a separate category of crime, distinct from other 'general crime' or assault. More than being considered distinct, domestic abuse is considered a 'priority' for the service[53] as part of the DPP's ambition to address violence against women and girls.[54] When pressed about why domestic abuse is a priority for the CPS there was consensus about the 'seriousness' of this type of offence, 'it's just commonplace for us to think of it as something that's serious. Women get killed every week by men in domestic relationships. It's serious'.[55]

Several prosecutors made a link to the seriousness of the offence and the part the CPS must play in ending domestic abuse. 'Well, I mean, obviously [laughs] dare I say, right, this is serious. It happens in private when people are vulnerable. It's not the sort of thing we can have in a civilised society, is it? It has to be stamped out and prevented'.[56] Prosecutor 3 added that effective prosecution and conviction through the criminal law can be a means of expressing actual and figurative condemnation of certain behaviour thereby having deterrent effect; the CPS must:

> put domestic violence in the public forum. It needs to try and stamp out domestic abuse. Basically, they have been identified as cases that we need to do everything we can to actually get justice and see that they are being looked at correctly and basically explore all sorts of avenues to try and stop it happening.[57]

The perceptions of the role and value of criminal prosecutions expressed here are reminiscent of Packer's Crime Control Paradigm[58] and of analysis by Michelle Madden-Dempsey. Specifically, they mirror Madden-Dempsey's assessment of prosecutorial action having consequential value insofar as it results in *actual* consequences; for example, it might result in conviction and successive punishment of perpetrators, the reduction of crime itself or

---

[53]Prosecutors 1, 3, 4, 9.

[54]Prosecutor 9 was the only prosecutor to mention domestic abuse in the context of the overarching VAWG strategy.

[55]Prosecutor 6.

[56]Prosecutor 2.

[57]Prosecutor 3.

[58]Herbert Packer, 'Two Models of the Criminal Process' (1964) *University of Pennsylvania Law Review* 1.

of people's anxiety about crime.[59] Prosecutions also articulate the expressive value of prosecuting which is not consequential but intrinsic. This is akin to the symbolic value of denouncing wrong-doing and exculpating the victim. The criminal 'charge', for example, has preliminary expressive value through accusatorial denouncement whereas conviction and sentence offers more finality through concrete condemnation.[60]

Both the consequential and intrinsic value of prosecuting domestic violence was reiterated by Prosecutor 6, 'Instead of going, oh yeah, let's get rid of this one. It's about looking at the implications of the wider community and the kind of rippling effect of how it will impact society as a whole'. It is noteworthy that I identified Prosecutor 6 as favouring tenacious prosecutions by regularly summonsing reluctant women to secure convictions. For this prosecutor, convictions were invariably considered the preferable outcome in domestic abuse cases. It is quite possible that her articulation of the part criminal prosecutions has in the greater pursuit of challenging the acceptability of intimate partner abuse in society generally has fuelled, or at least has supported, her commitment to obtain convictions, through the use of the summons whenever necessary. In addition to the social value of condemning the crime, Prosecutor 6 also believed that in being seen to take domestic violence seriously, the public's confidence in the CPS as an organisation would increase. The implications of this, according to Prosecutor 6's logic, are that victims would have increased confidence in and would rely more upon the criminal justice system.

(ii) Deferring to Management

Managerialism encourages 'effectiveness' by developing consistent working approaches to meet organisational goals. Consistency is typically achieved through the expansion of management personnel who are tasked with overseeing operations. If expectations about decision-making are clearly defined in policy, and discretion is set within restrictive parameters, decision-making can become routinised and can effectively result in a de-skilling or downgrading of the skilled worker's role (here the Crown Prosecutor).[61] Flynn describes this in terms of a shrinkage in 'work autonomy' or a

[59]Michell Madden-Dempsey, *Prosecuting Domestic Violence: A Philosophical Analysis* (Oxford University Press 2009) 60.

[60]Ibid., 68.

[61]Thomas Kilkauer, 'What Is Managerialism?' (2015) *Critical Sociology* 1103, 1103.

'de-professionalisation of expert labour'.[62] Where managers are ensuring reliable deployment of discretion in line with organisational objectives, their presence is likely to contribute to fewer decisions being made against the cultural grain and they might be seen to have a constraining effect on the workforce. Decision-making powers of professionals might also be curbed as a result of NPM if managers themselves make the decision. Due to the seriousness with which domestic abuse is viewed within the service, most of the prosecutors interviewed were required to consult with their line manager (the 'Level D') before taking any decision to discontinue or terminate domestic abuse proceedings. Prosecutor 5 expressed unease about the approach taken by her line managers,

> I think the decisions really have to be made on a case by case basis and these kind of blanket policies, I don't think are appropriate in domestic violence cases... sometimes of course it's going to be right to pursue a prosecution even if the victim doesn't want to support, of course it's going to be. But there are cases when I think perhaps there are other options available such as referring to other agencies, non-conviction restraining orders, some kind of intervention to help people lead safer lives rather than just this kind of, "No, we've got to prosecute".

Some more senior and experienced prosecutors informed me that they had previously been obliged to consult with their manager but recently were told that they were no longer required to do so. This apparent contradiction between expanding management personnel on the one hand and yet replacing hierarchical decision-making on the other[63] exposes how managerialism, just as its umbrella ideology, neoliberalism, may not operate rigidly according to theory. Rather, it might be considered instrumentalist, pragmatically embracing 'what works'[64] to streamline processes and save money. Managerialism thus 'thinks on its feet'; initially, insisting managers take the decision and then deciding to reduce 'hierarchical decision-making' to free-up valuable managerial time once the 'working practice' is established.

Whilst this may appear again to afford individual prosecutors discretion, the change appears to have taken place because these prosecutors were trusted by their line manager to exercise their discretion in accordance

---

[62]Rob Flynn, 'Managerialism, Professionalism and Quasi-Markets' in Mark Exworthy and Susan Halford, *Professionals and the New Managerialism in the Public Sector* (Open University Press 1999) 30.

[63]Carol Jones, 'Auditing Criminal Justice' (1993) 33(2) *British Journal of Criminology* 187, 188–189.

[64]Jamie Peck, 'Zombie Neoliberalism and the Ambidextrous State' (2010) *Theoretical Criminology* 104, 106.

with now-familiar CPS policies, targets and management expectations. Confirming this, Prosecutor 3 (who now had permission to take the decision herself) commented that one's line manager still set the tone for the decision you were likely to take; 'it tends to be, well, to be encouraged to apply for witness summonses, quite often. I think it depends who is, basically, the Level D at the time as towards the sort of approach you take'.

(iii) Streamlining Processes: Digitalisation

Streamlining processes in the interests of achieving cost-efficiency and the delivery of 'core quality standards' (or organisational objectives) is another key strategy of NPM. Jones has suggested that managerialism's 'three E's'—economy, efficiency and effectiveness—are responsible for a move away from traditional guiding principles of criminal justice such as procedural justice and fairness.[65] She describes a move towards 'managerial justice' where speed and finality are valued which requires routinised ways of operating to ensure quantity can be handled proficiently.[66]

In a bid to modernise and streamline efficient processes, the CPS has, relatively recently, introduced the 'digital file' and consequently eliminated the 'paper file'. Prosecutors are now allocated a digital caseload (Prosecutor 3 indicated hers included 145 files that day), and each prosecutor is presented with a digital task list every day (Prosecutor 3 indicated that her task list was 7 pages long and that many of those tasks were reviews that needed to be completed that day in readiness for the case appearing in court the following day).

Illustrating how NPM expects productivity, Prosecutor 6 had been told that there was an expectation that she would complete eight full file reviews daily and that managers were monitoring that this was achieved. She had reservations about the merits of such a demand and suggested that the system had to be 'played' by prosecutors to achieve the expected target,

> It's that kind of thing of, big brother is watching you. Can't be trusted. Sometimes if you've taken a long time on a file that is complex, you say, I can't put down that I spent three hours looking at this crazy nightmare. I've got to say I've done one and a half hours. Then I've got to try and do more work to fill in the hours I've got to put down on paper. It's crazy.[67]

[65]Jones (n 63) 187.

[66]Packer (n 58) 1.

[67]Prosecutor 6.

The same prosecutor had frustrations with the laboriousness of locating information on a digital case as compared to a physical paper file and suggested that only if she 'cut corners' could she complete the work expected on a digital file in the time allocated.[68] For Prosecutor 2, digital working was 'fine, as long as things are sent properly and legibly. It can be quite irritating when it's not. To pick up a paper file and look through and everything is there is nice. [Digital working] is not something I've been completely against... Whether it's improved efficiency or not, I am not so sure'.[69]

Decisions being made in domestic abuse cases must be considered in the light of the time constraints presented by the more laborious nature of working through a digital file and in the light of the expectation that prosecutors must manage a significant caseload and task list within the time allotted. Time pressures doubtless impact the thoroughness with which information can be collated and considered; 'There's never enough time to do anything... it sort of feels like you're working against [it] to get it all done quickly'.[70]

Garland and Packer highlight how the need for efficiency in the criminal justice system evolves routinised decision-making.[71] In domestic abuse cases, the use of summons represents an efficient solution to the obstacle of victim retraction because of the time saved avoiding a thorough victim risk assessment which requires consulting a variety of sources (victim retraction statements, police risk assessments, Independent Domestic Violence Advocates' representations or information known to police 'witness care' officers). Summons therefore achieves two NPM demands; it is time-efficient and it simultaneously espouses the organisational objective to actively condemn domestic abuse.

(iv) Austerity

Since 2010, the coalition and Conservative governments have governed through a political logic of austerity, a priority which, just as NPM, makes

[68]It should be noted that Prosecutor 6 did not suggest that she herself cut corners, just that if you did not, you had to make up the time elsewhere.

[69]Prosecutor 2.

[70]Prosecutor 2. Prosecutor 3 used the same words, 'I don't have enough time to do anything'. Prosecutor 4 said, 'There is never enough time'. Prosecutor 5, 'There just aren't enough hours in the day or enough prosecutors in the office to be doing the job that needs to be done'. Prosecutor 7, 'I don't feel I have enough time to prepare'. Prosecutor 8 stated that she did not have enough time to deal with DA. Prosecutor 9 stated that she did not always feel she had enough time to prepare for court.

[71]David Garland, *The Culture of Control: Crime and Social Order in Contemporary Society* (Oxford University Press 2001) 18; Packer (n 58) 1.

demands for 'economy'. As managerialism is specifically designed to facilitate cost-efficiency, NPM's methods gain particular credence in times of austerity. Austerity, a political rather than an economic concept,[72] aims to return economic stability through the seemingly common sense but arguably 'economically illiterate'[73] notion of spending within one's means. The policy has been closely linked to neoliberalism; indeed, it has been argued that austerity is not a peripheral neoliberal policy but its 'most important moment'.[74] The government itself rarely prefers the term, rather it is a label that is ascribed by others to describe the 'dramatic and severe spending cuts'[75] designed to significantly reduce budgetary deficits in preference to raising funds through taxation or borrowing.

The prosecutors I interviewed were under no doubt that budgetary 'cuts', attributed to austerity, contributed to the pressure they felt to work expeditiously. In the last chapter, I outlined the £185 million cut to the CPS budget between 2009 and 2015.[76] Such cuts represent the opposite of the stimulus plans associated with the Blair and Brown era which saw targeted spending plans in the public sector, notably in the area of criminal justice.[77]

Prosecutor 5 spoke of the reduced numbers of staff available to do the work in 2017, 'The majority of people working at the CPS are doing their absolute best. I know they are. But there just aren't enough hours in the day or enough prosecutors in the office to be doing the job that needs to be done'. Whilst Prosecutor 2 noted that, 'Lots of people have gone. It just seems to me that there is a smidgen of what was left. I mean, I know that you are told that there is less magistrate's work now, but it doesn't feel like it. It sort of still feels like you are working against the line to get it all done quickly'. Prosecutor 2 was correct that the numbers of cases brought to magistrates' courts nationwide declined by just over 100,000 in the period

[72]Rebecca Bramall, Jeremy Gilbert and James Meadway, 'What Is Austerity?' (2016) 87 *New Formations* 119–140.

[73]Ibid., 119–140.

[74]Alpar Losonc, 'Austerity: History of a Dangerous Idea by Mark Blyth' (2014) *Panoeconomicus* 389, 394.

[75]Bramall, Gilbert and Meadway (n 72) 119.

[76]Hansard online, 'Crown Prosecution Service: Funding' (2017) 619 available at https://hansard.parliament.uk/Commons/2017-01-11/debates/3CCEE460-C6B8-44B5-A7C3-677947ECEA19/CrownProsecutionServiceFunding accessed 18 September 2018.

[77]It should be noted that in August 2019, the Conservative, Johnson-led, government announced that the CPS will receive £85 million in additional funding. DPP Max Hill welcomed the move indicating that 'We will be able to invest the money, to try and make the process of going through court more efficient'. BBC, 'Law and Order: Extra £85 Million for CPS to Tackle Violent Crime' (2019) available at https://www.bbc.co.uk/news/uk-49314259 accessed 21 January 2020.

2010–2015, falling from 641,000 cases to 539,000.[78] Prosecutors are also likely to be accurate when they identify that they have no sense that the number of cases that must be prepared by each individual prosecutor has reduced. This is because between 2010 and 2015, 2400 members of staff left the service, largely through voluntary redundancies, in order to meet the 40% reduction in the staffing budget in the same period.[79]

In a further move, apparently motivated by a desire to reduce the amount of work both prosecutors and courts have to contend with in times of austerity, prosecutors reported that District Judges in their area were unilaterally and routinely issuing summonses at the first hearing in *every* contested domestic abuse case regardless of whether women had expressed reluctance. [80] These summonses would remain on file and were available for service should the reviewing lawyer deem them necessary in due course. This avoided the need for a separate CPS application to the court for a summons and appears to have been motivated by efficiency savings because the practice reduces the number of court hearings in a single case. Prosecutor 9 described the practice simply as a 'backstop summons'. However, Prosecutor 7 expressed more concern explaining that the availability of the summonses encouraged their service and gave a concrete example of one senior lawyer's quick readiness to use it. The message conveyed by District Judges here is that summonsing a reluctant complainant is ordinary, standard and not a-typical. Irrespective of whether District Judges are creating this climate or reflecting the CPS tendency to require victim attendance, the effect is surely one of normalising reliance by the CPS on the practice.

Austerity has also impacted another key actor working in the criminal justice system; the Independent Domestic Violence Advocate (IDVA) who works with survivors from the point of crisis towards longer-term well-being goals. The Home Office ceased direct funding of IDVAs in March 2017 and local Police and Crime Commissioners are now responsible for their provision. Working with those categorised as 'high risk', IDVAs work as a bridge between multiple agencies (including the CPS) within both civil and criminal courts. Their primary function is to ensure the victim's voice and safety

[78]Ibid. The reduction in cases being brought to court is arguably as a result of spending cuts, in times of austerity, experienced by the police.

[79]Ibid. At the time of writing, in January 2020, the CPS announced that it would be recruiting Crown Prosecutors nationally as a result of the £85 million additional funding promised by the Conservative government prior to the December 2020 general election.

[80]Prosecutors 7 and 9 (Prosecutor 5 alluded to the practice also—a court clerk had talked to her about it).

is fore-fronted at proceedings and prosecutors in my study spoke favourably of IDVAs' input. IDVAs advise, for example, on the appropriateness of defence applications to vary bail conditions or on the proposed conditions of a restraining order. For Prosecutor 9, the area domestic abuse lead, the presence of IDVAs in court had assisted her in developing and learning 'best practice' and Prosecutor 6 suggested such specialist knowledge set the tone in court. Prosecutors clearly considered IDVAs an important information resource when it came to deciding how best to proceed when a woman is no longer supportive of the prosecution, but only to the extent that they are available to prosecutors or that prosecutors have the time to locate and consult them.

(v) Statistical Analysis

Monitoring performance and target attainment through computerised bureaucracy is characteristic of NPM. To facilitate appraisal of domestic abuse cases (notably the conviction rate and the number of court hearings), domestic abuse must be 'flagged' on the CPS computer system. 'Flagging' a case means that a coloured marker appears on the digital case file so that it is readily identifiable as domestic abuse (as defined by the Home Office) and outcomes can be collated. All prosecutors in the sample were aware that 'flagging' enabled the CPS to compile statistics which were monitored 'as a measure of success'.[81] Statistics were largely considered a concern for managers but nonetheless prosecutors described how statistics 'filter through'[82] to them. Some prosecutors reported that managers emailed their teams statistics for information purposes only. Others received them with an explanation of how 'well' the team were doing in prosecuting domestic abuse and what prosecutors needed to be aware of 'moving forward' bearing in mind, recognised Prosecutor 7, that each of the 13 CPS areas is ranked. Tables are compiled comparing the 13 CPS area conviction rates and are readily circulated and available. Here, clearly visible, is evidence of how the CPS, in the absence of external competitors, is encouraged to compete with itself for best 'output' in line with the tenets of New Public Managerialism.

For one prosecutor, the culture that statistical analysis of cases imbued was not one that sat comfortably with her,

---

[81]Prosecutor 2.

[82]Prosecutor 2.

> I've never been a manager, so I don't - it's one of the reasons I get so frustrated with working for the CPS, I have to say. It's all about, to me it just seems like it is all becoming about targets and statistics and not about the individuals. There's not so much focus on victims. I've never been a manager, so I don't know what goes on in these management meetings and how much it is drummed into you but I always get the impression that it is very very important that targets are met and numbers of successful prosecutions are such and such.[83]

This seems to mirror the notion that New Public Managerialism constructs the public as consumer in the sense that what becomes prioritised is not so much meeting individual victim needs so much as meeting market demands for efficient 'output'[84] and performance. There was a sense amongst prosecutors that the CPS is always monitoring area performance, particularly as compared to other CPS areas. Prosecutor 8 explained,

> My experience is that the conviction rate is… there is a very close eye kept on that for obvious reasons… and obviously because you are flagging DV, if there is a conviction rate falling or dropping or whatever they are able to monitor it.

These auditing processes are also the means by which parliament can hold the Crown Prosecution Service to account. The government's Chief Legal Advisor, the Attorney General, oversees the work of the Director of Public Prosecutions and his organisation and is answerable to parliament for CPS performance. Rates of CPS convictions or discontinuances are also used by the Justice Select Committee that examines CPS expenditure, administration and policy. The Committee is tasked with publishing reports that the government must respond to, to explain or justify how it is spending taxpayers' money.

However, if it is the CPS as an *institution* that is being held accountable to parliament for conviction rates by virtue of such statistical tracking, how are decisions of *individual* prosecutors affected? I identified two ways individual prosecutorial decision-making is impacted by the monitoring of area or nationwide statistics.

The first way is through an institutional-wide response which might be triggered if a set of statistics indicated, for instance, a slump in conviction rates. In such circumstances, Prosecutor 2 suggested that the CPS might

[83] Prosecutor 5.

[84] Carol Jones, 'Auditing Criminal Justice' (1993) 33(2) *British Journal of Criminology* 187, 188–189.

react by rolling out compulsory training amongst prosecutors to address the issue. Such training has the potential to instil a wider cultural shift in the service, as evidenced in 2005–2008. This chimes with NPM's ability to set and implement organisational strategies which have the effect of controlling public servants (prosecutors) and regulating professional independence.[85]

(vi) Risk and Responsibility

In addition to prompting changes to institutional-wide practice and culture, the second way poor performance figures might affect prosecutorial decision-making is at an individual level. Prosecutor 7 understood that a poor monthly performance might prompt further investigation by managers into *particular* files. She understood that individual cases would be scrutinised and questions would be asked about why the case had been dropped. In addition to that, and in any event, a more thorough examination of prosecutorial decision-making takes place in all cases that have resulted in an 'adverse outcome'. An adverse outcome, explained Prosecutor 1, is, 'anything that doesn't result in the defendant being convicted of at least one offence [and] is an unsuccessful outcome; whether discontinued, withdrawn, offered no evidence, dismissed at half time or after full trial'.[86] All 'adverse outcomes' are studied by managers to establish the reasons for not obtaining a conviction and to see if 'improvements' could have been made.[87] Prosecutor 9 confirmed that:

> Adverse outcomes are particularly looked at to see why. Was it a case of a victim not coming to court and therefore we didn't have the evidence? Is it a case the victim came to court but didn't come up to proof [or] didn't give evidence very well? … It's that aspect of things that they look at as to why cases, for want of a better word, failed. Why didn't we secure that conviction? They look to see whether we can learn any lessons from it.[88]

That being so, prosecutors were mindful that any decision they take that might contribute to a reduction in the conviction rate, might be open to inquiry. If a case fails on the day of trial because a summons was

[85]Mark Exworthy and Susan Halford, *Professionals and the New Managerialism in the Public Sector* (Oxford University Press 1999).

[86]Prosecutor 1 by clarification email dated 28 July 2017.

[87]Prosecutor 6.

[88]Prosecutor 9.

not secured, then this may indicate inaction on the part of the prosecutor. Conversely, if a woman has been summonsed and fails to answer the summons, then the prosecutor has done everything within their power (short of issuing a decisions warrant for her arrest) and cannot be criticised.

One area domestic abuse 'champion' suggested that if a prosecutor did not summons, it would not lead to automatic criticism because of growing awareness that summonsing may not necessarily be preferable, particularly if it discourages women from seeking help from criminal justice agencies in the future. Nonetheless, she accepted that prosecutors realised that adverse outcome cases would be examined more rigorously than cases that resulted in conviction and that prosecutors would feel or could be held accountable for decisions leading to acquittals. In short, if a prosecutor fails to push for a domestic abuse conviction, the decision will be one that is scrutinised and the prosecutor will at least have needed to justify the decision in their written review of the case. Managerial appraisal of files therefore contributed to a sense of professional and personal responsibility to meet organisational objectives. Here, again, is evidence of the effect of NPM, which demands compliance with policy objectives (to 'take domestic abuse seriously') and, just as Chapter 3 outlined, holds those tasked with delivering standards and guidelines to account through regular monitoring and inspections.[89]

As a result, we see how NPM can create a culture of fear and insecurity. Prosecutor 4 confirmed that when making the decision to summons, '[Prosecutors] will think of themselves, individually, first of all. They are all civil servants and they want to cover their backs. First rule'. Prosecutor 1 agreed that relying automatically on summons is the least 'dangerous' option for prosecutors because they have demonstrated understanding that every option must be explored to obtain 'justice' for the domestic abuse victim and criminal sanctions for the defendant. Summons, he surmised, 'absolves their responsibility for making decisions [not to prosecute]'.[90]

Prosecutors feared repercussions from managers, not only in relation to professional criticism for 'inadequate' decision-making. The fear extended to criticism should something happen to the victim in the future where a case had been terminated 'prematurely': 'What always used to worry me was, you know, am I going to get one of these cases where it doesn't go ahead or we can't prosecute it properly… and then she's going to be murdered. People

[89]Garland, *The Culture of Control* (n 71) 120.

[90]Prosecutor 1.

are going to say, sorry you were the SCP.[91] Horrendous…'[92] When I asked Prosecutor 8 if that meant that blame might be apportioned to the individual prosecutor if a preceding case had been dropped, she replied, 'Isn't that the CPS to a fault though? They would just hang you out to dry, wouldn't they, I think'.

Indicating that he did not prefer the practice of routine summonsing, Prosecutor 1 suggested that this was because he had had some management experience and concluded that he was probably more self-assured in his decision-making than other people might be. However, even he recognised the potential for repercussions: 'Touch wood, I haven't had one that's come back to bite me yet'. When prompted to expand, he answered:

> I suppose if you really sat and thought about every case, you would have this slight concern that, you know, the victim could be, I don't know, subject to a further serious or even fatal assault. But, we are dealing with so many of these cases, you know, on a daily basis that you have to kind of just get on with it.

For this experienced and senior prosecutor, whilst being aware of the gravity of the decision he was taking, distancing himself from responsibility for any future harm that may come to the victim was the sensible and pragmatic approach to take.

As NPM demands efficiency and speed to achieve cost-effectiveness, prosecutors develop strategies of coping with the demands of heavy workloads. As domestic abuse caseloads require engagement with the cruelty and barbarity of others, one way in which productivity might be maintained is by resisting full engagement with the suffering contained in the victim's account. Prosecutors do not receive training to cope with emotional 'contagion' and must informally manage its impact.[93] By practising emotional detachment, prosecutors are able to minimise 'vicarious trauma', which allows them to step aside from feelings of guilt and responsibility,[94] perhaps evident with Prosecutor 1, cited above. Decision-makers can practise 'detachment, disbelief and denial of responsibility in order to avoid… becoming emotionally overwhelmed by the accounts of persecution and

[91]Senior Crown Prosecutor.

[92]Prosecutor 8.

[93]Louise Ellison and Vanessa Munro, 'Taking Trauma Seriously: Critical Reflections on the Criminal Justice Process' (2017) 21(3) *International Journal of Evidence and Proof* 183, 198.

[94]Ibid., 184.

violence routinely encountered'.[95] This emotional detachment or disengagement from shocking occurrences is a habit that understandably evolves for the purposes of self-protection, but it inevitably means that victim accounts feel unreal and the severity or even veracity of what has been experienced by the victim is diluted.

In the context of prosecuting domestic abuse within NPM constraints, crucial coping strategies avert the need to re-live or imagine the details of a crime, but this can result in a withdrawal from engaging with the needs of the victim or from a detailed assessment of what might facilitate her 'capability set'[96] (or options). In line with Ellison and Munro's assessment of the legal profession through a 'trauma-informed lens', routinely summonsing allows prosecutors to demonstrate a commitment to 'taking domestic abuse seriously' whilst ensuring a measure of emotional self-preservation. Detachment also preserves and permits clarity of thought, which facilitates efficient professional decision-making and task-completion. Withdrawing emotionally from the details of the abuse therefore serves the prosecutor in effecting expeditious decisions and assists in managing the pressures of managerial targets, high workloads and the impacts of austerity.

The Difficulty with Victimless Prosecutions

A number of prosecutors were alert to the fact that victim summons might not always be preferable, but as discussed, six out of nine prosecutors believed that summons was the typical way of proceeding following victim retraction. Concerns cited about routine reliance on summons included the potential for criminal proceedings to further endanger the victim,[97] the potential for secondary victimisation due to the trauma of giving evidence,[98] the damage that can be done through forcing someone to do something against their will[99] or the disincentive to the victim of calling on the criminal justice system in the future.[100] Prosecutor 3 perceived that the 'take

[95] Ibid., 198.

[96] Martha Nussbaum, *Creating Capabilities: The Human Development Approach* (Harvard University Press 2011).

[97] Due to the possibility of perpetrator harassment or retaliation.

[98] Prosecutor 5.

[99] Prosecutor 7.

[100] Prosecutor 9.

home' message from the training she received in 2017 was that where victimless prosecutions are possible, they are to be considered preferable to 'forcing her to come to court'. Through consideration of case studies, the training thus recognised some of the problems of summons.[101]

However, the reason that victimless prosecutions may still not be relied upon is that they are notoriously difficult to prove; 'nine times out of ten, I would say, probably as high as that, the opportunity to prosecute without the victim's support is quite limited'.[102] This is due to offences so often being committed in the privacy of the home out of the gaze of third-party witnesses or CCTV; forensic evidence being unlikely to assist given that the parties are known to each other; and the issue being tested at trial being a question of fact that must be determined between two opposing versions of events, thereby requiring the victim to give her side of the story. Even though the victim may have sustained ostensibly corroborating injuries, in her absence, the perpetrator may still be able to 'explain these away' by suggesting that they were suffered in the course of his legitimate self-defence.

Nonetheless, with the advent of police body-worn footage immediately following an incident, evidence such as damage to property, demeanour of the parties, impermanent but visible injuries sustained and even the victim's first account through the rule of res gestae might all be available. This, in conjunction with 999 calls and comments made by the defendant in interview, can be used to build the case against the suspect, absent the victim. The 2016–2017 training also reminded prosecutors to make use of the hearsay provisions contained in the Criminal Justice Act 2003 and the possibility of having the victim's statement read at trial in her absence.[103] The requirement to 'case build' absent the victim is clearly going to be more labour intensive than the simple issuing of a summons. As discussed above, time pressures imposed by managerial efficiency demands may also influence the decision.

Prosecutors in the sample were far less likely to reflect on the possibility of potential drawbacks or dangers of pursuing a victimless prosecution. Prosecutor 8, who considered summons 'very much … a last resort' said that she was impressed that her colleagues were doing everything they could to

---

[101]Prosecutor 2.

[102]Prosecutor 1.

[103]In the magistrates' court, the hearsay application is usually made on the day of trial. If unsuccessful, the prosecutor will inevitably be forced to offer no evidence and the case will be dismissed (an adverse outcome). The uncertainty surrounding this option and likely outcome means that, according to Prosecutor 3, prosecutors are likely to prefer summonsing the victim.

prosecute without the victim. She commented that the 2016 training made her 'really scrutinise the evidence to make sure I can't prosecute. No stone is left unturned to try and make sure we are doing everything we can'.[104] Doubtless, victimless prosecutions carry clear advantages; there is no risk of secondary victimisation through the ordeal of the trial process; the perpetrator knows that the victim is no longer supporting the prosecution and is therefore arguably less likely to be motivated to intimidate or retaliate; and the behaviour can be condemned and punished. Nonetheless, the risk remains that a criminal sanction is not the safest or desired outcome for the victim, perhaps particularly if parties wish to reconcile. The decision to pursue the case regardless of victim preference also has implications for the victim's sense of autonomy and may impact her decision to call on police again in the future. These risks appear to be factors that are either not considered at all or considered to be secondary to bringing the perpetrator to justice. It appears that meeting the organisational objective is, once again, key.

Domestic Abuse: Not an Issue of Gender for Prosecutors

The extent to which prosecutorial decision-making was influenced by an understanding of domestic abuse as gendered crime was negligible. Prosecutors all commented that domestic abuse victims were usually women. One prosecutor, the area lead in domestic abuse, even referenced domestic abuse prosecutions as part of the wider violence against women strategy.[105] Some were quick to observe that men could also be victims.[106] But there was a distinct lack of appraisal of domestic abuse as a gendered crime rooted in societal gender inequality, male privilege or sexist attitudes. Prosecutors spoke of the defendant's anger, excessive drinking or the couple rowing as potential triggers to abuse and did not connect the resulting use of male violence to a sense of entitlement as a result of male privilege. The notable absence of feminist explanations for domestic abuse speaks to Annette Ballinger's assessment that in dealing with domestic abuse primarily as crime, the effect is to ignore the gendered nature and causes of the behaviour.[107]

---

[104]Tense alteration.

[105]Area domestic abuse lead, Prosecutor 9.

[106]Prosecutors 3 and 7.

[107]Annette Ballinger, 'Lessons for the Coalition' (2011) *Criminal Justice Matters* 16.

Prosecutor 8 commented that 'I do see patterns [in who are the victims] not just in DV, but just that the vulnerable in society are preyed upon'. As part of the 2016 CPS training, stereotypes about who the victims of domestic abuse are were 'blasted away'.[108] Prosecutors were reminded that domestic abuse can happen to anyone.[109] Apparently being re-defined in gender-neutral terms, domestic abuse as a priority for prosecutors becomes part of broader aims of criminal justice, for example centring victims, reducing the number of court hearings and achieving efficient convictions. None of the prosecutors interviewed spoke about the part prosecutors might play in challenging patriarchal norms or sexist ideologies through consistent denouncement of domestic abuse. Despite recent neoliberal governments' explanations, at policy level, of violence against women being a symbol and strategy of patriarchy, evidenced here is how criminal justice agents construct these crimes as failed responsibilisation at an individual level (per neoliberal criminology) and not as evidence of gender inequality.

Conclusion

The principles and practices of New Public Managerialism have been evident in the English and Welsh criminal justice system since at least the mid-1990s.[110] Three key strategies have been deployed since then; modernisation, efficiency and financial prudence; target setting, performance monitoring and managerial accountability; and lastly increased standardisation in policies and practices which has the effect of curbing the decision-making autonomy of professionals.[111] This chapter has drawn out the ways in which NPM's strategies currently operate, often in unacknowledged ways, to influence how prosecutors make decisions in cases of intimate partner abuse where the victim no longer supports criminal prosecution.

The data uncovers a 'working practice', present in 2017 amongst the sample, that can be summarised as a tendency for Crown Prosecutors to

[108]Prosecutor 8.

[109]The empirical research pre-dated the first public statement dated 6 September 2017 by the CPS which openly acknowledged and supported male victims of domestic abuse. Crown Prosecution Service, 'Male Victims Covered by CPS VAWG Strategy' available at http://www.cps.gov.uk/publications/equality/vaw/public-statement-male-victims-crimes-covered-by-CPS-VAWG-strategy.pdf accessed 12 September 2017.

[110]McLaughlin et al. (n 2).

[111]Raine and Willson (n 3) 82.

routinely rely on summonsing reluctant victims of intimate partner abuse to give evidence at trial. This approach appears to have emerged since 2008. According to the majority of prosecutors interviewed, the 'working practice' appears closer to soft 'no-drop'[112] or 'social change'[113] strategies of prosecuting domestic abuse rather than the 'survivor-defined'[114] approach advocated in CPS policy and guidelines. The potential consequences for victims of routinely relying on summons include overlooking risks to her safety during the course of proceedings or immediately afterwards[115] the risk that she no longer trusts the criminal justice system to act in her best interests in the future[116] or the risk that the coercive behaviour of her abuser is simply replaced with coercive practices of the state[117] thereby undermining her own emotional well-being and belief in her ability to be autonomous.[118]

The chapter proposes some of the possible reasons for the emergence of the 'working practice' to the extent that it is identified amongst the sample. It uncovers how concealed, tacit and hitherto unacknowledged strategies of New Public Managerialism contribute to a prosecutorial reliance on summons. At its core NPM seeks efficiency and service delivery in line with organisational objectives and targets. As achieving high rates of convictions in domestic abuse cases is celebrated,[119] the article explains that the routine use of summons serves as an expeditious yet effective way of meeting managerial demands for efficiency whilst effecting CPS policy objectives.

Prosecutorial analysis about the importance of committed prosecutions remained gender-neutral and extended to an understanding that prosecutions send a 'message' that domestic abuse is wrong, and the behaviour should not be left unchallenged. A feminist narrative about the causes of domestic abuse may be woven into CPS policy but prosecutors do not make

---

[112]Eve Buzawa and Carl Buzawa, *Domestic Violence: The Criminal Justice Response* (3rd edn, Sage 2003) 194–203.

[113]Andrea Nichols, 'No-Drop Prosecution in Domestic Violence Cases: Survivor-Defined and Social Change Approaches to Victim Advocacy' (2014) 29(11) *Journal of Interpersonal Violence* 2114, 2114.

[114]Ibid., 2114.

[115]Lauren Catteneo, Lisa Goodman, Deborah Epstein, 'The Victim-Informed Prosecution Project: A Quasi-Experimental Test of a Collaborative Model for Cases of Intimate Partner Violence' (2009) *Violence Against Women* 1227, 1229–1230.

[116]Buzawa and Buzawa (n 112) 194–203.

[117]Linda Mills, 'Killing Her Softly: Intimate Abuse and the Violence of State Intervention' (1999) *Harvard Law Review* 550.

[118]Bruce Winick, 'Applying the Law Therapeutically in Domestic Violence Cases' (2000) 69 *UMKC Law Review* 33.

[119]CPS, 'Violence Against Women and Girls Report' (n 52).

decisions in an effort to confront or destabilise pre-existing gender hierarchies. Prosecutors in this sample also failed to consider how routinised decisions to summons disproportionately affect the lives of women. The belief in the criminal justice system as a force for good and the consequent commitment to achieving perpetrator convictions also appears to support the decision to summons. Such faith in the criminal justice system seems to confirm Ford's assessment of 'prosecution ideology'[120] (that prosecutors consider their role as inherently 'good' as it represents the state's interest in preventing crime) and prosecutors' attachment to Packer's 'Crime Control' model (which expresses that crime can be reduced by the consistent arrest and punishment of offenders).[121]

If the primary research reveals a prosecutorial practice habitually disinclined to adhere to a victim's request to terminate proceedings, the sample also reveals preliminary indications that the 'working practice' may not enjoy wholehearted support from many prosecutors. Moreover, following recent training in 2016–2017, three out of nine prosecutors were reluctant to accept that routine summons was *de rigueur*. Instead, they suggested that 'victimless prosecutions' were being encouraged and each case was being reviewed on its own terms. Whilst there remained a presumption in favour of prosecuting domestic abuse cases, they indicated a nuanced balancing exercise based on information provided from victims, police and third parties was taking place where complainants were unsupportive. Thus, there is some evidence from the research that positive and sensitive change—towards a more nuanced or 'survivor-defined' approach to prosecuting domestic abuse—is afoot. This marks a move towards the CPS policy approach to prosecuting domestic abuse[122] and appears to be taking place, albeit at a preliminary stage, **despite the pressures and demands of NPM**. The following chapter considers the consequences for abused women from the prosecutorial praxis described here.

---

[120] David Ford, 'Coercing Victim Participation in Domestic Violence Prosecutions' (2003) 18(6) *Journal of Interpersonal Violence* 669, 679.

[121] Packer (n 58) 1.

[122] Crown Prosecution Service, 'Domestic Abuse Guidelines for Prosecutors' (2014) available at https://www.cps.gov.uk/legal-guidance/domestic-abuse-guidelines-prosecutors accessed 9 February 2018.

References

Bramall R, Gilbert J and Meadway J, 'What Is Austerity?' (2016) 87 *New Formations* 119–140.

Burton M, *Legal Responses to Domestic Violence* (Routledge Cavendish 2008).

Buzawa E and Buzawa C, *Domestic Violence: The Criminal Justice Response* (3rd edn, Sage 2003).

Catteneo L et al., 'The Victim-Informed Prosecution Project: A Quasi-Experimental Test of a Collaborative Model for Cases of Intimate Partner Violence' (2009) *Violence Against Women* 227, 1229–1230.

Cretney A and Davis G, 'Prosecuting Domestic Assault: Victims Failing Courts, or Courts Failing Victims?' (1997) *The Howard Journal of Crime and Justice* 146.

Crown Prosecution Service, 'A Statement of Prosecution Policy: Domestic Violence' (CPS Policy Group 1993).

———, 'Code for Crown Prosecutors' (HMSO 1992).

———, 'Domestic Abuse Guidelines for Prosecutors' (2014) available at https://www.cps.gov.uk/legal-guidance/domestic-abuse-guidelines-prosecutors accessed 9 February 2018.

———, 'Evaluation of the National Domestic Violence Training Programme 2005–2008' available at https://www.cps.gov.uk/publications/equality/evaluation_of_national_domestic_violence_training_programme.html accessed 29 June 2018.

———, 'Prosecuting "Domestic" Assault' (1996) *Criminal Law Review* 162.

———, 'Violence Against Women and Girls Report, 2016–17' (2017) available at http://www.cps.gov.uk/publications/docs/cps-vawg-report-2017.pdf accessed 16 October 2018.

Edwards S, *Policing Domestic Violence: Women, the Law and the State* (Sage 1989).

Ellison L, 'Prosecuting Domestic Violence Without Victim Participation' (2002) 65(6) *The Modern Law Review* 834.

Ellison L and Munro V, 'Taking Trauma Seriously: Critical Reflections on the Criminal Justice Process' (2017) 21(3) *International Journal of Evidence and Proof* 183.

Exworthy M and Halford S, *Professionals and the New Managerialism in the Public Sector* (Open University Press 1999).

Fionda J and Ashworth A, 'The New Code for Crown Prosecutors: Part 1: Prosecution, Accountability and the Public Interest' (1994) *Criminal Law Review* 894.

Ford D, 'Coercing Victim Participation in Domestic Violence Prosecutions' (2003) 18(6) *Journal of Interpersonal Violence* 669.

Garland D, *The Culture of Control: Crime and Social Order in Contemporary Society* (Oxford University Press 2001).

Goodman L and Epstein D, *Listening to Battered Women: A Survivor Centered Approach to Advocacy, Mental Health and Justice* (American Psychological Association 2008).
Gottschalk M, *The Prison and the Gallows: The Politics of Incarceration in America* (Cambridge University Press 2006).
Hall M, *Victims of Crime: Policy and Practice in Criminal Justice* (Willan 2009).
Hansard online, 'Crown Prosecution Service: Funding' (2017) 619 available at https://hansard.parliament.uk/Commons/2017-01-11/debates/3CCEE460-C6B8-44B5-A7C3-677947ECEA19/CrownProsecutionServiceFunding accessed 18 September 2018.
Hoyle C, *Negotiating Domestic Violence: Police, Criminal Justice and Victims* (Clarendon Press 1998).
Hoyle C and Sanders A, 'Police Response to Domestic Violence: From Victim Choice to Victim Empowerment' (2000) 40(1) *British Journal of Criminology* 14.
Jones C, 'Auditing Criminal Justice' (1993) 33(2) *British Journal of Criminology* 187, 188–189.
Kilkauer T, 'What Is Managerialism?' (2015) *Critical Sociology* 1103.
Losonc A, 'Austerity: History of a Dangerous Idea by Mark Blyth' (2014) *Panoeconomicus* 389.
Madden-Dempsey M, *Prosecuting Domestic Violence: A Philosophical Analysis* (Oxford University Press 2009).
McLaughlin E, Muncie J and Hughes G, 'The Permanent Revolution: New Labour, New Public Management and the Modernization of Criminal Justice' (2001) *Criminal Justice* 301.
Mills L, 'Killing Her Softly: Intimate Abuse and the Violence of State Intervention' (1999) *Harvard Law Review* 550.
Nichols A, 'No-Drop Prosecution in Domestic Violence Cases: Survivor-Defined and Social Change Approaches to Victim Advocacy' (2014) 29(11) *Journal of Interpersonal Violence* 2114.
Nussbaum M, *Creating Capabilities: The Human Development Approach* (Harvard University Press 2011).
Packer H, 'Two Models of the Criminal Process' (1964) *University of Pennsylvania Law Review* 1.
Peck J, 'Zombie Neoliberalism and the Ambidextrous State' (2010) *Theoretical Criminology* 104.
Raine J and Willson M, 'Beyond Managerialism in Criminal Justice' (1997) 1(3) *The Howard Journal of Crime and Justice* 80.
Winick B, 'Applying the Law Therapeutically in Domestic Violence Cases' (2000) 69 *UMKC Law Review* 33.

5

Women Survivors and Legal Consciousness: A Thematic Analysis

Introduction

Whilst trying to avoid an essentialist conception of 'women' or 'law', I have, thus far, provided a generalised account of violence against women and the CPS response.[1] I have highlighted feminist explanations that link the causes of violence against women to systemic gender subordination (i.e. the pervasive privileging of men's interests over women's). I have suggested that neoliberal governments' narratives and policies conspicuously deploy aspects of feminist discourse as a means of justifying a reliance on the criminal law to end violence against women.[2] And I have argued that, as part of this orientation, the Crown Prosecution Service now practises 'tenacious prosecutions'. In this chapter, I turn attention to 'particularity'[3] and the empirical insights offered by eleven women who have experienced domestic abuse. In so doing, the chapter highlights how discourses speaking to 'generality' risk enacting a totalising account of what women who have been abused require.

A focus on 'particularity', through analysis of the eleven women's stories in this chapter, allows us to 'describe the complexity of women's experience

[1]For Elizabeth Schneider, the account thus far represents a 'move to generality'. Elizabeth Schneider, *Battered Women and Feminist Lawmaking* (Yale University Press 2000) 59.

[2]For an explanation of 'carceral feminism' see Elizabeth Bernstein, 'Militarized Humanitarianism Meets Carceral Feminism: The Politics of Sex, Rights, and Freedom in Contemporary Anti-trafficking Campaigns' (2010) 36(1) *Signs: Journal of Women in Culture and Society* 45–71.

[3]Schneider, *Battered Women & Feminist Lawmaking* (n 1).

A. Porter, *Prosecuting Domestic Abuse in Neoliberal Times*, Palgrave Socio-Legal Studies,
https://doi.org/10.1007/978-3-030-61369-3_5

non-simplistically, accurately and in greater detail'.[4] The chapter draws together commonalities which lend weight to women's individual voices, but examination of the 'particular' also reveals contradictions and incongruities between them. These tensions lend support to the post-modern feminist conception that there is no one way to be a woman, resonant with intersectional[5] and post-intersectional[6] theorisations. Subjectivity is messy and, as Nash warns, there are not even 'prototypical intersectional subject[s]'.[7] Rather, women's lives are diverse with myriad truths, roles and realities necessarily requiring prosecutors to be more attentive and responsive to the textured and multi-faceted lives of women, as revealed by this sample.

Difference need not preclude collectivity, however, and deploying the collective category of 'women' here recognises women's commonality as a 'blurred concept'[8]; non-uniform, yet with shared aspects. Women's collective experience can be discerned from a complex network of criss-crossing, intersecting and overlapping likenesses.[9] By examining and being alert to the 'particular', recurrent strands overlay to produce 'a thread of considerable strength' and political strategy is not impeded.[10] These 'particular' themes, that may or may not repeat, must still be considered within the 'general'[11] or 'contextual'[12] dimensions because domestic abuse exists within wider societal gender subordination. By focusing on the particular accounts of these women, my ambition is not, therefore, to ignore broader or general contexts in which these experiences are situated.

---

[4]Elizabeth Schneider, 'Particularity and Generality: Challenges of Feminist Theory and Practice in Work on Woman-Abuse' (1992) 67 *NYUL Review* 520.

[5]Kimberle Crenshaw, 'Mapping the Margins: Intersectionality, Identity Politics, and Violence Against Women of Color' (1991) 43 *Stanford Law Review* 1241–1299.

[6]To displace the notion that identity is merely a neat intersecting or formulaic grid which produces stable and predictable identities Kwan speaks not in terms of 'intersectionality' but in terms of 'cosynthesis' in Peter Kwan, 'Complicity and Complexity: Cosynthesis and Praxis' (2000) 49 *DePaul University Law Review* 673–690. Hutchinson speaks of 'multi-dimensionality' in Darren Hutchinson, 'Identity Crisis: "Intersectionality," "Multidimensionality," and the Development of an Adequate Theory of Subordination' (2001) 6 *Michigan Journal of Race and Law* 28–50. Whilst Valdes considers 'interconnectivity' in Francisco Valdes, 'Sex and Race in Queer Legal Culture: Ruminations of Identities and Interconnectivities' (1995) 5 *Southern California Review of Law and Women's Studies* 32–46.

[7]Jennifer Nash, 'Re-thinking Intersectionality' (2008) 89(1) *Feminist Review* 1, 4.

[8]Vanessa Munro, *Law and Politics at the Perimeter: Re-evaluating the Key Debates in Feminist Theory* (Hart 2007) 127.

[9]Ibid., 130.

[10]Ibid., 128.

[11]Elizabeth Schneider, *Battered Women and Feminist Lawmaking* (n 1) 71–73.

[12]Rebecca Dobash and Russell Dobash, 'The Context-Specific Approach' in David Finkelhor et al. (eds), *The Dark Side of Families: Current Family Violence Research* (Sage 1983) 261–276.

Deploying a legal consciousness lens, the chapter explores how women who have experienced intimate partner abuse consider, understand and make sense of (criminal) law in their lives.[13] This enquiry supplements the question of how prosecutors approach decision-making in cases of domestic abuse as examined in Chapter 4. This chapter confronts prosecutorial culture and working practices by spotlighting how criminal law interacts with women's everyday lives. It underlines how prosecutorial decisions made quickly, based on frequently scant and second-hand information, may lack the detailed scrutiny required to understand the complexity of women's constraints and what they need. This chapter goes beyond standard approaches to legal consciousness that interrogate how specific laws (or decisions made by legal actors) are functioning for ordinary people.[14] In using legal consciousness, my intention is to unpick the more theoretical question of how law is able to sustain its hegemony and institutional power despite its frequent failure to live up to its liberal promises. What is it that gives law 'legitimacy'? A legal consciousness study which focuses on how, why and by whom the law is used thus brings the potential to understand the way the law sustains cultural norms and structures of power and inequality. Moreover, by exposing the gap between the law as intended and the law in action, legal consciousness has the potential to reveal 'the justice *possible* through law'.[15]

Both legal consciousness and feminist legal theory have the potential to destabilise law's claim to legitimacy. Just as Carol Smart sought to de-centre law and the belief that improvements to existing laws could advance women's status, this feminist legal consciousness study similarly draws out the shortcomings of a resort to law by exposing that women's legal victories are often pyrrhic.[16] Furthermore, both methodologies (feminism and legal consciousness) challenge law's assertion that it is a bordered system, separated from the 'everyday' or from intrinsic social inequality.[17] The project therefore contributes to scholarship that challenges legal positivism's assertion that law is closed, sealed or self-referential and that its internal logic leads to predetermined 'correct' decisions. The stories in this chapter show that, just as Conaghan has argued, law is not detached from social ordering

---

[13]Patricia Ewick and Susan Silbey, 'Conformity, Contestation, and Resistance: An Account of Legal Consciousness' (1992) *New England Law Review* 731, 731.

[14]Susan Silbey, 'After Legal Consciousness' (2005) 1 *Annual Review Law and Social Science* 323–368.

[15]My emphasis. Ibid., 325.

[16]Carol Smart, *Feminism and the Power of the Law* (Routledge 1989).

[17]Nicola Lacey, *Unspeakable Subjects: Feminist Essays in Legal and Social Theory* (Hart 1998) 1–15.

nor, it follows, can it be assumed that law is a neutral or gender-free space; law is distinctly masculine.[18] Socio-legal scholarship of the kind entered into in this chapter offers the possibility to challenge law's patriarchal inheritance. By blurring the boundaries between law in its 'splendid isolation' and what lies beyond—in people's homes, lives and relations—the gendered nature of law and legal processes becomes visible.

In more concrete terms, I begin by outlining legal consciousness as a technique of socio-legal scholarship. Having identified Ewick and Silbey's three broad schemas of legal consciousness (people who appear positioned *before*, *with* or *against* the law[19]), I deploy these groupings to thematically analyse the particular accounts revealed in the qualitative research.[20] Women positioned *before* the law reify its objectivity and fairness, find the law intimidating and consider it something that exists for the benefit of others. Feeling less distanced from the process is particularly key if these survivors are going to engage the criminal law. Women *with* the law consider the law their ally and resource and are likely to prove least 'problematic' in terms of their continued support for the prosecution. Yet these women can frequently be disappointed or have their safety compromised by the outcome unless their expectations are managed. Those *against* the law expect little from the criminal law and invariably resist its intervention. Criminal justice agents might try to support these women into being *with* the law whilst accepting that it may not always be attainable or, indeed, desirable. These observations highlight that criminal justice agents owe a duty to every woman, regardless of her expectations and legal consciousness, to assist her in recognising her victimhood whilst simultaneously respecting the ways in which she may be exercising agency. Therapeutic jurisprudential considerations repeatedly emerge as a theme that can be deployed by practitioners in pragmatic terms to improve survivors' experiences.

The women in the sample, with one exception, volunteered to be interviewed after I approached three different domestic abuse charities.[21] All eleven women, without exception, had had interactions with the police as a result of their abusive partners. Seven out of the eleven women supported prosecutions on at least one occasion and all of these now had partners or ex-partners with criminal convictions for offences committed against them.

---

[18]Joanne Conaghan, *Law and Gender* (Oxford University Press 2013).

[19]These three positionings are discussed in detail below.

[20]See Chapter 1 for clarification about my empirical methodology.

[21]The reader is referred to Chapter 1 for methodology.

Of the four women whose partners had not been prosecuted in court, three had not wanted to press charges from the outset and, for one, a police harassment warning, pre-charge, had proved sufficient deterrent thereby circumventing the need for court proceedings. Only one perpetrator had been convicted as a result of a victimless prosecution whilst three women had had to attend court to give evidence at trial following a not guilty plea.

1. What Is Legal Consciousness?

Law pervades everyday life.[22] This is perhaps especially obvious for women who experience intimate partner abuse in relation to *criminal* law. For even where invocation of criminal law is resisted, the police can be called in an emergency. Law has meaning, even in its absence, in abused women's lives.[23] The stories and reflections of the eleven survivors in this chapter analysed through the lens of legal consciousness, reveal what the criminal law represents for them and how they situate themselves in relation to it. This is more than the simple process of extracting women's attitude towards the law, but an uncovering of their understanding of it, their engagement with it and the way they *imagine* the law operates.[24] Legal consciousness is thus a way of tracing 'the ways in which law is experienced and interpreted by specific individuals as they engage, avoid, or resist the law and legal meanings'.[25]

Ewick and Silbey's rendering of legal consciousness exposes how law is socially constructed by asking how it operates for ordinary people. Law is understood as a structural component of society in the sense that legality forms part of social relations and is at the interface of social interaction.[26] Legal consciousness might therefore be considered a type of social practice which not only reflects but also constructs social structures incrementally

---

[22]Patricia Ewick and Susan Silbey, *The Common Place of Law: Stories from Everyday Life* (University of Chicago Press 1998) xi.

[23]Ibid., 34.

[24]Two articles that explore domestic violence victim's use of the law go some way to exploring aspects of their legal consciousness. David Ford, 'Prosecution as a Victim Power Resource: A Note on Empowering Women in Violent Conjugal Relationships' (1991) *Law and Society Review* 313; Ruth Lewis et al., 'Protection, Prevention, Rehabilitation or Justice? Women's Use of the Law to Challenge Domestic Violence' (Domestic Violence: Global Responses) 179. However, no studies directly use legal consciousness to understand how women experience the criminal justice system and prosecutorial decision-making in their lives.

[25]Susan Silbey 'Legal Consciousness' in Peter Cane and Joanne Conaghan (eds), *The New Oxford Companion to Law* (Oxford University Press 2008).

[26]Ewick and Silbey, *The Common Place of Law* (n 22) 43.

over time.[27] Legal consciousness is, then, less a study of law *and* society in an instrumentalist sense (tracking the causal relationship between law and society), and more a study which presents law *in* society as constitutive (tracing the presence of law *in* society).[28] The task of the researcher becomes one of locating the place of law in women's lives, exploring law's 'complex and contradictory fabric'.[29] If legal consciousness is understood as individuals' participation in the construction of legality and law's legitimacy, such an appraisal might motivate prosecutors to respond sensitively to survivors' varying subjectivities and preconceptions about the role of criminal prosecution.

In drawing out the legal consciousness of those interviewed, my thematic analysis uses as its starting point the three interpretive frames of legal consciousness that Ewick and Silbey identify as representing and shaping how people experience legality.[30] As legality is understood as 'an internal and emergent feature of social life',[31] formal legal events need not be the focal point. By describing and analysing legal consciousness as *before* the law, *with* the law or *against* the law (see below), we begin to understand how each woman positions herself in relation to the law and her understanding of what the law can achieve for her.

Most of the women interviewed indicated that their relationship to law, before their abuse, broadly fell within the frame of being *before* the law. In this conception, law is considered separate to one's social life. People *before* the law indicate a sense of deference to a set of institutions, rules and practices that are considered both authoritative and impartial.[32] Law and legal constructions are reified and accepted as rational and ordered offering the promise of just arbitration in a sphere that is 'majestic'[33] and objectively fair. This conception of law embodies the same qualities that liberal law asserts for itself. Darcey indicated her position being *before* the law in plain terms, 'I abide by the law and I am going to do as I am told. And I am just going to swallow it [the outcome]'. Later on she indicated her belief that law provides moral judiciousness: 'If you tell a lie, if you don't tell the truth, you

[27]Ibid., 44.

[28]Rosie Harding, '"Dogs Are 'Registered', People Shouldn't Be": Legal Consciousness and Lesbian and Gay Rights' (2006) *Social and Legal Studies* 511, 513.

[29]Ewick and Silbey, *The Common Place of Law* (n 22) xii.

[30]Susan Silbey and Patricia Ewick, 'The Rule of Law—Sacred and Profane' (2000) *Society* 37(6) 49, 50.

[31]Patricia Ewick and Susan Silbey, *The Common Place of Law* (n 22) 23.

[32]Ibid., 47.

[33]Silbey and Ewick, 'The Rule of Law—Sacred and Profane' (n 30) 50.

will face the consequences and you could go to prison'. For others describing a *before* the law conception, the law represented the possibility of validation or an alternative moral order to that expressed by those around them,

> [Law] is basically someone standing up and saying, look, your behaviour is not on… If I was to say something about his behaviour, he denies it. He's told [our son] that he hadn't done anything wrong… I think it's an authority isn't it. Somebody is there if your family is not standing up to him. Who else have you got? It's the law. I think it was the law that really kind of put the nail in the coffin [of the abusive relationship].[34]

The law here is described as an objective and impartial arbiter that presides over those in its jurisdiction. However, if people conceive of law as hierarchical, unfailing and steady in the way Irie above describes, then they may begin to feel powerlessness, frustration or even anger at their own perceived insignificance in relation to it.[35] Diane illustrated this sense when she confirmed: 'I would still report [future abuse], but it's just you wonder what the effect of it is going to be and whether it's actually going to make you feel slightly undermined'. Diane seems to describe law here as being distant, impenetrable or inert; something that will 'happen' to her and over which she has little control. Being *before* the law, therefore, does not mean that individuals are unaware of law's downsides.[36] Specifically, with regard to the criminal law, the shortcomings may include disappointing outcomes, complicated and unexplained procedures, the intimidating theatrics of a trial or the use of impenetrable technical legal language. Such aspects all contribute to law's remoteness and impersonality and can offer insight into why those who identify as *before* the law often fail to call upon it for their own assistance. This tension between reification and disenchantment with the law is more fully explored in the subsequent thematic analysis.

Legal consciousness understands that individuals contribute to the process of shaping legality and this process of legality construction is perhaps most plainly in evidence through the *with* the law identification.[37] For a *with* the law conception recognises that whilst law and legal rules pre-exist, they can also be moulded and manipulated to suit one's ends.[38] Described as a

[34]Irie.

[35]Ewick and Silbey, *The Common Place of Law* (n 22) 47.

[36]Ibid., 71.

[37]Ibid., 45.

[38]Ibid., 48.

game, an individual who plays *with* the law understands that 'the boundaries thought to separate law from everyday life are… relatively porous'.[39] The law becomes a 'terrain of contest',[40] utilised by the individual to serve specific ends and achieve specific goals. Law is not considered lofty or revered for its power per se, but its facility is understood and deployed for self-interest. For Karen, the law was considered a resource constantly available to her, it was important that the law was on her side and aware of all events pertaining to her then separated husband: 'I just phone the police all the time now. Every time something happens… I need to tell them what's going on because unless I tell them then it's not all recorded'. For this woman, her concrete knowledge and experience of the criminal justice system meant that she knew how best to build the evidence against her violent ex-husband to prove his harassment of her. Karen thus described being *with* the law; using or directing the law for her own ends.

This means that, unlike those *before* the law who accept law's claim as a natural, inevitable and determinant phenomenon, those *with* the law recognise that law's actors, organisations, rules and procedures can be engaged and manoeuvred. Moreover, in recognising the law as a resource, those *with* the law consciously position themselves in relation to it and in so doing assert culturally identifiable markers about themselves. For Karen, by actively reporting every transgression of her now separated partner, she asserted a number of things; firstly, 'I am being harassed', secondly, 'I will not accept this' and thirdly and perhaps most powerfully, 'I know how to call upon the law to hold you to account'. Recognising that the law can be engaged for her benefit, Karen made identity claims pertaining to herself and her agency. Karen described invoking the law in this way as a way of moving on from 'years of him putting me down or hitting me or telling me that I ain't no good - you start to believe it yourself'. Being *with* the law became an enabler for her and intrinsic to her sense of empowerment as she endeavoured to move on from the relationship.

The third and final variety of legal consciousness, being *against* the law, describes people's sense of being caught in law's net or being in opposition to it.[41] Law is not something to be trusted and legality is a dangerous consequence of law's seemingly arbitrary power.[42] Those *against* the law often

[39]Ibid., 48.

[40]Harding (n 28) 514.

[41]Patricia Ewick and Susan Silbey, *The Common Place of Law* (n 22) 48.

[42]Ibid., 192.

describe being unable to keep law at a distance from their everyday life and they oppose its reach and potential for disciplinary power. They recognise that society is hierarchically structured and often consider themselves the 'underdog' up against a socially, economically and legally privileged adversary. Not wishing to engage *with* the law strategies, they often use their initiative to subvert law and its ordered systems to their advantage; methods used include minor deceptions, failures to say or do things, reticence, deliberately 'acting up' or making light of the seriousness of the situation.[43] The key characterisation here is the sense that law's rules cannot be played by them. Renata most clearly expressed herself as situated *against* the law,

> I come from a background where there is kind of a lot of interaction with the Criminal Justice System. We are multi-generational prison people... But we don't have much faith in it in as much as you don't really expect it to do anything for you... can you imagine if I go to court for anything? They would rip me apart. I can never rely on it. It's let me down when I was young and it continues to let me down now.

The aims and purposes of defiantly resisting the law can be various; self-preservation, an attempt to maintain one's dignity or perhaps simply as a means to maintain the separation between oneself and the law. For Renata there was a clear sense that the law would not help her, and her motivation for not engaging the law appeared to be to avoid being disbelieved, judged, treated badly and ultimately let down:

> I don't think there is a big enough recognition that people who have committed crimes can also be the victims of crime... When I think about like [my] arrest for soliciting and stuff like that, it was a relatively minor crime. But because of that crime, I don't feel like I can ever access the Criminal Justice System [as a victim].

Later on she confirmed that as 'the system is not set up to help me' she set up her own ways of policing her violent intimate relationships that demonstrated skilful negotiations and adroit insight into how best she might keep herself and her children safe.

I have outlined three positions here but individuals' relationships with the law are not fixed or static. Legal consciousness describes a fluid process of

[43] Silbey and Ewick, 'The Rule of Law—Sacred and Profane' (n 30) 53–54.

social practices and an ongoing construction of legality.[44] Nor need a single 'type' of legal consciousness be described in a single narrative; there is no requirement for mutual exclusivity and an individual might express all three positions within one story.[45] Bearing in mind the potential for fluidity of legal consciousness, the next part of the chapter uses the three standpoints to interrogate their impact on how abused women use or do not use the criminal law.

2. Women '*Before*' Law: Preferring to 'Go It Alone'

For abused women *before* the law, the law is seen as something distant and separate to one's own life; it is conceived as existing for the benefit of other people. This conception carries the potential that women will not call upon the law, even at times of crisis. Irie grew up in a family in which her father was physically abusive, mainly to her mother but sometimes she too would be beaten. She observed how her own mother never engaged family lawyers or the criminal justice system and for her, law and those who knew the law, appeared to operate in a sphere that dealt with matters more important than her own troubles. There was an assumption that the coercive, controlling and aggressive strategies that her own husband employed against her should or would be of no concern to criminal justice professionals and, prior to leaving her husband, she had never once called police regarding his treatment of her. The way she spoke about the law, combined with her actions in failing to invoke the criminal law or in failing to take family legal advice regarding child contact arrangements, paint a *before* the law positioning.

When eventually her child's school called police on her behalf and subsequently directed her to a family solicitor for advice, Irie described how 'the turning point was knowing that I was going to get support from the law, the lawyer, and the police as well. My God any support from the law is good'. Highlighting the way she held 'the law' in lofty esteem, she spoke of how shocked she was that her now separated husband, whom she described as 'a pillar of society', had been so irreverent to the family lawyer: 'He spoke disrespectfully. And I am thinking, he's a lawyer. [My husband] might have two parts of a degree but what has he done with it? The lawyer has a degree. He's

[44]Ewick and Silbey, *The Common Place of Law* (n 22) 50.

[45]Ibid., 224–225.

put it to good use. It's just disrespectful… you have to listen to the lawyer'. The reverence and regard for the lawyer's standing and his legal professional education seemed to render him superior to those not versed in the law. Her deference to law and legal knowledge was exemplified when she explained why she had not called the police herself, 'I heard that the law changed from whatever it was. I didn't call police'. There was a sense from Irie that even if she could recall why she thought the law had changed, it would not be something she would expect to understand. Law was something produced and practised by an elite group with specific and inaccessible knowledge.

Having always considered the law something which helped other more creditable people with meritorious claims, Irie reified law. She appeared to accept law's own imposing claims to neutrality and fairness. By not wishing to bother the police, she played her part in constructing law as something that is detached from everyday life. The law was described 'as having ontology and authority that is severed from the multiple concrete practices and relationships that enact it'.[46] When finally calling upon law to assist her, the law and its agents on this occasion did not let her down. She felt the police had been 'really really good' and had supported her by issuing an informal harassment warning which her husband did not breach. On this occasion, 'Law' lived up to its promise and successfully intervened to secure her safety.

Another woman who, during the period of her abusive relationship, appeared positioned *before* the law was Darcey. She conceived the law as an authority to be complied with and whose decisions were determinative. Darcey's relationship with her now ex-husband had been characterised by his drink and drug misuse. His behaviour ranged from angry tirades, verbal aggression, criminal damage, threats made to her with a kitchen knife and marital rape, to sincere apologies, heart-to-hearts and promises to change.[47] In ordinary life, Darcey's most evident characteristic was her proactive agency. She was self-employed and the chairwoman of a local charity. In her typically resourceful way, Darcey had sought relationship counselling services from Relate, had been to the Citizen's Advice Bureau and had familiarised herself with the domestic violence leaflet provided. She had also made

[46]Ewick and Silbey, *The Common Place of Law: Stories from Everyday Life* (n 22) 75.

[47]Liz Kelly defines all forms of violence against women and girls perpetrated by men and boys as 'sexual violence'. She notes that studying 'battering' or 'rape' separately denies the continuum of elements and events—be they physical assaults, verbal abuse or sexual coercion—that characterise men's abuse of women. Liz Kelly, 'How Women Define Their Experiences of Violence' in Kersti Yllo and Michele Bograd (eds), *Feminist Perspectives on Wife Abuse* (Sage 1990) 114–115. Andrea Nichols has also called these latter behaviours 'apologetic manipulations' in Andrea Nichols, 'No-Drop Prosecution in Domestic Violence Cases: Survivor-Defined and Social Change Approaches to Victim Advocacy' (2014) 29(11) *Journal of Interpersonal Violence* 2114.

her mother aware of her situation: 'I was trying to like put safety things in place. The safeguarding training that I had delivered in the charity - I was resourcing it. It was just like, I've got a problem here and I need to do something. I need to make myself safe and I need to know what to do if… because it had escalated that much'. When asked why she had not contacted police during the time of the abusive relationship, she indicated, 'I didn't want to trouble police. What was I going to tell them? I had no proof. I had no evidence. I had nothing to show them. Even that night [the violent night that proved to be the end of the relationship] when I knew that I was in big serious trouble… I phoned my friend'.

Three points arise from this. The first is the link to what Nielsen has termed the 'impracticality paradigm' of law. This speaks, inter alia, to the difficulty people recognise in legal enforcement in the absence of proof. The paradigm is particularly associated with acts committed in the private sphere.[48] The second is that Darcey, like Irie, demonstrated that in being *before* the law, law felt like a distant entity, so aloof that Darcey did not want to bother it with her self-perceived trivialities. This view of law as something which exists for others perhaps stems from the way in which law presents itself as transcending the immediate and particular; 'law houses itself in monumental buildings of marble and granite and arranges its agents behind desks, counters and benches. It expresses itself in a language that is arcane and indecipherable to most citizens'.[49] The perceived immensity, impersonality and complexity of the law gives rise to a sense that the law is something too serious and weighty to invoke in one's own life. Involving the law means that one's intimate relationship has reached a point that requires third party intervention, determinations about one's life will be made and consequences will follow with little scope, according to the *before* the law conception, for one's own input or negotiation as to strategy.

The third point is that these women *before* the law may have failed to engage the criminal law due to anxiety about not being believed by criminal justice agents, 'Why was anybody else going to believe what was happening? … This was the stuff of movies'.[50] This fear about not being believed, according to the *before* the law schema may have been, in part, to do with a sense of insignificance in relation to the law or the perceived impenetrability and impersonality of it.

[48]Laura Beth Nielsen, 'Situating Legal Consciousness: Experiences and Attitudes of Ordinary Citizens about Law and Street Harassment' (2000) 34 *Law and Society Review* 1055, 1081.

[49]Ewick and Silbey, *The Common Place of Law* (n 22) 106.

[50]Darcey.

(i) Women Before the Law: Importance of Therapeutic Jurisprudential Considerations

Yet it would be incomplete to suggest that these women's concerns about not being believed would only have been to do with their perceived insignificance in relation to law's grandeur. These women's fear of not being believed may also have had something to do with profound matters of self-identification and the impact of their abusive relationship on their mental health. Women in abusive relationships have often sustained a reign of terror, repeated episodes of physical violence or isolation and been told of their 'inadequacies'. The victim of domestic abuse might therefore feel shame, a diminished sense of self-esteem or self-efficacy and depression.[51] Strategies to cope might include denying to oneself that the abuse is occurring or minimisations that seek to normalise the abusive experiences.[52] Even where the level of danger appears to be rising (as Darcey described), if an abuser has told her she is 'crazy' or blameworthy, this can lead to self-doubt and an unwillingness to call the police.[53]

It is for that reason that when Darcey's friend called the police on her behalf that pivotal night, the police's ability to communicate to Darcey that they understood and believed her formed a crucial part of the evolution of Darcey's life journey and, in turn, legal consciousness. Darcey described that night when she hid in the bedroom with her 3- and 5-year-old children whilst her husband 'went berserk' outside. When he saw from the window that police had arrived, he went out to meet them.

> *R*: Then someone come upstairs and I was just literally 'like that' and frozen. The [police]man said, just come out a minute and just leave the children there a minute. I just need to come and speak to you. He literally put his hands on me like that [gets upset].
>
> *I*: It's really hard isn't it.
>
> *R*: It was a key moment. And he said, 'You do understand this is domestic violence, don't you?' I was like, 'Yeah'. I am so glad he did that. Literally, he just stopped me like that, because I was bouncing off the walls. He just

[51] Bruce Winick, 'Applying the Law Therapeutically in Domestic Violence Cases' (2000) *UMKC Law Review* 33, 60.

[52] Lenore Walker, *The Battered Woman Syndrome* (4th edn, Springer 2016) 291; Liz Kelly, 'How Women Define Their Experiences of Violence' in Kersti Yllo and Michele Bograd, *Feminist Perspectives on Wife Abuse* (Sage 1990) 124–128.

[53] Walker (n 52) 291.

> put his hands gently on either side of me. He said, 'You do know?' and I am like, 'Yeah, I get it'.

The policeman here, in a single gesture, perhaps through the tone of his voice and with explicit recognition of the victim's situation demonstrated compassion and understanding, not blame. He effectively conveyed that he believed her.

Such a response is consistent with that advocated by therapeutic jurisprudence scholars who recognise law's potential to operate as a 'therapeutic agent'.[54] The approach, which I explore in more detail in Chapter 6, brings a humanising emphasis to legal practice; an approach that recognises the law can and ought to promote emotional and psychological 'well-being' where it can.[55] As well as seeking to influence laws and procedure, therapeutic jurisprudence urges *legal actors* to recognise their capacity to work in ways that can produce 'healing potential' for those who come into contact with the law.[56]

Therapeutic jurisprudence invites legal professionals to be animated by concern for the victim and to focus on her needs, just as the police did in Darcey's story.[57] Darcey explained that the policeman's colleague played with the children whilst she completed a risk assessment in another room. By acting with kindness and sympathy criminal justice agents can help contribute to the process of improving psychological and emotional strength that might be considered critical for building a survivor's long-term deliverance. Sensitive responses from criminal justice agents that 'do not perpetuate her sense of discontrol'[58] might contribute to a reduced sense of being *before* the law and may encourage a woman to feel that she could be *with* the law. For Darcey above, this interaction with police led her to terminate the relationship.[59] She was telephoned daily from a victim support charity who encouraged her to obtain a civil non-molestation order and she subsequently engaged the family courts regarding the separation and child contact arrangements.

---

[54]David Wexler, 'Applying the Law Therapeutically' (1996) *Applied and Preventive Psychology* 179, 179.

[55]Christopher Slobogin, 'Therapeutic Jurisprudence: 5 Dilemmas to Ponder' (1995) *Psychology, Public Policy and Law* 193.

[56]Bruce Winick, 'The Jurisprudence of Therapeutic Jurisprudence' (1997) *Psychology, Public Policy and Law* 184, 185.

[57]Winick, 'Applying the Law Therapeutically in Domestic Violence Cases' (n 51).

[58]Ibid., 62.

[59]Darcey did not recall the police taking a statement following this incident but she explained that she felt they achieved what she needed them to, namely to make her and her family safe that night.

For those *before* the law, reluctance to bring one's private family life, ordinarily secreted behind closed doors, into the public legal domain, is common; the decision to do so can be a significant turning point. The intrusion into private life must then be handled with particular sensitivity. Karen explained why it was particularly difficult for her to make the transition from her abusive relationship being a private matter to it being a public one.

> And also, do you know what else? It's embarrassment… so many people go through it, but no-one will tell you. If you see me day to day walking down the street, you would never have been able to tell what my home life was like… but it's embarrassing to tell people like, oh yeah, well, my life is crap and every time I go home I don't know whether he's going to beat the shit out of me or not. He takes my money and he takes everything I've got and I just have to get on with it.

Hirschmann similarly describes how women are often ashamed of their abuse because they have been made to feel responsible for making a success of their relationships; this can be why they do not seek help from third parties.[60] Yet once called upon, criminal justice agents are in a unique position to minimise any embarrassment and signpost additional support. With appropriate empathy, the intrusion into a person's private life can be felt less keenly and practitioners can support women not to feel shame and to understand that she is not the only one suffering in this way. Moreover, by acting with the therapeutic consequences in mind, criminal justice agents can diminish reluctance to call upon the law in the future.

The following two extracts are indicative of the ways that sensitive, therapeutic treatment of victims by criminal justice agents during the court process can assist the woman to feel that the law is *with* her and not too imposing, remote or distanced to be concerned with the particulars of her life. They show how, by treating women respectfully, compassionately and courteously, criminal justice agents can reduce a woman's sense of being *before* the law, with the law operating in a sphere separate to herself and for the benefit of other people.

Having been through a magistrates' court trial, Jen's ex-partner appealed his conviction for his harassment of her. Jen found herself warned to attend the Crown Court for an appeal hearing de novo[61]: 'It is daunting. I mean,

[60]Nancy Hirschmann, 'Freedom, Power and Agency in Feminist Legal Theory' in Margaret Davies and Vanessa Munro (eds), *The Ashgate Research Companion to Feminist Legal Theory* (Ashgate 2013) 61.

[61]When a defendant appeals a conviction from the magistrates' court to the Crown Court, the appeal hearing requires all witnesses to give evidence again (for a second time).

especially when you get to Crown Court and the barristers and with the wigs'. She explained that despite the fact that the prosecution barrister was clearly busy, he had been able to sit with her and show her his 'human side';

> They have to be a certain person to do that job, obviously. They must be very, they are very tough. It was seeing that other side… and I know it was ridiculous in the scheme of things… but he was going through all [the papers - Jen indicates that the barrister sighed and shook his head in disbelief]. You could see he actually felt something about the situation rather than, 'I am here. This is just another case. Just another job'.

By connecting with Jen in this simple but personal way, 'a little bit of empathy or something, it goes a huge way… I felt confident in him'.

Karen described a very similar experience in the witness room waiting to give evidence:

> She [the woman at court from victim support] was good. She was sort of like, she was having a bit of a laugh about it with me, actually. [The prosecutor] was a gentleman which he said to me, like, "Are you okay if it's a gentleman?" I am like, "Yes, that's fine". So they do think about those things. And he was really funny as well… had a laugh. They said, "We've read his history. Jesus. Poor you, you have had to deal with this all over the years". I am like, "God, I know". They just made … me feel like it wasn't a bad thing. You didn't feel judged. You felt it was humanised.

Similarly, Sasha spoke of her affirmative experience of giving evidence, via live-link, at trial. She did not dwell on the potentially unpleasant process of giving evidence to the court but rather her recollection focused on how the witness support staff at court had been 'absolutely fantastic'. I asked why she had thought they had been so good and she simply stated,

> Conversation. Not necessarily all about the court hearing. It was just general conversation… and they were prepared to give their time. Offered drinks all the time. It was just a nice experience… to walk in there and not feel like I was being judged… they made you feel comfortable and welcome.

This focus on how comfortable she had been made to feel waiting to give evidence seemed to dominate the event. She contrasted this positive experience with that of the appeal in the same case where there were no victim support staff/volunteers, only court ushers. She felt that there had been 'massive problems' that day; 'It was awful… I don't feel like the people I spoke to at court were supporting me, they were just doing a job… If I had to give evidence from anywhere again, I would travel. I would go to [town A police station, despite the distance]. I would never do it from [local town B court] again'. Had her only experience of giving evidence been like that of the appeal hearing in town B, one wonders if Sasha would have ever agreed to give evidence again.

If prosecutors are to assist women to feel that the law is *with* them, then being aware that they can play a part in transforming victims into survivors is key. Notably for Jen, Karen and Sasha, recalling the respect and thoughtfulness with which they were treated at court was poignant not only for the way it facilitated their experience of the criminal procedure and the likelihood of their using the criminal courts in the future but also, more broadly, for the way that it contributed to their forward journey. Having others treat them as credible witnesses, respectfully and with understanding, assisted these women to re-draw their narratives about what had happened and allowed them to move towards feeling that the law, and perhaps society generally, was *with* them.

3. Women *'With'* the Law: Law as a 'Power Resource'

The following section considers those women positioned *with* the Law. All of the women I spoke with indicated that the charities they were being supported by had all discussed, indeed encouraged, them to work *with* the law to bring about satisfactory arrangements for managing their perpetrators' abuse.[62] However, what is also clear from the primary research is that any promise that law will achieve a conclusive and beneficial end result for those *with* the law, can often lead to disappointment. For that reason, these women's stories reflect the argument that it would be, 'a mistake to resort to the law as a panacea' and that, instead, 'the law must be seen as just one of the other available services'.[63] Legal intervention frequently fails to end the abuse as promised and there can be negative consequences for women's safety and healing, as I explore below, as a result. If women were to cut out

[62]David Ford, 'Prosecution as a Victim Power Resource: A Note on Empowering Women in Violent Conjugal Relationships' (1991) *Law and Society Review* 303.

[63]Susan Maidment, 'The Law's Response to Marital Violence: A Comparison Between England and the USA' in John Eekelaar and Sanford Katz (eds), *Family Violence: An International and Interdisciplinary* (Butterworths 1978) 110.

the legal 'middle man' and go straight to feminist (charitable) support networks, Carol Smart suggests this might be preferable as she considers the law is often unable to keep pace with women's lived realities.[64] By exposing law's shortcomings, the primary research inherently demands improvements to both the legal and non-legal response. The research also carries a cautionary lesson about the need to temper expectations and to be realistic about what law might be able to accomplish for survivors. These findings appear to be in line with Smart's assessment that the risks of going to law might only be worthwhile if the risks are 'acknowledged and weighed in the balance'.[65]

Recall how Ewick and Silbey's model of being *with* the law describes the 'law as a game' that can be played to secure one's end goals. This legal consciousness articulation presents law as a 'positive framework with rules, tactics and positions'[66] that individuals play to win. There are two problems that arise for abused women from the 'law as a contest' schema. First, the analogy brings with it the danger that the 'playing' is seen to be done for sport or to enjoy the upper hand in a dispute. Cooper consequently cautions that this representation can de-centre law's substantive legitimacy.[67] The characterisation also risks playing to discourses that female victims are incredible complainants who only involve the law unmeritoriously, out of spite or by way of pay back.[68] In the context of a domestic abuse victim who's ongoing safety is paramount and who's meaningful quality of life is in the balance, the notion that she might be 'playing' for personal amusement is unfitting.

The second problem of understanding being *with* the law as a 'game' is that it implies that strategic engagement with the law is likely to produce a benefit or an end result. For abused women encouraged to engage the law, the reality is that frequently law will not be beneficial. Whilst those *before* the law often anticipate law's potential to frustrate—proceeding in

[64]Carol Smart, 'Reflection' (2012) *Feminist Legal Studies* 161, 162.

[65]Carol Smart, *Feminism and the Power of the Law* (n 16) 161.

[66]Davina Cooper, 'Local Government Legal Consciousness in the Shadow of Juridification' (1995) 22 *Law and Society* 506, 513.

[67]Ibid., 513.

[68]The CPS provides for guidance in how to deal with false allegations in two types of offences; rape and domestic abuse. These are both offences in which the victims are overwhelmingly female. The indication from the CPS appears to be that the problem of the incredible complainant is gendered. CPS, 'Guidance for charging perverting the course of justice and wasting police time in cases involving allegedly false allegations of rape and/or domestic abuse' (2017) https://www.cps.gov.uk/legal-guidance/guidance-charging-perverting-course-justice-and-wasting-police-time-cases-involving accessed 7 February 2020.

an impersonal way or making decisions without due consideration of their specific needs—those *with* the law often expect benefits. The challenge for women positioned *with* the law then is not to become disillusioned should the law not produce the desired outcome and to recognise that law might only be part of the solution they seek.

Particularly in the context of intimate partner abuse, Ewick and Silbey's *with* the law paradigm might be modified to conceive of law not as a contest but as one available 'facilitator and resource'.[69] This still describes a *with* the law schema, akin to law as a game, but without suggesting foul play or gaming for personal entertainment. It recognises the value of the law is both its normative and strategic capacities, without invoking suggestions that 'winning' the game (or court case) is the end goal. Considering law as *a* resource also expresses law's potential to support those who seek it without suggesting it is everything. It suggests law's role in educating parties both morally and in practical terms and ultimately its role in *beginning* a shift in the balance of power in the relationship.

Women in the sample had experience of three different domestic abuse charities set up to assist them. Every woman I spoke with explained that the charity had outlined how the law can be *with* them; law both as a facilitator and resource. The entry point to the charity for four of the women was the 'one stop shop'[70] weekly facility. This is a drop-in service that is free and, in one place, offers advice, information and support from various agencies such as housing representatives, family solicitors, Independent Domestic Violence Advocates, Citizen's Advice and the police.

Charlie explained that the domestic abuse charity that supported her had encouraged her to reposition her legal consciousness to be *with* the law. Prior to attending the one-stop-shop, Charlie had called the police only once before and that was during an emergency situation; a particularly violent assault where she had just received a serious head injury. She had been able to get away from her husband, lock the door of the bathroom and recalls, 'I was that upset. I thought, well I've got no-one else to phone. I will ring the police. That is what I did'. Despite her husband pleading guilty at court and being sent to prison, when he assaulted her after his release, she did not call the police again but reported the matter at the hospital. She explained, 'I knew that I wanted that action on record, just in case it ever

[69]Cooper, (n 66) 515.

[70]Jen, Danielle, Diane, Darcey, Charlie and Sasha spoke of accessing various 'one stop shop' facilities.

happened again' but that she did not think to involve the police at that time because it was not an 'emergency'. Charlie was someone typically *before* the law who had only chosen to call the police on the one occasion she found herself in acute danger. Being *before* the law, Charlie stated that even after experiencing ongoing persistent coercive controlling and aggressive behaviour, instead of reporting it to the police, 'in the end, I went to the one-stop-shop ... he kept threatening to stab me and they were quite concerned... they passed me on to talk to a policeman that was there'. Despite being persuaded that providing an eight-page statement to police would likely result in prosecution, no prosecution was brought because the evidential test was not met; 'It was just insufficient evidence. That's what I was told'. But, whilst criminal law came down as a barrier to her aid, she was then assisted by the family lawyer at the one-stop-shop to obtain a non-molestation order which her husband consistently breached. In repositioning Charlie to use the law to her advantage in an attempt to end his persecution of her, she was advised to report to the police every infraction of the order; 'I record everything. I've been told to report everything, so I have'.[71]

By encouraging women to engage the law, the domestic abuse charities in the sample continue a long-standing tradition of demanding that the state provides 'pragmatic responses' to confronting violence against women.[72] Great strides have been made by the state since the 1970s, in terms of proactive criminal justice intervention. However, just as MacKinnon has observed that 'equality is valued nearly everywhere but practised almost nowhere',[73] the following section highlights how legal interventions can fail to live up to their promise, as they ultimately did for Charlie.

Of the seven women who had supported criminal proceedings, none were identifiably positioned *against* the law. Nonetheless, all spoke without exception about aspects of the process that disappointed. Victim satisfaction with the criminal justice system and the treatment of victims during the criminal process can be 'an important pathway between victimisation and emotional recovery'.[74] Poor experiences can notably increase stress or even be

[71]Similarly, Jen confirmed that the charity supporting her had told her to 'report it, just to be on the safe side'.

[72]Rebecca Emerson Dobash and Russell Dobash, *Women, Violence, and Social Change* (Routledge 1992) 1.

[73]Catherine MacKinnon, *Women's Lives: Men's Laws* (Harvard University Press 2005) 45.

[74]Maarten Kunst, Lieke Popelier and Ellen Varekamp, 'Victim Satisfaction with the Criminal Justice System and Emotional Recovery: A Systematic and Critical Review of the Literature' (2015) 16(3) *Trauma, Violence and Abuse* 336–358. See also Lauren Bennett Cattaneo and Lisa Goodman, 'Through the Lens of Therapeutic Jurisprudence: The Relationship between Empowerment in the Court System and Well-Being for Intimate Partner Violence Victims' (2010) 25(3) *Journal of Interpersonal Violence* 481.

experienced as secondary victimisation—where the criminal process is likened to a 'second assault'. Improved participation and satisfaction, by contrast, can assist recovery.[75] Ensuring that women enjoy positive experiences of the criminal process is paramount not only to enhance emotional well-being but also to ensure that women situate themselves *with* the law so that they feel able to call on it in the future. More widely, poor experiences might also lead to a loss of confidence in the system for other future users and have the effect of undermining law's legitimacy. From a legal consciousness perspective, the effect of a poor experience might turn a woman *against* the law.

(i) The Importance of Good Communications

A recurring theme amongst the women in the sample was that they received inaccurate, unreliable or insufficient information and communications from criminal justice agents. Communications with witnesses have been an area particularly targeted for improvement since 2005. This is when witness care units were established in police stations and, within those units, witness care officers now support and guide each and every victim and witness through the court process.[76] Keeping victims and witnesses informed of the progress of their case is also included as part of the 'overriding objective' of the criminal procedure rules.[77]

Karen explained the importance of keeping survivors informed about the case:

> You live every day not knowing if it's going to be your last, if today is the day they are going to kill you. And then you try and do something about it and... when you are not listened to... or no-one is there to support you, it's really really difficult... Some people just need a phone call once a week to say, right, this is where we are at with this - even if you have made no progress at least you know someone is there trying for you.

Karen explained that in the lead up to the trial, she experienced months of radio-silence from the police and witness care staff and that it was only

[75] Kunst et al. (n 74).

[76] Crown Prosecution Service, 'Victims and Witnesses' available at http://www.cps.gov.uk/southwest/victims_and_witnesses/ accessed 8 December 2017.

[77] 1.1(2)(d) of The Criminal Procedure Rules 2015 available at https://www.legislation.gov.uk/uksi/2015/1490/article/1.1/made accessed 11 December 2017.

just before the trial date that, 'all of a sudden people want to talk to you'. Jen also received insufficient information. She recalled how she had not been informed about the possibility of an appeal against conviction and the fact that this would require her to give evidence a second time: 'He appealed. But again, I was never told. I thought once he was convicted [that would be the end of it]. Had I known he could appeal, I would have prepared myself, because I knew he would'.

Other women found themselves disarmed when they were not told about a defendant's release on bail[78] or release from custody.[79] Charlie thought that Witness Care were, 'very very good… until he was prosecuted and then they didn't want to know. I got nothing once he'd [received a custodial sentence]. He was released and nobody told me. I got a knock on my door and it was him'. Charlie had clearly been unprepared for her husband's re-appearance and chided herself about her response, 'They all said I was really stupid for having him back. I am a sucker for a sob story, aren't I? I can't help myself'. Had she been told in advance of her perpetrator's release date, she felt that she could have prepared herself and put protections in place in readiness.

The women in the sample also recalled occasions when police officers had erred in communicating with them. These centred on a tendency to set overly high expectations about what could be achieved from supporting a prosecution. Having been 'talked round' by police into making a statement about the offences committed against her, the police told Diane that charges of Assault Occasioning Actual Bodily Harm would be brought against her husband. In fact, no prosecution was ever brought.[80] Diane explained that when she realised no action would be taken against her abuser, 'It was just really disappointing… to have that assurance from an officer to say that, "Tell us everything and we will get him" to then not have anything [charged] really put me in a really vulnerable situation. So yes, I did find that quite difficult because I did feel let down'.

Another woman recalled making a statement to police because she had been told by an officer at the 'one-stop-shop' that, 'we can arrest him and

---

[78]Karen.

[79]Darcey and Charlie.

[80]The charging lawyer assessed that the physical abuse amounted to a series of common assault level offences and the complaint had been being made outside of statutory charging time limits for summary proceedings; s127 Magistrates Court Act 1980 imposes the statutory limitation of 6 months from summary incident to charge. This experience occurred prior to the availability of s76 of the Serious Crime Act 2015 (an either-way offence) which legislated against controlling or coercive behaviour amongst intimates. A series of common assault offences might now be chargeable after the statutory 6-month time limit under the new offence.

we can put him in prison for what he is doing to you'.[81] The perpetrator was duly arrested and interviewed but he was released the same day on bail pending further enquiries. Whilst he was put on police bail with conditions not to contact her, he proceeded to text her 'like 50 times a day' and whilst he was brought before the court for breach of bail, he was quickly readmitted to bail. Ultimately no charges were brought because 'it was basically his word against mine and he denied it... but they [had] told me that they actually could [prosecute]'.

Overpromising by the police can leave women more vulnerable as they are given a legitimate expectation that a certain course of action will follow their report. Without proper awareness that 'no further action' may be taken, women may fail to take alternative action to keep themselves safe. A thoughtless initial police response, with insufficient caveats, can also be detrimental to the victim's emotional state.[82] Poor advice might also have the effect of moving a survivor towards being *against* the law and the consequences of this positioning are discussed in detail below.

(ii) Experiencing the Court Process

'Procedural justice' refers to court processes that are perceived by participants to be fair. Where there is procedural justice, victim satisfaction can be enhanced and negative psychological effects reduced.[83] Experiencing 'procedural justice' has been consistently shown in social justice and victimology literature to assist the victim moving forward from a crime.[84] When victims perceive that their voice has been heard, stress and anxiety can be diminished whilst positive impacts can include increased self-esteem, faith in the future, belief in a just world and the ability to cope.[85] The following section evidences how perceived procedural *in*justice can mean victims try to avoid or disengage from the process because they consider the process

[81]Charlie.

[82]Kunst et al. (n 74) 355.

[83]Tom Tyler, 'Procedural Justice, Legitimacy, and the Effective Rule of Law' (2003) 30 *Crime and Justice* 283.

[84]Uli Orth, 'Secondary Victimization of Crime Victims by Criminal Proceedings' (2012) 15(4) *Social Justice Research* 313; Malini Laxminarayan, 'Procedural Justice and Psychological Effects of Criminal Proceedings: The Moderating Effect of Offense Type' (2012) *Social Justice Research* 390.

[85]Malini Laxminarayan, 'Procedural Justice and Psychological Effects of Criminal Proceedings: The Moderating Effect of Offense Type' (2012) *Social Justice Research* 390, 390.

is a nuisance or, more seriously, traumatic.[86] At worst, the criminal process and proceedings can cause psychological harm (what is known as secondary victimisation).[87] In addition to receiving poor communications, women reported other factors about the court process that took its toll; the length of time waiting for proceedings, the apparent complexity of the process and the strain of providing a victim personal statement.

Women reported that reducing the delays in proceedings would lessen associated stress. For Jen, proceedings had been lengthy due to a double booking at court on the day of trial, due to an appeal and due to the defendant's failure to attend court on two occasions. She described the process as, 'Extremely stressful. It's all the waiting. Like I said, you get yourself all psyched up - as you can ever be - and then it doesn't happen'. Despite having just achieved a successful conviction on appeal, when the perpetrator further harassed Jen just before his sentencing hearing, she decided not to report the matter to police:

> I thought, here we go. It's my word against his again. It's going to be court. It's going to be a trial. It's going to be an appeal. I can't stand another year of this. It didn't seem fair on me. It didn't seem fair on my children, because however much you try and hide it and carry on as normal, you can't, because it is affecting you. I wasn't sleeping. I was really teary. I was on anti-depressants.

This woman commented that she was also confused about what had happened to conclude the criminal proceedings. She understood that her perpetrator had been sent to prison but she did not know why, 'as I say I don't know if he was found guilty. I don't know if he pleaded guilty. I don't actually know whatever happened. And that's a bit strange. I wasn't even 100% [sure] what they meant about the sentence'. Giving proper information about the offence charged, how the defendant pleaded and why they were sent to prison would assist the victim to understand not only unfamiliar processes but also what behaviours had been punished and why. This will have implications for her therapeutic journey.

Finally, women spoke of the demands of providing a victim personal statement. Everyone I spoke with appreciated the merits of doing so (giving the sentencing judge insight into the impact of the offending). However,

---

[86] Rob Mawby and Sandra Walklate, *Critical Victimology* (Sage 1994) 33.
[87] Orth, (n 84).

two women spoke of how the statement was hard to write because it was 'draining and upsetting',[88] because it forced one to 're-live'[89] the abuse again. Karen explained that she felt able to write the statement because over the years she had grown strong, 'but for other people a personal statement can also be embarrassing. You are giving the person the knowledge that they have ruined you. Some people [perpetrators] get a kick out of that and that's the problem'. On balance, however, those in the sample who provided a victim personal statement felt that the opportunity had been positive. One woman had even chosen to attend court to read out her victim personal statement in person at the sentencing hearing and had described the experience as empowering because she was able to show her abuser that she was strong enough to stand up to him.[90]

(iii) Sentencing Outcomes: A Victim's Perspective

Unfavourable sentencing outcomes can feel like a betrayal of victim expectations.[91] A number of the women in the sample perceived sentences to be too lenient: 'How many times does a person have to be given a community order before someone says, "No, you've had your chance and enough is enough now"?'[92] Danielle was of the view that her perpetrator repeatedly escaped prison because he had a mortgage and a good job. She suggested that for someone like him (someone who might ordinarily be considered *before* the law) a custodial sentence would serve as a wake-up call and future deterrent. However, of the four women interviewed whose partners were imprisoned as a result of their domestic abuse offending, all four men had, on release, continued their abuse. Pertinently, all four of those men had a history of involvement, as defendants, with the criminal justice system and all four had previously served custodial sentences for other matters. This suggests that these men, described by their partners in terms of being positioned *against* the law, did not consider imprisonment something to fear or to seek to avoid, more it was seen as an inevitable part of their lives.

---

[88] Karen.

[89] Jen.

[90] This was 'Isabelle' whose audio recording failed but about whom brief notes had been taken by the researcher.

[91] Orth, (n 84) 315.

[92] Danielle.

Another outcome available at the conclusion of the case is a restraining order.[93] An order typically includes a condition prohibiting the defendant from contacting the victim directly or indirectly. Breach of such an order carries with it a maximum sentencing option of five years imprisonment.[94] The seven women in the sample whose partners had received a criminal restraining order (or who had earlier obtained a civil non-molestation order[95]) overwhelmingly expressed exasperation with it; 'What's the point [of an order]? It's a piece of paper and I might as well put it in the bin'.[96] A number of the women expressed the fact that they felt helpless when the order was breached. This runs counter to the intended effect of the order which ought to afford a victim protection and a reassertion of control in the relationship.[97]

There were three reasons why court orders seemed to exacerbate women's sense of vulnerability or powerlessness. First, some women did not believe that any action would be taken by the police. Charlie described the police response to her husband's breaches of the order as being, 'Naff all, really, "There's nothing [we] can do" is basically what I am getting... It's really getting me down'. Charlie understood that this was due to there being insufficient evidence and described the impact on her physical health due to the stress of feeling helpless. Danielle noted that police inaction was not due to lack of evidence but rather a failure to take breaches seriously.[98]

The second reason court restraining orders caused distress was the sense that even when the police acted on a breach it would result in or, in their experience, had resulted in the perpetrator being released without real consequence to him. Karen said that, 'even when you've got that restraining order, they break it once, they are released. They break it twice, they are still released... and someone can, you know, beat the crap out of you and they are still released... Then they [the perpetrator] know how vulnerable you

[93]A restraining order is available on conviction or acquittal where it is deemed 'necessary': s5 Protection from Harassment Act 1997.

[94]S1(5)a Domestic Violence, Crime and Victims Act 2004.

[95]Civil orders can be obtained by virtue of s42(2) or s45(1) (ex parte applications) Family Law Act 1996.

[96]Karen.

[97]Jen, 'He just totally ignored the orders'; Danielle, 'He was kind of harassing me, breaching the order'; Diane, 'I ended up getting a non-molestation order and that was breached several times... so he got a restraining order... he's never served any time'; Karen, Darcey and Charlie confirmed repeated breaches, whilst Sasha said, 'I've got a non-molestation order in place and a restraining order in place but they are both useless'.

[98]This view was based on her experience in around 2010. Danielle was also someone I identified as being situated *against* not *with* the law, as discussed in detail below.

are. You are the vulnerable one who is like, "Where does it end?"'. Sasha agreed that her ex-partner breached the order because, 'he knows he can get away with stuff… [once convicted of breaching the order twice] all he got was the restraining order to stay in place and a court fine'.

The third reason that court orders had the effect of making women feel vulnerable was that for a significant number of the women, reporting a breach of the order was likely to aggravate their ex-partner and put them at increased risk.

> If they went round and said to him, "We've had a report that you've breached the order", they don't do anything except a slap on the wrist, "Don't do it again". He would go mad and god knows what he would do [to me]. It was easier not to report it to police, because nothing was going to happen.[99]

Karen, Charlie and Sasha all agreed that more than the order merely being ineffectual (and therefore the harassment continuing as before) its imposition had had the counter effect of antagonising their assailant.

Despite the problems associated with enforcing the order, the ineffective penal outcomes and the possibility of triggering aggressive behaviour, women found themselves in a quandary; 'Breaking a non-molestation order is nothing to him. I am really worried about when it runs out'.[100] On the one hand, the non-molestation order had been systematically breached and had even, for this woman, exacerbated her partner's harassment of her, but on the other hand she could not imagine being without it. Women felt they had nowhere else to turn but to the criminal justice system in their ongoing struggle to end the abuse, short of moving out of the area.[101] Having the order, despite its shortcomings, gave her moral assuredness that his behaviour was not acceptable and that the state was, at least in principle, on her side. To that extent at least, restraining orders contributed to her ongoing journey to living abuse free.

Women in the primary research also expressed dismay with the probation service. Specifically, there was concern about the effectiveness of the Integrated Domestic Abuse Programme (IDAP) run by the probation service. The course had been undertaken by four of the perpetrators in the sample. Officially, the programme delivers a 13.3% reduction in recidivism in

[99]Danielle.

[100]Charlie.

[101]Lana felt that moving away was the only way the abuse would ever stop and had done so. Diane felt the same but could not face leaving her support network of family and friends.

the following two years.[102] All four of the women in the sample whose partners had completed the course, however, reported that the programme had done nothing to change their perpetrator's behaviour.

The above narratives illustrate that even when a woman has done everything in her power to work *with* the criminal justice system—she has reported the offence, supported the prosecution and requested a restraining order—women still report being unsafe, harassed or intimidated. Perpetrators often violate restraining orders and harass the victim,[103] convictions are appealed,[104] and sentences do not change the defendant's behaviour.[105] If professionals encourage women to be *with* the law, that must make the survivor aware that it may not be a 'quick fix' solution and that law must be considered only part of the process. Managing women's expectations about law's potential to provide 'closure' is crucial because, as the sample evidences, a turn to criminal law frequently disappoints. Ultimately, for some abusers according to Jen, 'Court orders, court, prison doesn't stop him. The worst thing is, I think the only thing that would stop him is finding somebody else'.

4. Women '*Against*' the Law: The Myth of the 'Superman Police'

Standing in contrast to the *with* the law schema, being *against* the law often means that individuals endeavour to keep law at a distance from themselves. Being *against* the law does not necessarily describe an active opposition to the law but can describe a feeling that one is unable to keep a comfortable separation from the law in one's life. Those that sense law's omnipresence often seek to avoid law and its effects.[106]

---

[102]National Offender Management Service, 'An Outcome Evaluation of the Integrated Domestic Abuse Programme (IDAP) and Community Domestic Violence Programme (CDVP)' (2015) available at https://www.gov.uk/government/uploads/system/uploads/attachment_data/file/449008/outcome-evaluation-idap-cdvp.pdf accessed 12 March 2020.

[103]Jen, Danielle, Diane, Karen and Sasha all described having non-molestation or restraining orders in place that were being ignored by the perpetrator. 'He just totally ignored the orders' (Jen) 'He would breach everything. All the time' (Danielle).

[104]Jen and Sasha had to go through the trial process a second time on appeal.

[105]Karen told me that the effect of her husband attending the probation service Integrated Domestic Abuse Programme was: 'Nothing as far as I am aware. He never stopped'. Danielle told me that: 'probation, prison- nothing changed' and Diane said of the probation order: 'It didn't really change anything, I don't think'.

[106]Patricia Ewick and Susan Silbey, *The Common Place of Law* (n 22) 48–49.

Within the primary research, those women who described an *against* the law positioning were in the minority; only Danielle and Renata consistently fell within this final typology. For Danielle, who frequently called the police in emergencies, this manifested in repeatedly failing to support a prosecution. For Renata, her reluctance to engage the police at all meant that the police and the criminal justice system never became involved at her instigation. The stories in this section uncover some of the failings of the criminal justice response as they were experienced by these two women positioned *against* the law; these deficiencies can be split into two broad themes.

The first deficiency is the failure of criminal justice professionals to recognise and respond to victimhood where it is not immediately disclosed or displayed by a victim. Victimhood can present in diverse ways and professionals must be particularly sensitive and attuned to recognising abuse even where it is not openly disclosed. If criminal justice agents understood the dynamics, patterns and strategies of domestic abuse, they would be pre-disposed to treat survivors with requisite therapeutic jurisprudence considerations, however they presented, remembering that every interaction has the potential to have a beneficial therapeutic outcome.

The second deficiency of the criminal justice system that emerges from these women's stories is a failure to understand that even where a woman is exercising agency in ways that are not, objectively, congruent with attaining her 'thrivership', women may be best placed to know what will keep her safe in her particular circumstances. This means that criminal justice professionals should not dismiss, ignore or deride a woman who appears to be exercising her agency in ways which do not mesh well with notions of one-size-fits-all 'rationality'.

(i) Against Law: Recognising Victimhood Whilst Understanding Agency

Before examining the particular events and recollections that contributed to Danielle's evolving resistance to legal intervention, I want to recall the shortcomings of the victim/agent dichotomy outlined in Chapter 2. This is because criminal justice agents' perceptions about the binary appear to have contributed to Danielle's growing disillusionment with the law and her belief that it would not serve her best interests. Laced throughout the account of Danielle (and, as I explore later, Renata), are deficiencies in the way the dualism functions for the police and their treatment of abused women.[107] The dichotomy between 'victimhood' and 'agency' is overdrawn. 'Victims' are considered those who have been 'harmed', who are vulnerable and who lack strength due to a one-way exercise of power from the perpetrator.[108] Passive and helpless, they are expected to express gratitude for assistance. 'Agents' on the other hand are those displaying a capacity to make proactive decisions—for example not to choose criminal justice intervention—and are, as a result, less likely to appear to need empathetic support from criminal justice professionals. In fact, the victim/agent dichotomy obscures the ways in which survivors can both be simultaneously subjected to domestic abuse (as a 'victim') and yet practice acts of resistance (as an 'agent').

Intimate partner violence occurs complexly 'in the context of love, responsibility, work and obligation, commitment and uncertainty'[109] and the decision to decline criminal justice intervention and/or to stay within an abusive relationship does not mean that a survivor should be considered incompetent, irrational or pathological. Even if a woman is being intimidated into withdrawing her support, her decision is hers, and is being made within the constraints of a survivor's particular material, relational and emotional existence. Hirschmann has described this as making 'movements to create freedom within a context of oppression'.[110] If a woman does not wish to accept state help, this does not make her 'difficult' or 'unreasonable' and her resistance should not prevent her from benefitting from sensitive state assistance at that moment or in the future.

Danielle's abuse was both extensive and shocking. She described the slow crescendo of abuse that, at the start of the relationship, was infrequent but towards the end of the relationship became a daily occurrence. The behaviours were often triggered by what she described as his 'binge drinking' and ranged from anger, physical beatings, kickings, woundings with knives and on one occasion knocking her off a ladder (breaking her arm). She

---

[107]Two authors that draw out the problems of the dichotomy are Martha Mahoney, 'Victimization or Oppression? Women's Lives, Violence and Agency' in Martha Fineman and Roxanne Mykitiuk (eds), *The Public Nature of Private Violence: The Discovery of Domestic Abuse* (Routledge 1994); Elizabeth Schneider, 'Feminism and the False Dichotomy of Victimization and Agency' (1993) 38 *NYL School Law Review* 387.

[108]Martha Mahoney, 'Victimization or Oppression? Women's Lives, Violence and Agency' in Martha Fineman and Roxanne Mykitiuk (eds), *The Public Nature of Private Violence: The Discovery of Domestic Abuse* (Routledge 1994) 62.

[109]Ibid., 60.

[110]Nancy J Hirschmann, 'Freedom, Power and Agency in Feminist Legal Theory' in Margaret Davis and Vanessa Munro (eds), *The Ashgate Research Companion to Feminist Legal Theory* (Ashgate 2013) 59. See also Martha Mahoney, ibid.

also described what she called 'torturous' behaviour such as her husband throwing objects at her whilst she slept, putting oil on the stairs so that she slipped, smearing the sheets with tomato sauce and mayonnaise and throwing boiling or freezing cold water over her in bed. This highly coercive, controlling and violent abuse became more frequent and severe over time. This man's undertaking to control Danielle was supported by his traditional attitudes towards women and gendered role expectations (though Danielle worked he spent the money). Danielle's description of her partner made him 'rank high on measures of emotional dependency and jealousy'.[111] Danielle explained that though family and friends knew about police attendances at the home, they could not believe her husband would be capable of such behaviour because he always managed to be a 'charmer' around them. She explained that, 'I didn't have any idea that what was happening was domestic abuse at the time'. Mahoney explains that a woman's failure to recognise her own victimhood can stem from a 'woman's belief in herself as an actor in her own life [which] can prevent her from identifying her experiences as similar to that of other women who experience oppression'.[112]

At the beginning of her abusive relationship, Danielle was not someone likely to have identified her relationship with the law as oppositional. However, as her abusive relationship progressed and the police were called out to assist in moments of crisis (she estimated 'well over' 50 police call outs during the course of her 12-year relationship) her legal consciousness became more and more entrenched in an *against* the law conception. It seems that the more the police and criminal justice system became involved, the less desire she had to engage them and, indeed, the more she feared and resented their involvement.

Danielle provided a number of examples where police had either failed to acknowledge her victimhood at all or had acknowledged it, but had assumed that her refusal to bring a prosecution meant that their job was done and that she no longer required a therapeutic or supportive response from them. Recalling the first time she called out the police and the first time she had felt let down by them for failing to recognise her vulnerability, Danielle considered they had done nothing to assist her, 'They didn't do a risk assessment. They didn't ask what was going on. It was just they were called to this

[111]Michael Johnson, *A Typology of Domestic Violence: Intimate Terrorism, Violent Resistance and Situational Couple Violence* (Northeastern University Press 2008) 26 and 32 describes that this pattern of abuse is overwhelmingly perpetrated by men.

[112]Mahoney, 'Victimization or Oppression? Women's Lives, Violence and Agency' (n 108) 62.

incident. The incident was dealt with. And then they went away and left you'.

More than merely failing to acknowledge Danielle's vulnerability, on one occasion in 2008 police openly blamed *her* for creating the incident. Police handling on this occasion was typical of her experiences, explained Danielle, in that it lacked empathy, sensitivity and constructive handling of the situation. It occurred one night when her husband was drunk and hammering on the back door to be let in, making threats to hurt her. Danielle called the police believing that the disturbance would prompt neighbours to call the police anyway. On arrival, having spoken to both parties, the police suggested to Danielle that the disturbance had been caused by her because she should have unlocked the door and let him into the property. They understood that he only wanted to collect some beer from the fridge and some clothes to take to a friend's house. The police's solution was to tell the perpetrator to leave and not return until the morning:

> They let him out of the back gate and as they were walking out of the front door, he was already at the back door, kicking off, going absolutely mad. And I thought at that time - and I got really badly hurt that night - I remember thinking, what is the point in me phoning the police. What is the point? They came out and said it was *my* fault.

The police in this account failed to acknowledge Danielle's victimhood, perhaps because they already knew that she was someone who had not previously wanted to support a prosecution. Yet, we know that when women feel respected and heard by helping professionals, this can form an important part in trauma recovery and the journey to thrivership.[113] Moreover, trust can develop between the parties which is likely to mean that a victim feels more inclined to take advice.[114] Even when the abuse was becoming more regular, Danielle recounted that, 'I didn't think that what was happening was wrong. Because they [police] never said to me, "This is really bad and [you] need to do something"'. On two occasions a 'domestic abuse unit' had telephoned Danielle the day after a police call-out, but she felt that they were simply carrying out a tick box exercise and were audibly relieved when she told them that everything was 'fine'.

---

[113] John Wilson, *Trauma, Transformation, and Healing: An Integrative Approach to Theory, Research and Post-traumatic Therapy* (Brunner/Mazel 1989) 212–216 cited in ibid., 120.

[114] Linda Mills, *Insult to Injury: Re-thinking Our Responses to Intimate Abuse* (Princeton University Press 2003) 13, 199–220.

Danielle did not recognise that she was being abused and police interventions played no part in supporting her to identify that she was; the police failed to recognise that her agency in deciding not to provide prosecution statements, did not preclude her victimhood and they did not address her appropriately. The persistent failure to respond to Danielle's victimhood sits in contrast to the experience of Darcey (detailed above) who found the police's empathetic response pivotal; Danielle's *against* the law positioning became entrenched by the very professionals tasked with assisting her.

Danielle had in fact, on three occasions, provided witness statements to the police towards the beginning of the relationship. On one of these occasions, before the police took 'no further action' against the suspect, he was released on bail pending further investigation. He was released with conditions not to contact Danielle, but he had a total disregard for the bail conditions and he escalated his threats and physical violence because she had involved the police. No charges were ever brought against the perpetrator because there was 'insufficient evidence' against him. This was confirmation, for Danielle, that she was not being abused. On the final occasion she provided the police with a statement, she quickly withdrew her support out of fear about what he might do but also because she felt that the prosecution would come to nothing in any event. She was never asked the reason why she was withdrawing her support.[115] Unsurprisingly, after these initial experiences of providing a statement in support of prosecution, Danielle stated that on subsequent occasions she thought, 'there is no way I am doing this… it doesn't do anything. And actually it makes him worse… nothing is going to happen to him and he gets let out and then it makes him really violent'. Here she describes assessing her situation and manoeuvring within the constraints she lived with 'to produce a slightly less bad outcome, an outcome that she dislike(d) a little less than the alternative on offer'.[116]

The benefits of prosecution and achieving a criminal conviction cannot always be presumed. Danielle found that criminal justice involvement provoked and escalated her partner's violence which was exacerbated by his indifference to the law and its sanctions. She felt that her perpetrator's familiarity with the criminal justice system meant that he knew what to say in a police interview and how to manipulate the situation to his advantage. Any threat of sanctions did not present a deterrent as, 'He's not scared of police.

[115] This was in 2003.

[116] Hirschmann, 'Freedom, Power and Agency in Feminist Legal Theory' (n 110) 59.

He's not scared of being interviewed. He's not scared of going to court. He's not scared of any of that'. Her story highlights the difficulty of assuming that if only a conviction could be achieved through the cajoling of the witness to give evidence, a net benefit for the victim will be achieved. In fact, poor criminal justice interventions can diminish a woman's safety in tangible terms and increase her vulnerability.

Nonetheless, Danielle continued to use the criminal justice system to the extent that she required it. In calling the police in emergencies but in never supporting a prosecution, she simultaneously assured her immediate safety, diminished the risk of exacerbating her partner's violence whilst fulfilling her inclination to maintain the relationship. On this basis her agency, within the confines of her situation, becomes clear. Danielle was able to use the police as a 'power resource',[117] but in acknowledging the costs of continued prosecution to her, she exercised some control through non-cooperation. Danielle's objective victimhood should not therefore preclude acknowledgement of her agency or any dismissal that she was not acting with 'reason'.

In fact Danielle's perpetrator eventually received a custodial sentence for Grievous Bodily Harm to her by way of a victimless prosecution (the serious photographed injuries and state of the house on that occasion provided the requisite corroborative evidence) yet the relationship continued on his release from prison. It was only after a visit from a health visitor and social services in which they spoke to Danielle about the situation and the unacceptability of bringing up a child in a violent home that Danielle sought advice from the 'one stop shop' with the intention of obtaining strategies for protecting her son.[118] Finally, after speaking with professionals there she recognised her victimhood and chose to terminate the relationship and moved out of the family home. She described her contact with the 'one stop shop' becoming, 'much more than I thought it would be'. This was clearly because professionals were available, able and willing to listen, supported her and gave her advice about the relationship. This appears to have been the first time that someone spoke with Danielle effectively about her situation with sensitive and practical suggestions. Following their separation, he continued to harass her but, despite now having support from the domestic abuse charity,

[117]David Ford, 'Prosecution as a Victim Power Resource' (n 62) 313, 319–320. Many *against* the law expressed that they felt invocation of the law was 'not worth it' in Ewick and Silbey, *The Common Place of Law* (n 22) 197. Danielle was clearly *with* the law to the extent that she needed it in emergencies but was *against* having the law further involved.

[118]On reflection Danielle commented that her health visitor encouraged her to go to the one-stop-shop under the auspices of helping her son but with the clear hope she would obtain support for herself.

she remained resolute in her *against* the law positioning, that there would be no criminal justice involvement because no good would come of it.

Danielle was keen to impress that she felt she had been part of the reason that the criminal justice system had achieved little for her (aside from the immediate emergency protection that sparked her frequent calls to the police) as she had failed to support prosecutions and to tell them the details of what was happening. However, she was clear that although she did not blame anyone and that it was always her decision to stay, 'I think there were loads of opportunities for somebody to recognise that something wasn't right, really with the relationship… not one of them spoke to me about it'. She described how she felt that the police were not on her side, 'I just had this real fear of them and I didn't want to talk to them about anything at all. I knew that he was good at making me look [a liar]… no evidence and no witnesses… and then they wouldn't believe me anymore. I think that was the fear'. Police responses appear to have been guided by her reputation as someone who did not support the prosecution (her 'agency'). A therapeutic response, which understood her victimhood and the reasons she chose not to support prosecutions, could have shifted both her legal consciousness positioning, her victimhood and her vulnerability.[119]

Unlike Danielle, Renata's resistance to the law was well developed prior to her three abusive marriages. Her presentation as someone *against* the law appears to have meant that when she had contact with the police, they consistently failed to acknowledge her victimhood. Growing up in a 'traveller'[120] family and community where, she reported, intimate partner abuse was pervasive, Renata understood that as soon as the police left, 'You are going to get the hiding you were going to get anyway, plus another one for phoning police, because that's not what you do'. Throughout her interview, Renata repeatedly expressed her relationship with the police and the criminal justice system in uncompromisingly hostile terms.[121] What becomes clear from Renata's story, however, is how, in the absence of the criminal justice system recognising her victimhood, due to her presentation as a strong woman exercising agency, she learned to navigate her safety in ways that did not depend on the 'superman police' (her ironic and therefore denigrating description).

[119]Hirschmann, 'Freedom, Power and Agency in Feminist Legal Theory' (n 110) 59.

[120]This was how Renata self-identified her childhood community.

[121]'They [the police] weren't my friend'. 'I didn't really expect the police to do anything for me'. 'You don't assume that they [police] are going to be helpful'.

Just as Ewick and Silbey describe in their *against* the law schema, Renata's resistance to the law manifested as her seeking to avoid it. For her, law was a product of arbitrary power and it was therefore unsafe to invoke.[122] Consequently, Renata was typical of those *against* the law in that she deployed self-help strategies and used her own initiative to keep herself safe. Her resistance also clearly 'inhere[d] in the telling of the story and passing on the message that legality can be opposed'[123] and even spilled into recounting how she was able to create her own fixes and, on occasion, exact revenge in order to protect herself.

In contrast to Danielle, Renata's agency manifested in a failure to ever call on the criminal justice system for assistance. Being married as a teenager to a man who sold her services as a sex-worker, her 'killer pimp'[124] would regularly deliver 'serious beatings' for the purposes of controlling her and keeping her 'in line'. Renata lamented that, during her time as a prostitute in the mid-1980s she did not present as an archetypal 'victim' and that consequently, 'a couple of times I can remember getting arrested and I was visibly bruised. Nobody asked me about the bruises. They were charging me for soliciting… but also showing signs of, like, physical abuse. There was quite a lot of opportunity there for people to intervene and nothing was done'. Throughout the interview she repeatedly reflected that '[police] were not my friends… they weren't helping me'. She reflected that she was not received sympathetically as a victim of intimate partner abuse because of the nature of the work she was doing and the way she presented. It was only when her then husband (and pimp) was imprisoned for a serious assault on a male in a public place (and this irony was not lost on Renata) that she was able to leave.

The importance of Renata's account is not just her reflections about her victimhood, it is the police's failure to recognise it, their antipathy towards her as a low-level offender and the reminder that there is no one way to present as 'vulnerable'. Renata had complex and intersecting presentations. The rest of her story, relating to her second and third husbands, is also key because it overtly highlights that criminal justice intervention will not always be the most appropriate way to proceed for victims of intimate partner abuse. Moreover, just because a woman does not engage the criminal justice system, it does not mean that she is not exercising agency, and making herself safe, in other ways.

[122]Ewick and Silbey, *The Common Place of Law* (n 22) 192.

[123]Ibid.

[124]A term she used to describe her then husband.

On leaving her second husband, Renata's decision not to involve the police following his serious assault of her was not solely due to her distrust in the police and her lack of belief in the effectiveness of criminal justice outcomes. Nor was it just her sense that she would not be believed due to her previous convictions and her failure to present as a vulnerable and compliant victim. It was also motivated by an astute strategy. Having 're-invented' herself, putting her previous convictions behind her, she did not want to bring her new family to the attention of children's social services or provoke her partner in such a way that he would withdraw the 'decent' maintenance allowance they had agreed in advance.

For very different reasons, involving the criminal justice system during her third marriage would also have been deleterious. Renata's third husband was an exceptionally violent man who operated within criminal networks and his friends were similarly so. When he started to exert violence towards her at moments of anger, Renata immediately knew that she would not continue the relationship. When the police became involved following his public use of violence (where a witness called the police), she was told that there could be no prosecution of him without her support. She reflected, 'In a way, them not prosecuting—it's kind of unforgivable [there had been witnesses] but it's worked out better for me. In a way, them not prosecuting [her husband] made me realise how vulnerable I was' and this motivated her to exercise 'damage limitation' and take steps to protect herself.

Whilst her husband was recalled to prison on licence (prompted by police involvement following the public assault on her), Renata recorded her perpetrator threatening her on the telephone so that she could serve a civil injunction on him (which she reflected offered her *some* protection). Furthermore, she began to spread rumours amongst his fraternity so that they began to lose sympathy with him (thereby limiting the likelihood they would take action against her on his behalf). She reported his stashing of illegal items at her home, via her probation officer, and was relieved that when police attended and 'kicked the door in' this provided evidence that she was not complicit in reporting the stash to police (this was her hope when she had reported him to her probation worker). When a police-issued panic alarm was retrieved by them only a week after the public assault, she installed a private security alarm which would prompt immediate security staff attendance. Furthermore, 'Not long after that, I went into [addiction] recovery. And I started [a new career]. On some level, I made the decision that I was never going to let myself be that vulnerable again. And now I am passionate about it'. The consequences of a prosecution, even if victimless, would have been to put her safety at very real risk due to the threat of retribution by either her husband or his network. The difficulty for a prosecutor to appreciate the complexity of Renata's situation is obvious.

Discussion

If the CPS routinely prefer to proceed with cases against a victim's wishes, with the intention of meeting their overriding policy objectives of taking violence against women 'seriously'[125] and if 'success' equates to 'bringing more perpetrators to justice',[126] the stories in this chapter act as a reminder that women's experiences are diverse and require sensitive appraisal. These CPS policy objectives might now appear crude 'headlines' in what requires careful handling and nuance. Leaving sweeping policy objectives aside, this chapter draws out how in fact the CPS domestic abuse Guidelines—advocating a 'survivor-defined',[127] case-by-case approach—is well founded.[128] Whilst the current presumptions that police arrest and the CPS prosecute are commendable starting points, what is most clearly exposed by the narratives in this chapter is that criminal prosecution may not always serve abused women in the way prosecutors imagine.

The accounts presented here do not present any unified narrative of what constitutes the best course of action to take for a woman who has experienced domestic abuse. Rather, they highlight the need for prosecutorial caution. For a woman situated *before* the law, interactions with the criminal justice system must emphasise her importance and centrality. Summonsing attendance at court for a woman positioned *before* the law may serve to confirm that the law orbits without sufficient regard for her, thereby confirming the reservations she has about her own agency. By summonsing or proceeding with the case against her wishes, prosecutors risk alienating the victim and replacing the coercive strategies of the abuser with the coercive strategies of the state. For a woman positioned *with* the law, criminal justice professionals must set reasonable expectations and encourage women to

---

[125]Crown Prosecution Service, 'Domestic Abuse Guidelines for Prosecutors' (2014) available at https://www.cps.gov.uk/legal-guidance/domestic-abuse-guidelines-prosecutors accessed 22 January 2018.

[126]Crown Prosecution Service, 'Violence Against Women and Girls' Report 2016–17' available at https://www.cps.gov.uk/publications/docs/cps-vawg-report-2017.pdf accessed 22 January 2018.

[127]Andrea Nichols, 'No-Drop Prosecution in Domestic Violence Cases: Survivor-Defined and Social Change Approaches to Victim Advocacy' (2014) *Journal of Interpersonal Violence* 2114–2142.

[128]The guidance urges prosecutors to 'consider the impact on the complainant if they are to be compelled, [as] compelling attendance at court may cause the complainant further distress', CPS, 'Domestic Abuse Guidelines' (n 125).

conceive of law as only part of the journey to living abuse free. If the law disappoints, it may only serve to make the victim feel that she has 'lost'. A woman *with* the law is least likely to withdraw her support for the prosecution but if she does, the police might use techniques of therapeutic jurisprudence to explore her reasons for doing so which may, in turn, assist prosecutors to decide whether proceeding with the case is the best course. Procedural justice and therapeutic interactions are more likely to foster a woman's trust in being able to call upon the police in future emergencies. For a woman *against* the law, criminal justice agents should be encouraged to recognise her victimhood and speak with her appropriately (in the next chapter I explore this further through an examination of the trauma-informed perspective). Yet, particularly for women *against* the law, recognising that women, as agents, might be best placed to navigate their future safety is necessary before deciding whether summons would best serve her.

If a key advantage of a criminal justice response centres around the availability of individuals trained to recognise a woman's specific needs, then, as Smart questions, need she rely on law at all?[129] It is accepted that when women feel heard and visible during the court process they can enjoy emancipatory benefits; however, 'life changing effects are often little to do with the result of a prosecution'.[130] Heather Douglas has suggested that the benefit of a criminal justice response is that women gain access and referral to feminist agencies and networks. Such organisations, she posits, have the potential to assist women to leave their violent men and to construct an alternative reality to the one presented by law (where law can serve to support violent men's narratives and minimise the extent of the harm caused to women). If the result of going to law sees women being signposted to women's support organisations—such as the three charities accessed by the women in the primary research—then, Douglas suggests, perhaps that is the law's value?

This chapter has drawn out some of the problems and even dangers that might still exist for women who engage the criminal justice system. These empirical insights accord with the arguments of feminist academics who have drawn attention to how male perpetrators might be better at navigating the 'masculine requirements of law'[131] and legal process; or that involving the justice system might 'create distress, disadvantages and disillusionment for

[129]Carol Smart, 'Reflections' (n 64) 160.

[130]Heather Douglas, 'Battered Women's Experience of the Criminal Justice System: Decentring Law' (2012) *Feminist Legal Studies* 121, 132.

[131]Carol Smart, 'Reflections' (n 64) 160.

women that overrides hope or safety that might be gained'.[132] Unsympathetic responses, dashed legitimate expectations, inconsequential sentences, orders that are ignored and abuse that continues or exacerbates are all reasons to pay heed to Smart's assessment that law's self-proclaimed 'truths' may not accord with women's experience and that sometimes victories may not be worth the price paid. Nonetheless, the chapter has also shown that, despite some obvious shortcomings of a criminal justice response, when women consider their voices to be heard, their narratives to be believed and their centrality to be key emancipatory progress can be made for them.[133]

Conclusion

Placing 'women's experience, and the perspective from within that experience, at the center'[134] is arguably the ambition of feminist legal study. The empirical work in this chapter undertakes this endeavour. It exposes the absence of a unified account of how women think about criminal law and how they expect it to act on their behalf. Nonetheless, by identifying women's broad positionalities in relation to law (legal consciousness), layers of commonality surface and implicitly demand attention. Within the narratives of the individual or groups of individuals, Schneider urges that the 'general', or broader context of gender inequality, is not forgotten and that the 'particular' be situated in the 'general'. In doing this, 'the particular illuminates the general, and the general provides context and depth to our understanding of the particular',[135] meaning that women's seemingly individual experiences of violence are always situated and understood to operate as an aspect of women's subordinate position in society. Moreover, the inadequacy of law to discursively accommodate feminist knowledge and subjects is underlined.[136]

---

[132]Douglas (n 130) 121.

[133]See also Lauren Bennett Cattaneo and Lisa Goodman, 'Through the Lens of Therapeutic Jurisprudence: The Relationship Between Empowerment in the Court System and Well-Being for Intimate Partner Violence Victims' (2010) 25(3) *Journal of Interpersonal Violence* 481; Carol Smart, 'Law's Truth/Women's Experience' in Regina Graycar (ed), *Dissenting Opinions: Feminist Explorations in Law and Society* (Allen and Unwin 1990) 1–20; and Douglas (n 130) 121.

[134]Catherine Mackinnon, *Towards A Feminist Theory of the State* (Harvard University Press 1989) 38.

[135]Elizabeth Schneider, *Battered Women and Feminist Lawmaking* (n 1) 5.

[136]Rosemary Hunter, 'Contesting the Dominant Paradigm' in Margaret Davies and Vanessa Munro (eds), *The Ashgate Research Companion to Feminist Legal Theory* (Ashgate 2013) 25; Carol Smart, *Feminism and the Power of the Law* (n 16) 88.

Through this exploration of women's legal consciousness, aspects of the criminal justice system that can be damaging or disappointing for female victims of domestic abuse have been revealed. Through empirical narrative, the chapter has shown that law may not prove to be a site of refuge or resolution for women who have experienced domestic abuse. The chapter therefore challenges Madden-Dempsey's philosophical appraisal that effective prosecutions of domestic violence offences would be a sound feminist strategy[137] and responds to Hunter's critique that Madden-Dempsey's abstract work fails to consider lived lives.[138] Smart's post-modern feminist project of de-centring law was never intended to mean that feminists and women should ignore law or write it off.[139] Rather, instead of 'colluding with law's overinflated view of itself' Smart encouraged feminists to concentrate on the law in practice.[140] As such, this chapter adheres to 'a more modern version [of feminist jurisprudence], taking the form of a complex, tentative, questioning engagement with law as a continuous process'.[141] From this, Smart encouraged, a valuable 'discursive struggle' would ensue. The following chapter responds to her call.

References

Bernstein E, 'Militarized Humanitarianism Meets Carceral Feminism: The Politics of Sex, Rights, and Freedom in Contemporary Anti-trafficking Campaigns' (2010) 36(1) *Signs: Journal of Women in Culture and Society* 45–71.

Cane P and Conaghan J, *The New Oxford Companion to Law* (Oxford University Press 2008).

Cattaneo L and Goodman L, 'Through the Lens of Therapeutic Jurisprudence: The Relationship Between Empowerment in the Court System and Well-Being for Intimate Partner Violence Victims' (2010) 25(3) *Journal of Interpersonal Violence* 481.

Conaghan J, *Law and Gender* (Oxford University Press 2013).

Crenshaw K, 'Mapping the Margins: Intersectionality, Identity Politics, and Violence against Women of Color' (1991) 43 *Stanford Law Review* 1241.

[137]Michelle Madden-Dempsey, 'Toward a Feminist State: What Does "Effective" Prosecution of Domestic Violence Mean?' (2007) 70(6) *The Modern Law Review* 908–935.

[138]Rosemary Hunter, 'Michelle Madden Dempsey: Prosecuting Domestic Violence: A Philosophical Analysis' (2010) 18(2) *Feminist Legal Studies* 195.

[139]Ibid., 162.

[140]Smart, *Feminism and the Power of the Law* (n 16) 25.

[141]Smart, 'Reflections' (n 64) 164.

Crown Prosecution Service, 'Domestic Abuse Guidelines for Prosecutors' (2014) available at https://www.cps.gov.uk/legal-guidance/domestic-abuse-guidelines-prosecutors accessed 22 January 2018.

———, 'Violence Against Women and Girls' Report 2016–17' available at https://www.cps.gov.uk/publications/docs/cps-vawg-report-2017.pdf accessed 22 January 2018.

Davies M and Munro V, *The Ashgate Research Companion to Feminist Legal Theory* (Ashgate 2013).

Douglas H, 'Battered Women's Experience of the Criminal Justice System: Decentring Law' (2012) *Feminist Legal Studies* 121, 132.

Ewick P and Silbey S, 'Conformity, Contestation, and Resistance: An Account of Legal Consciousness' (1992) *New England Law Review* 731.

———, *The Common Place of Law: Stories from Everyday Life* (University of Chicago Press 1998).

Finkelhor D et al., *The Dark Side of Families: Current Family Violence Research* (Sage 1983) 261–276.

Ford D, 'Prosecution as a Victim Power Resource: A Note on Empowering Women in Violent Conjugal Relationships' (1991) *Law and Society Review* 313.

Graycar R, *Dissenting Opinions: Feminist Explorations in Law and Society* (Allen and Unwin 1990).

Harding R, '"Dogs Are 'Registered', People Shouldn't Be": Legal Consciousness and Lesbian and Gay Rights' (2006) *Social and Legal Studies* 511.

Hunter R, 'Michelle Madden Dempsey: Prosecuting Domestic Violence: A Philosophical Analysis' (2010) 18(2) *Feminist Legal Studies* 195.

Hutchinson D, 'Identity Crisis: "Intersectionality," "Multidimensionality," and the Development of an Adequate Theory of Subordination' (2001) 6 *Michigan Journal of Race and Law* 28.

Kwan P, 'Complicity and Complexity: Cosynthesis and Praxis' (2000) 49 *DePaul University Law Review* 673.

Lacey N, *Unspeakable Subjects: Feminist Essays in Legal and Social Theory* (Hart 1998) 1.

Lewis R et al, 'Protection, Prevention, Rehabilitation or Justice? Women's Use of the Law to Challenge Domestic Violence' (Domestic Violence: Global Responses 179.

Mackinnon C, *Towards A Feminist Theory of the State* (Harvard University Press 1989).

Madden-Dempsey M, 'Toward a Feminist State: What Does "Effective" Prosecution of Domestic Violence Mean?' (2007) 70(6) *The Modern Law Review* 908.

Munro V, *Law and Politics at the Perimeter: Re-evaluating the Key Debates in Feminist Theory* (Hart 2007).

Nash J, 'Re-thinking Intersectionality' (2008) 89(1) *Feminist Review* 1.

Nichols A, 'No-Drop Prosecution in Domestic Violence Cases: Survivor-Defined and Social Change Approaches to Victim Advocacy' (2014) 29(11) *Journal of Interpersonal Violence* 2114.

Nielsen L, 'Situating Legal Consciousness: Experiences and Attitudes of Ordinary Citizens about Law and Street Harassment' (2000) 34 *Law and Society Review* 1055.

Schneider E, *Battered Women and Feminist Lawmaking* (Yale University Press 2000).

———, 'Particularity and Generality: Challenges of Feminist Theory and Practice in Work on Woman-Abuse' (1992) 67 *NYUL Review* 520.

Silbey S and Ewick P, 'The Rule of Law—Sacred and Profane' (2000) 37(6) *Society* 49, 50.

Slobogin C, 'Therapeutic Jurisprudence: 5 Dilemmas to Ponder' (1995) *Psychology, Public Policy and Law* 193.

Smart C, *Feminism and the Power of the Law* (Routledge 1989).

———, 'Reflections' (2012) *Feminist Legal Studies* 160.

Valdes F, 'Sex and Race in Queer Legal Culture: Ruminations of Identities and Interconnectivities' (1995) 5 *Southern California Review of Law and Women's Studies* 32.

Walker L, *The Battered Woman Syndrome* (4th edn, Springer 2016).

Wexler D, 'Applying the Law Therapeutically' (1996) *Applied and Preventive Psychology* 179.

Winick B, 'Applying the Law Therapeutically in Domestic Violence Cases' (2000) *UMKC Law Review* 33.

———, 'The Jurisprudence of Therapeutic Jurisprudence' (1997) *Psychology, Public Policy and Law* 184.

Yllo K and Bograd M, *Feminist Perspectives on Wife Abuse* (Sage 1990).

6

Thrivership: Moving Legal Subjectivity Beyond the Agent/Victim Dichotomy

> [Prosecutors] need to think about survivors' voices… Because we, as professionals, can sit here and have this conversation, but actually there is an empty chair there and that's a survivor who is actually best placed to tell us what they need. Whether it's through participation or consultation - we [support workers] will always try to bring the victim and survivor into the room. They best know their story and what they need.[1]

Introduction

The liberal legal subject of criminal law inadequately describes women's lives and the experiences of living with an abusive partner. The notion of a highly autonomous and socially de-contextualised actor produces an exaggerated dichotomy where domestic abuse survivors are perceived either to align with this paradigmatic capable agent, or not. Feminists have traditionally critiqued the liberal legal subject for its invocation of a genderless, judicious and unconstrained version of agency and for its potential in legal practice to imply that the alternative is a failed, irrational and non-credible subject. In recent times (as Chapter 4 explored), the Crown Prosecution Service has endeavoured to respond to this critique and instead of conceiving the unsupportive victim as inconsistent and unreliable and dropping the case

[1]Focus Group (hereafter FG) 2, Participant support worker 4.

A. Porter, *Prosecuting Domestic Abuse in Neoliberal Times*, Palgrave Socio-Legal Studies,
https://doi.org/10.1007/978-3-030-61369-3_6

accordingly, prosecutors now frequently identify the domestic abuse victim as a particularly vulnerable subject who lacks agency and requires protection (through ongoing prosecution).

In this chapter, through the observations and reflections of seventeen domestic abuse support workers consulted in five focus groups in 2019, I develop alternative modes of analysis to assist prosecutors to think about domestic abuse complainants.[2] The extensive and specialist experience of these support workers provides illustrative and illuminating examples from practice and grounds the theoretical discussion. From these insights, my intention is to provoke prosecutors to make decisions and act in ways that support survivors to move towards a life in which they are no longer defined by the abuse perpetrated on them.

Transcending the liberal legal subject requires a nuanced consideration of the person. I first acknowledge our ontological vulnerability which imposes a responsibility on the part of the state's criminal justice system to prosecute domestic abuse. Yet my approach also accepts that a human desire for self-determination and autonomy, contextually situated, is a universal truth. The job of prosecutors should be to help survivors to attain autonomy (relationally conceived) and self-determination, rather than assuming either that they have it or they don't have it. That attainment is an important part of 'thrivership' as I discuss below. In order to support survivors to 'thrive', I encourage prosecutors to be trauma-informed and to develop tailored therapeutic legal praxis.[3]

1. Victimhood and 'Vulnerability'

I have suggested that, in an effort to demonstrate that they are taking domestic abuse seriously, prosecutors routinely frame the victim as 'vulnerable' and in need of protection (through prosecution). Indeed, the CPS requires prosecutors to mark any domestic abuse victim as 'vulnerable' on their files and CPS policy describes domestic abuse victims as 'particularly

[2]Support worker participants in the sample were employed by five different charities in the South of England. All were, or had been, employed as key workers assigned to support survivors, two were now employed as trainers and trained key workers and other professionals who encounter victims of domestic abuse as part of their employ, and three were no longer key workers but now worked in policy, lobbying government for improvements.

[3]David Wexler, 'Therapeutic Jurisprudence: An Overview' (2000) 17 *TM Cooley Law Review* 125.

vulnerable'.[4] This depiction follows a concerted political effort to re-centre the victim in criminal proceedings and also the demands of violence against women campaigners for the criminal justice system to take domestic abuse seriously. But this blanket categorising of the 'vulnerable' victim lacks nuance. In its everyday usage, 'vulnerability' is a descriptor which refers to someone's susceptibility to potential harm or damage and implies the need for special care, support, or protection.[5] This understanding of 'vulnerability' has pervaded public policy and official rhetoric not only in the area of domestic abuse; it has also been used to describe 'virtually every group facing a difficult predicament'.[6] Furedi has even suggested that 'vulnerability' has become the defining condition of our time.[7]

The political rubric of 'vulnerability', however, is not comprehensive or consistent and nor is there a common theoretical understanding of what it is. Munro and Scoular refer to vulnerability's common usage as a 'flat' understanding of vulnerability that fails to interrogate the complexity of the condition, its relations and narratives.[8] I showed in Chapter 5, for example, that the description obscures the victim's simultaneous capacity for agency. Nonetheless, the everyday use of the term enjoys ethical appeal across political agendas; it has been used as a means of justifying state intervention in people's lives.[9] Caution should therefore be exercised before relying on 'vulnerability' as a legitimising call to action because the fluidity and malleability of 'flat' vulnerability terminology renders it susceptible to being applied to meet the political ends of any range of mainstream political groupings under the guise of state altruism.[10]

Whilst naming 'vulnerability', therefore, has the encouraging potential to support social justice ameliorations by prompting state responsiveness, there

[4]See Chapter 4 and Crown Prosecution Service, 'Domestic Abuse Guidelines for Prosecutors' (2014) available at https://www.cps.gov.uk/legal-guidance/domestic-abuse-guidelines-prosecutors accessed 9 April 2020.

[5]'Vulnerability' comes from the Latin, 'to wound'.

[6]Frank Furedi, 'Fear and Security: A Vulnerability Led Policy Response' (2008) *Social Policy and Administration* 645, 656.

[7]Ibid., 656.

[8]Vanessa Munro and Jane Scoular, 'Abusing Vulnerability? Contemporary Law and Policy Responses to Sex Work in the UK' (2012) *Feminist Legal Studies* 189, 189.

[9]Ibid., 189.

[10]Ibid., 191. Alexandra Trimmer (Utrecht University School of Law) referred to 'vulnerability' as a 'chameleon concept', able to change to suit its surrounds at 'A Workshop on Vulnerability and Social Justice' (2016) Leeds University.

is potential for its use to extend neoliberal governance.[11] For example, in response to our vulnerability to terrorism, stronger surveillance policies are green lighted. In response to vulnerable sex workers and migrants, securitisation through border controls and criminalisation is implemented and in response to the vulnerable victim of domestic violence the perpetrator must be brought to justice and future risk to the victim must be managed by the state (through, inter alia, criminal prosecution). Objections to using 'vulnerability' to effect these ends are concerned with oppressive paternalism resulting in expanded state control and the stigmatisation and exclusion of those so labelled.[12] Objections might also include how identifying individuals as 'vulnerable' has implications for their personal liberty and autonomy which, as I argue below, are vital ingredients for 'thrivership'.

The desirability and attainability of liberal autonomy and its attendant ideals of individualism, self-reliance and achievement have been criticised. Anderson has suggested that the traditional liberal ideal of autonomy is unachievable, and Fineman has branded the autonomous subject, a 'myth'.[13] The state typically identifies vulnerable individuals and groups that do not meet this standard and uses identity-based interventions to target named vulnerabilities. Framing domestic abuse complainants as 'wounded subjects'[14] at risk of future harm and 'suffering bodies in need of protection',[15] the UK government's action plan to end violence against women and girls confirms that 'protecting women and girls from violence, and supporting victims and survivors, is a key priority for this government'.[16] As such,

[11]'Neoliberalism' is discussed in detail in Chapter 3. Briefly, 'neoliberalism' (in so far as it might ever be reduced to an identifiable value system) describes a political and economic paradigm shift away from post-war Keynesianism towards a privileging of markets; privatisation, economic efficiency, austerity and reduction in welfarism are all characteristic. 'Neoliberalism' has also been linked to the criminalisation of poverty and the expansion of criminal regulation—see, for example, Loic Wacquant, *Punishing the Poor: The Neoliberal Government of Social Insecurity* (Duke University Press 2009).

[12]Kate Brown, '"Vulnerability": Handle with Care' (2011) *Ethics and Social Welfare* 313, 316.

[13]Pamela Anderson, 'Autonomy, Vulnerability and Gender' (2003) *Feminist Theory* 149, 157; Martha Fineman, *The Autonomy Myth* (The New Press 2005).

[14]Wendy Brown, *States of Injury: Power and Freedom in Late Modernity* (Princeton University Press 1995).

[15]Alice Miller, 'Sexuality, Violence Against Women and Human Rights: Women Make Demands and Ladies Get Protection' (2004) *Health and Human Rights* 17, 24.

[16]HM Government's 'Ending Violence Against Women and Girls Action Plan 2016–2020: Progress Update' (HMSO 2019) available at https://assets.publishing.service.gov.uk/government/uploads/system/uploads/attachment_data/file/783190/VAWG_Progress_Update_Web_Accessible.pdf accessed 10 April 2020.

women and girls become 'positioned firmly as 'victims' and hence outside the 'we' who would be acting on their behalf'.[17]

Fineman proposes a compelling alternative way of conceiving the legal subject which, I contend in the context of domestic abuse, equally justifies and sets the expectation that domestic abuse will be proactively and effectively prosecuted. Fineman's conception takes us beyond the usual identity and discrimination paradigms and beyond 'them' and 'us' targeted policy interventions. Instead, she invites the state to recognise and be responsive to *vulnerability* per se by considering vulnerability as *the* defining universal human condition. The 'vulnerable subject' is embodied and Fineman's analysis foregrounds the fleshiness of what it is to be human; requiring nourishment, hydration and sleep whilst being susceptible to harm and illness. This human subject is also exposed to environmental threats such as famine, flood or fire. These biological processes on the one hand and external threats to the body on the other highlight our 'embodied vulnerability'.[18] These inescapable realities render us ontologically vulnerable.

Yet, whilst vulnerability might be universal, it will not manifest in the same ways for everyone. Differences emerge because our embodied vulnerability is also 'embedded' in time and place, and our bodily vulnerability can thus be compounded by the vagaries of institutions and relationships.[19] Butler similarly recognises that 'the body is constitutively social and inter-dependent'[20] whilst Mackenzie, Rogers and Dodds' recognise that vulnerability is 'situational', context specific, and can be exacerbated by social, political, economic and environmental situations.[21] 'Embedded vulnerability' differs across geographies[22] and it may come, go or endure.[23] Vulnerability, however, is always experienced in the body regardless of its

[17]Rosemary Hunter, 'Constructing Vulnerabilities and Managing Risk: State Responses to Forced Marriage' in Sharron FitzGerald (ed), *Regulating the International Movement of Women* (Routledge 2012) 25.

[18]Fineman does not use the term in her writing; she refers to 'embodied humanity' and 'bodily vulnerability' in Martha Fineman, 'The Vulnerable Subject: Anchoring Equality in the Human Condition' (2008) 20 *Yale Journal of Law and Feminism* 1, 9. However, she used this term speaking at 'A Workshop on Vulnerability and Social Justice' (2016) Leeds University.

[19]Martha Fineman speaking at 'A Workshop on Vulnerability and Social Justice' (2016) Leeds University.

[20]Judith Butler, *Frames of War: When Is Life Grievable?* (Verso 2009) 31.

[21]Catriona Mackenzie, Wendy Rogers and Susan Dodds, *Vulnerability: New Essays in Ethics and Feminist Philosophy* (Oxford University Press 2014) Introduction.

[22]Butler (n 20) 31.

[23]Mackenzie et al. (n 21) 7.

cause[24] and, urges Butler, we must attend to it, even abide by it when we begin political thought.[25]

The state's first priority according to Fineman's theory of the vulnerable human condition is to confront its own contribution to enhancing or diminishing individuals' resilience. Our vulnerability will vary according to the quality and quantity of resources we possess or can command to be resilient.[26] It is the inequality of resilience, not vulnerability, that is at the core of Fineman's vulnerability theory.[27] In times of crisis, such as when violence is inflicted by a partner, one's accumulated resources impact one's realistic options. So, whilst vulnerability is ontological, the extent of our agency, autonomy and freedom is dependent on our resilience.[28] Starting with this realisation as foundational requires the state to be responsive to the conditions which exacerbate our vulnerabilities—not in ways which are authoritarian but in ways which 'empower' subjects.[29]

In the past, the state could have been accused of enabling violence against women in the home to persist because criminal justice agents were reluctant to intervene. Contemporary criminal justice responses now appear, prima facie, to meet the state's responsibility to support the resilience of abused women. The 'presumption to arrest',[30] the ostensible 'presumption to prosecute'[31]

---

[24]Ibid., 8.

[25]Butler (n 20) 29.

[26]Martha Fineman, 'The Vulnerable Subject and the Responsive State' (2010) 60 *Emory Law Journal* 251.

[27]Stu Marvel, 'Vulnerability Theory and Sexual Assault on Campus' presented at 'A Workshop on Vulnerability and Social Justice' (2016) Leeds University.

[28]Our resilience depends, according to Fineman, on at least five resource areas or 'assets'; physical (material goods, assets affecting our economic quality of life), human (our capability to make the most of a situation, dependent on education, knowledge, resources and experience), social (our family, social networks and communities), ecological (our natural or physical environment) and existential (our beliefs, religion, culture, art, politics which allow us to see the beauty in life) in Martha Fineman, 'Equality, Autonomy and the Vulnerable Subject in Law and Politics' in Martha Fineman and Anna Grear (eds), *Vulnerability: Reflections on a New Ethical Foundation for Law and Politics* (Ashgate 2013) 22–23.

[29]Martha Fineman, 'The Vulnerable Subject: Anchoring Equality in the Human Condition' (2008) *Yale Journal of Law & Feminism* 19.

[30]Carolyn Hoyle and Andrew Sanders, 'Police Response to Domestic Violence: From Victim Choice to Victim Empowerment' (2000) *British Journal Criminology* 14, 17, identifies that there have been pro-arrest policies operating in many police services since 1993.

[31]In cases where the evidential test is met but the complainant withdraws her support for the prosecution, 'it will be rare for the public interest stage not to be met' in Crown Prosecution Service, 'Domestic Abuse Guidelines for Prosecutors' (2014) available at https://www.cps.gov.uk/legal/d_to_g/domestic_abuse_guidelines_for_prosecutors/ accessed 26 April 2020.

and the tenacious pursuit of convictions[32] now operating in England and Wales are commendable steps taken by the state's criminal justice system to support abused women. These working practices attend to the conditions in which domestic abuse occurs—and therefore contribute to abused women's resilience—in a number of ways.

Firstly, at a structural level, pushing for committed prosecution of domestic abuse offences means that when prosecutors (representatives of the state) so act, they can contribute to constituting their communities as less patriarchal.[33] This is because, as Madden-Dempsey asserts, domestic violence often tends to sustain and perpetuate patriarchy; that is, the perpetrator's behaviour bears the hallmarks of stereotypical gender expectations, for example, the man's designation as the head of the family and the woman's assignment to caring responsibilities; the perpetrator's control of the finances or the woman's access to work opportunities; and the perpetrator's restriction of the victim's social life and other movements (often accompanied by threats or the use of force).[34] If domestic abuse has its aetiology in patriarchy (the 'patriarchal force' theory discussed in Chapter 1[35]), tenacious prosecutions will denounce patriarchy by confronting the patriarchal norms that permit the abusive behaviour.[36]

In the primary research, participant support worker 1 confirmed that domestic abuse often exists where male violence is deemed culturally acceptable: 'Women come from households where domestic abuse was prevalent… where family or friends might not necessarily see it as wrong… [a conviction] is wider society [saying] this isn't ok, it shouldn't have happened, and there are consequences'.[37] Some women, according to Participant 3, choose to engage the criminal law precisely for its educative value because 'it sets an example to their children' that the abuse was unacceptable.[38] If prosecutions

[32]Antonia Porter, 'Prosecuting Domestic Abuse in England and Wales: Crown Prosecution Service Working Practice and New Public Managerialism' (2019) 28(4) *Social and Legal Studies* 493.

[33]Michelle Madden-Dempsey, *Prosecuting Domestic Violence: A Philosophical Analysis* (Oxford University Press 2009) 45–99.

[34]In her response to commentators, Madden-Dempsey asserts that the 'vast majority' of domestic violence tends to sustain and perpetuate patriarchy; Michelle Madden-Dempsey, 'A Response to Commentators' (2010) *International Journal of Law, Policy and Family* 24.

[35]Claire Houston, 'How Feminist Theory became (Criminal) Law: Tracing the Path to Mandatory Criminal Intervention in Domestic Violence Cases' (2014) *Modern Law Review* 217.

[36]Madden-Dempsey, *Prosecuting Domestic Violence* (n 33) 165.

[37]Participant 1, Focus Group (hereafter FG) 1.

[38]Participant 3, FG 1.

are consistently pursued, what follows is a 'norm cascade'[39] in which societal standards shift because the attitudes that oppose and challenge patriarchal performances are demonstrably supported. A presumption to prosecute, and doing so tenaciously, evidences how the state is being responsive to our 'embedded vulnerabilities' by challenging patriarchal ideology that incubates domestic abuse.

Linked to the educational value of 'condemning the behaviour and being very clear that there is no tacit approval of it',[40] others in the focus groups echoed observations from Packer's Crime Control Model; that consistent and ready pursuit of the criminal law has the potential to repress criminal conduct.[41] Deterrence occurs not just because of shifts to acceptable cultural and attitudinal norms, but also from the perspective that punishing those who commit offences discourages the individual and other individuals from committing the same crime. Support workers commented that the deterrent effect of sentencing the perpetrator to custody, whilst being immediate and absolute because of his physical removal, is often only effective for the period of detention.[42] None of the participant support workers expressed the view that a perpetrator's own experience of imprisonment would prevent future abuse (though clearly this is also the intended effect of custodial punishment). However, many of the support workers expressed the view that the probation service rehabilitation programme—Building Better Relationships—could be effective in 'helping [offenders] understand what domestic abuse is and why it's wrong and… can be really powerful [in changing his behaviour]'.[43] Support workers also widely acknowledged that restraining orders *could* have deterrent effects because of the 'repercussions' of breach; here, they referred to the police and courts taking the behaviour more seriously due to there being a breach of a court order.[44] The deterrent aspect of the conviction and restraining order were also thought by support workers to be symbolic because the perpetrator is finally made accountable for his behaviour and has to take responsibility for his future actions.[45]

---

[39]Cass Sunstein, 'Social Norms and Social Roles' (1996) *Columbia Law Review* 903, 909.

[40]Participant 1, FG 1.

[41]Herbert Packer, 'Two Models of the Criminal Process' (1964) *University of Pennsylvania Law Review* 1.

[42]FG 2.

[43]Participant 16, FG 5.

[44]FG 1, 3 and 5.

[45]FG 2.

Lastly, committed and successful domestic abuse prosecutions can help build the resilience of domestic abuse victims by validating their experience. For many women who give evidence at trial and whose abuser is convicted, the experience and outcome can be defining; 'It's recognition for her. It wasn't just in her head. It wasn't how a relationship [should be]... that's really empowering for them'.[46] When a woman gives her account and has it believed, it is especially significant for women whose abuser has repeatedly undermined, belittled and swept aside her version of events as part of the abuse.

Support workers were able to describe the part that criminal prosecutions can play in supporting survivors' resilience and resources by shifting the conditions in which domestic abuse manifests. Here, the state ostensibly meets its responsibilities in Fineman's account of vulnerability. Nonetheless, participants in the focus groups were keen to make the point that these 'gains' for victims all assume a 'best case scenario' assessment of the criminal process. For, even when outlining the gains that can be made from the system, support workers were caveating these benefits with comments that they could be achieved 'in theory'[47] or in an 'ideal world'[48]; 'There is a difference between what they [victims] will gain, to what we hope they will gain'.[49] Expanding on that, Participant 10 explained that the criminal process 'can [also] be completely demoralising, can completely destroy your faith in state institutions and it can make you feel like you haven't been believed and that you are being revictimised... or if you are believed... the sentence can be really frustrating and actually insulting'.[50] The criticisms support workers in the focus groups levelled at the criminal justice system in practice were extensive and echoed the disappointing and even safety-compromising experiences recounted by many of the survivors in the preceding chapter.[51]

---

[46]FG 3.

[47]FGs 1, 3 and 5 all suggested the advantages of engaging the criminal justice system were 'theoretical' or 'in theory'.

[48]FGs 1, 3 and 5 all used this phrase.

[49]FG 3, Participant 10.

[50]FG 3, Participant 10.

[51]The downsides support workers recounted about the criminal process included the following: the length of time a survivor waits for conclusion of the case—referred to by one support worker as 'legal limbo'—which is often compounded by the woman receiving inadequate information (FG 1); that the police, the CPS and the courts are 'outcome driven' and the women sitting at home trying to safeguard themselves and their children are forgotten by those professionals (FG 1); that bail conditions and court orders are breached and ineffective (FG 1, 3 and 5); that criminal justice professionals display attitudes of 'victim blaming' (FG 5) and that acquittals 'completely destroy their self-esteem, confidence and makes them really reluctant to ring the police in emergencies when they really need to' (FG 2).

In sum, a presumption and commitment to prosecute might, prima facie, demonstrate state willingness to challenge the ideological conditions that condone domestic abuse on the one hand and support the personal resilience of domestic violence survivors on the other. To that extent, there is merit in endorsing a presumption and commitment to prosecution; such a criminal justice approach meets Fineman's call for the state to be responsive to vulnerability. Yet there will be occasions when prosecution will not be preferable for individual women; for example where the risk of retaliatory violence is increased, where proceedings are preventing a desired reconciliation between parties or, conversely, where the victim has moved away from the relationship and terminating the case frees her from his abuse continuing to dominate her life. When a woman withdraws her support for a criminal prosecution, conceiving of the ontological vulnerable subject grounds the presumption and commitment to prosecute but it will not further assist prosecutors who work within the existing structural and institutional constraints to know how to exercise their discretion. If prosecutors are to make decisions which best support a reluctant victim's resources and resilience—and notably her immediate and long-term safety—I consider next what lessons can be learnt from support workers who work closely with survivors on a daily basis. I begin by outlining what support workers ultimately want for survivors; what do they consider 'thriving' to mean for abused women?

2. What Does It Mean to Thrive?

A theory of 'thrivership' is emerging, particularly in the fields of psychology[52] and health,[53] as a way of understanding what we might want for those who have experienced domestic abuse. In this section, I want to contribute to that body of work by outlining how domestic abuse support workers conceive of 'thriving' for women, post-abuse. Thrivership is distinct from 'survivorship'. Surviving is a vital stepping stone en route to recovery but, unlike 'thrivers', survivors still feel defined by the abusive experience, struggle with the emotional pain of it, have only just learned to name the abuse and are

[52] Paula Poorman, 'Perceptions of Thriving by Women Who Have Experienced Abuse or Status-Related Oppression' (2002) 26(1) *Psychology of Women Quarterly* 51.

[53] Isobel Heywood, Dana Sammut and Caroline Bradbury-Jones, 'A Qualitative Exploration of "Thrivership" Amongst Women Who Have Experienced Domestic Violence and Abuse: Development of a New Model' (2019) 19 *BMC Women's Health* 106, 109.

only beginning to find and rely on supportive networks.[54] The journey of moving on from 'managing' the experience of domestic abuse is not linear, the process often fluctuates and spirals but, ultimately, 'thrivership' is transformative.[55] 'Thriving' has been characterised as reclaiming a sense of self, enjoying health and well-being, benefiting from a social network and having a positive outlook.[56]

As a basic requirement, the support workers in my focus groups were clear that for the women they worked with, 'thriving' would require women to be 'free of violence',[57] 'safe'[58] and that they and their children would not be living in 'constant fear'.[59] Support workers explained that this would mean that the women they worked with were physically, psychologically and emotionally safe. Support worker 15 suggested that safety is foundational for abused women's thrivership and referred to this as being the first requirement in their 'hierarchy of needs'.[60] Heywood and others have also identified safety as the first building block or 'fundamental requirement' on the road to thriving, post-abuse.[61]

When probed about whether women could 'thrive' whilst remaining within a relationship that had been/continues to be abusive, Participant 3 expressed the concerns of most participants; she was not sure that it was possible: 'There would have to be a huge amount of couples counselling and working together to change the dynamic of abuse'.[62] Participant 1 retorted that she did not think that counselling would work, 'if one person has the power in the relationship. How can you speak?'. For others, being able to thrive within what was/is an abusive relationship meant that women would have to know, in practical terms, how to stay safe, access support and effect choices if they needed to.[63] Participant 13, a refuge worker, explained that

[54]Barbara Whitfield, 'From Victim, to Survivor, to Thriver' (2003) available at https://survivor2thriver.files.wordpress.com/2012/01/www_cbwhit_com_victim_to_survivor_htm2.pdf accessed 23 April 2020.

[55]Ibid.

[56]Heywood et al. (n 53) 106.

[57]FG 5.

[58]All groups.

[59]FG 1 and 2.

[60]Participant 15, FG 5 referred to Maslow's hierarchy of needs: Abraham Maslow, 'A Theory of Human Motivation' (1943) 50(4) *Psychological Review* 370–396 in which 'physiological' needs (hydration, food, sleep and breathing) are foundational. Once that is satisfied, according to Maslow, a person needs 'safety', followed by 'belonging and love', 'esteem' and 'self-actualisation'.

[61]Heywood et al. (n 53) 117.

[62]FG 1, Participant 3.

[63]FG 3.

when a woman leaves the refuge to return to the relationship they fled, she works with the woman to,

> Put in a safety plan… you'll have your things packed ready to go… you need to keep your phone charged… you need to keep money in the bag with your papers… you make sure you know how to get out the window or the safe way out of the house… or you have got a safe room. These little things will save your life if it goes wrong. They go armed with all of that because that's all we can do, not with our blessing, but with our help. "I can protect myself. I know what I am going to do".

The practical steps and advice given by this support worker have been found, across a number of studies, to impact women's sense of safety and ability to stay safe.[64] Nonetheless, in the context of a woman returning to what has been an abusive relationship, support workers tended to describe the potential for the woman to 'survive' rather than to 'thrive'.

Following on from 'safety', the next stage, which marks a significant move towards thriving, is when women are able to *recognise* and name their partner's abuse. When survivors no longer hide or minimise the abuse and begin to tell their story, support workers explained that having others listen and recognise the abuse, can give women resolve to pursue a forward trajectory.[65] All of the charities consulted in the primary research run group programmes with women in which, through collective narrative and storytelling, women begin to understand that what has happened to them is not altogether unique and that abusive behaviours frequently follow similar patterns; fast-moving and intense courtships, the slow creep of undermining and controlling behaviours and the escalation into more frequently occurring and severe abuse.[66] One charity had developed a course called 'Triple R' in which women first learn to 'recognise the abuse'.[67] As well as hearing experiences from the peer group, women learn to recognise the strategies of abusers—the common techniques and underlying attitudes of power

[64]Lisa Goodman, Lauren Bennett Cattaneo, Kristie Thomas, Julie Woulfe, Sui Kwan Chong and Katya Fels Smith, 'Advancing Domestic Violence Program Evaluation: Development and Validation of the Measure of Victim Empowerment Related to Safety (MOVERS)' (2015) 5 *Psychology of Violence* 355; Cris Sullivan, 'Examining the Work of Domestic Violence Programs within a "Social and Emotional Well-being Promotion" Conceptual Framework' (2012) National Resource Center on Domestic Violence 2014.

[65]FG 4. See also, Heywood et al. (n 53); Whitfield (n 54).

[66]Charities in the sample named the following courses that they ran: 'Freedom', 'The Power to Change', 'Liberty', 'Phoenix', 'Family Now', 'ARISE'.

[67]FG 2.

and control—from the course facilitators. Following on from 'Recognition', 'Triple R' teaches women how to 'Recover from the abuse and to build a safe sustainable future (Resilience)'.[68] Ultimately, support workers described that 'what we want for women [from these courses] is for them to recognise that they deserve more'[69] and that 'moving forward, they are able to recognise what a healthy relationship is'.[70]

Some of the group programmes described by participants run in collaboration with the mental health charities, Mind and Insight. Participant 12 explained that particularly for women with children, being able to do something that puts themselves first, to relax and have some head space, is an important part of reclaiming the self.[71] All five domestic abuse charities in the research organised activities for women such as gardening, sewing, yoga, running and beauty therapy which women accessed through the provision of one-stop-shops, support groups or at their refuge. Returning to skills and hobbies or jobs and education can remind women of their self-worth, to know who they are and what they want.[72] All of the charities in the research also made one-to-one talking therapies available to women who needed it because, as Participant 10 explained, so often women are struggling with their mental health but they don't meet the NHS thresholds and/or the waiting list is too long.[73] This provision of counselling services is another opportunity for women to come to terms with what has happened by sharing their story free from judgement but, as well as 'recognition', psychotherapy also helps to build survivors' self-confidence which is vital for their thriving.

All participants were clear that building self-confidence in survivors did not mean that they would direct women in any particular direction. Rather, supporting women to thrive requires that women have the 'ability and the confidence to make choices about their own and their children's lives and to understand that they have the power and the independence to do it'.[74] Having a sense of control and being able to make choices for oneself is a survivor's 'right', according to Participant 14.[75] Participant 15 expressed why support workers were so committed to being 'client-led':

---

[68]FG 2.

[69]FG 1, Participant 2.

[70]FG 3.

[71]FG 3 and 4.

[72]Heywood et al. (n 53) 117.

[73]FG 3.

[74]FG 4, Participant 12.

[75]FG 4.

> We understand that women have had their choices taken away from them through their experiences of abuse and we don't want to replicate that. We will never tell them what they have to do. We will present them with choices… but we won't tell them to follow a particular path, unless we are safeguarding children [or the woman is assessed as being at immediate/ high risk on the DASH] then obviously we have to escalate that [to MARAC or MASH].[76]

Support workers considered their professional role was to explain survivors' options but not to advise what the best course of action was; 'Chances are, they won't have been able to exercise their own independent decision-making for quite some time'[77] and encouraging women to make decisions that positively affect their lives is edifying.

Therapeutic jurisprudent, Bruce Winick, also advocates the benefits of enabling individuals' 'choice' to support beneficial therapeutic outcomes. Drawing from cognitive and social psychology, Winick contrasts the damaging psychological effects of state imposed decision-making with the psychological gains made when individuals are afforded choice.[78] Behavioural psychologists researching 'self-determination theory' have found that 'deep holistic processing is facilitated by a sense of choice, volition and freedom from excessive external pressure toward behaviour or thinking in a certain way'.[79] This means that strong intrinsic gratification can be derived from self-determination. The resulting positive attitude fostered from choice can mobilise psychic or cognitive resources that facilitate goal attainment through motivation.[80]

In the context of an abused woman who requests termination of the prosecution, the benefits of acceding to her request, according to self-determination theory, seem clear. By treating her as a competent adult and allowing her to effect her choice, self-determination theory indicates that her individual effort and self-motivation will increase which will in turn animate her competence to evaluate, self-monitor and react to the course of events following her decision. In short, 'choice' can promote a sense of control which

[76]MARAC (Multi-Agency Risk Assessment Conferences held with professional such as social workers, police, housing, mental health and IDVAs) and MASH (Multi Agency Safeguarding Hub which brings together professionals such as children's social care, education, IDVA, health workers, police, youth offending teams) come together to discuss what is in the best interests of the survivor and her family.

[77]FG 4, Participant 13.

[78]Bruce Winick, 'On Autonomy: Legal and Psychological Perspectives' (1992) *Villanova Law Review* 1705, 1755

[79]Richard Ryan and Edward Deci, 'Self-Determination Theory and the Facilitation of Intrinsic Motivation, Social Development and Well-Being' (2000) *American Psychologist* 68.

[80]Winick (n 78) 1760.

is associated with self-efficacy and persistence. Acting in pursuit of our own goals and being able to take responsibility for our own behaviour assists us to gain mastery of our lives and to develop a cohesive sense of self that is necessary for thriving.[81]

Contrast this with a failure to accede to victim choice. Negative psychological by-products—pressure, resentment and frustration of goal attainment—are all associated with being directed and consequently failing to feel personally committed or responsible for events.[82] Being dictated to can contribute to a sense of helplessness, passivity and depression, which means that not adhering to a woman's request can have negative psychological impacts and diminish her optimal functioning.[83] Victims who are led to believe that their view will be taken into account—because, for example, their victim withdrawal statement contains their reasons for not wanting the prosecution—but find their request is then actively rejected, can also feel a personal sense that their opinion is invalid, discounted or unmeritorious, further stripping them of having a sense of control. Ultimately, those who are decided for often merely 'go through the motions', deriving no real or long-lasting benefit through attitudinal or behavioural change.[84]

But it is not simply the case that *actual* choice is the only way a person can feel in control. Psychologists studying self-determination have uncovered that having a *sense* of choice has the same effect. A *belief* in personal control whether or not rightly held has 'an intriguing self-fulfilling nature' where people go out into the world 'in a vigorous fashion' and begin to control situations that may have previously eluded them.[85] Respecting and responding to victim preference where a decision is going to be taken in opposition to it, rather than disengaging with the woman and making her feel coerced, will be central to affording her a *sense* of self-determination and emotional well-being.[86] For, even when a course of action is the one forwarded by the prosecutor, when a survivor understands the reasoning behind it, they can come to congruently endorse it. When that happens, it

---

[81]Edward Deci and Richard Ryan, *Handbook of Self-Determination Research* (University Rochester Press, 2004).

[82]Ibid., 1756.

[83]Ryan and Deci (n 79).

[84]Ibid., 1768.

[85]Christopher Peterson, 'Personal Control and Well-Being' in Daniel Kahneman, Ed Diener and Norbert Schwartz (eds), *Well-Being: The Foundations of Hedonic Psychology* (Russell Sage 1999) 288.

[86]Bruce Winick, 'Applying the Law Therapeutically in Domestic Violence Cases' (2000) *UMKC Law Review* 60, 64.

is quite possible for her to autonomously enact those behaviours; that is she can perceive that she is the origin or source of the action.[87]

When making decisions that affect survivors' lives, prosecutors have the potential to reduce the pathogenic side effects of by-passing victim preference. By taking a humanistic approach to their interactions with survivors—discussing, explaining, empathising and listening—prosecutors can promote women's participation and sense of agency in the decision being made. By conveying respect, courtesy and understanding prosecutors can therefore contribute to her sense of participation thereby minimising the negative impacts of proceeding with a case against her wishes.[88] Doing this in advance of the trial date—by telephone or in person—would further allow the survivor time to understand and come to 'own' the decision and potentially reduce the need to summons her to court to give evidence.

Support workers were also clear that whilst they felt a woman's autonomy and sense of control over her life is essential to her thriving, this should not be at the expense of thinking about women as independent actors. Women's thrivership includes autonomous self-determination but it does not preclude her relationality (her reliance on others and others' reliance on her). Participant 3 described that, 'Thriving means being able to have your say and being able to have your own opinion, to feel validated, to feel connected to yourself, so that you have the ability to then connect with others'.[89] In Poorman's empirical work, survivors themselves described that the quality of one's connections with others and one's interpersonal environment contributed to their physical, emotional and spiritual 'healing'.[90] Support workers in my study commented that when charities run group courses, the benefits extend beyond the content of the skills being taught; these organised activities encourage women to leave the house, to meet other people and develop positive social interactions. Participant 10 emphasised that this is particularly valuable for women whose partner has been controlling and who may have been prevented from having friendships 'bloom'.[91] Being connected to others is vital not only in terms of the practical advice and guidance that

---

[87]See Richard Ryan and Edward Deci, *Self-Determination Theory: Basic Psychological Needs in Motivation, Development, and Wellness* (The Guilford Press, 2017).

[88]Jo-Anne Wemmers, 'Victims in the Criminal Justice System and Therapeutic Jurisprudence: A Canadian Perspective' in Edna Erez, Michael Kichling and Jo-Anne Wemmers, *Therapeutic Jurisprudence and Victim Participation in Justice* (Carolina Academic Press 2011) 77.

[89]FG 1, Participant 3.

[90]Poorman (n 52) 57.

[91]FG 3, Participant 10.

could be offered from others but also in developing feelings of connectedness, oneness and community that are important for one's mental health and, ultimately, positive outlook.

The observations of these support workers are mirrored in the work of academics who recognise that there is value in autonomy, but only when it is relationally conceived. 'Relational autonomy' is distinct from the 'hyper-individualism'[92] of the traditional liberal subject.[93] Relational autonomy recognises diverse personhood and that subjectivity is 'socially embedded and that agents' identities are formed within the context of social relationships and shaped by a complex of intersecting social determinants such as race, class, gender [and] ethnicity'.[94] We are both constituted from and shaped by networks of relationships; friendships, intimate relationships, family, community, economic markets and political policies.[95] Nedelsky explains that society readily acknowledges this reality for children; children's development and character is impacted by circumstances and particularly by their parents (be they neglectful and abusive or supportive, loving and nurturing). To suggest that on attaining the age of 21 we are no longer affected by our environment and support networks and that we automatically become independently operating, rational and aspirational agents seems disingenuous.[96] For that reason, most contemporary philosophers of autonomy share the view that we are fundamentally and irreducibly relational.[97]

---

[92]John Christman, *The Politics of Persons: Individual Autonomy and Socio-Historical Selves* (Cambridge University Press 2009) 165.

[93]Relational individualism' was first conceived by Nancy Chodorow, 'Toward a Relational Individualism: The Mediation of Self through Psychoanalysis' in Thomas Heller, Morton Sosna and David Wellberry (eds), *Reconstructing Individualism: Autonomy, Individualism and the Self in Western Thought* (Stanford University Press 1986); and successive feminist ethicists have developed the concept of 'relational autonomy', e.g. Catriona Mackenzie and Natalie Stoljar (eds), *Relational Autonomy: Feminist Perspectives on Autonomy, Agency and the Social Self* (Oxford University Press 2000); and Jennifer Nedelsky, *Law's Relations: A Relational Theory of Self, Autonomy and Law* (Oxford University Press 2011).

[94]Catriona Mackenzie and Natalie Stoljar (n 93) 4.

[95]Jennifer Nedelsky, *Law's Relations* (n 93) 19.

[96]Ibid., 20.

[97]Marilyn Friedman, 'Autonomy, Social Disruption and Women' in Catriona Mackenzie and Natalie Stoljar (n 93) 40. Relational autonomists charge liberal autonomy with being inherently masculinist with a notion of selfhood and agency that impedes feminist aims of equality. Liberal autonomy has often been considered 'inhospitable' to women because the pursuit of self-sufficiency is at the expense of human connection, notably at the expense of men's connection with family. The notion is arguably therefore a fundamental cause of women's subjection. Relational autonomy reconfigures the West's typically individualistic model of the self into a relational one, whilst resisting submersion of the individual entirely into the collective.

A relational approach to autonomy identifies that our ability to exercise choice and attain self-realisation will be contingent on our social arrangements and relationships. Our success is not down to simply being a determined individual. Yet, just as Rawlsian liberals, relational autonomists value and promote our individual capacity and desire to exercise self-determination. Meyers suggests that when people are able to express 'what they truly want, who they deeply care about, what they genuinely believe in and so forth, and when they are able to act on those desires, affections and values, they may attest to their own autonomy'.[98] Valuing, rather than rejecting our individual capacities for 'self-realisation' means that the state must aim to secure an 'autonomy-supporting culture'[99] that simultaneously recognises the value of social relationships that promote autonomy and that facilitates our access to resources and opportunities that do the same.[100]

Support workers advocated the benefits prosecutors would reap should they routinely obtain information from a woman's key worker prior terminating a case; 'We are a support service and people are much more inclined to speak to us and… disclose the degree of complexity [of their case]'. Prosecutors would therefore be able to get a better sense of how well supported a woman is; her friendships, her employment or the professional services she receives. Prosecutors could also learn how dependent or not she remains on her partner (both emotionally and financially), the caring responsibilities she may have to children and the progression of any family court proceedings. One support worker reflected on the success of the specialist domestic violence court when it was in operation in her area.[101] She explained that she would attend the court weekly and 'actually being able to have that dialogue with the prosecutors and give them information. It just felt safer. It felt more victim focused to anything we have got now,

[98]Diana Meyers, 'Intersectional Identity and the Authentic Self? Opposites Attract!' in Catriona Mackenzie and Natalie Stoljar (eds), *Relational Autonomy: Feminist Perspectives on Autonomy, Agency and the Social Self* (Oxford University Press 2000) 151.

[99]Catriona Mackenzie, 'The Importance of Relational Autonomy and Capabilities for an Ethics of Vulnerability' in Catriona Mackenzie, Wendy Rogers and Susan Dodds (eds), *Vulnerability: New Essays in Ethics and Feminist Philosophy* (Oxford University Press 2014) 45.

[100]Ibid., 45.

[101]Specialist domestic violence courts (now specialist domestic abuse courts) were rolled out in England and Wales in 2006. They represent a collaborative and co-ordinated community response to domestic abuse with information collated for court from the police, health professionals, social services and independent domestic violence advocates with the intention of increasing the number of successful convictions and improving victim safety and satisfaction. They no longer run in every region of England and Wales.

I think'.[102] The sharing of information with the prosecutor at court, collated from a range of community partners—social workers, police, housing, health and independent domestic violence advisors—enables the prosecutor to understand what part a criminal prosecution might play in a woman's life. At the termination of a criminal case, support workers said that victims should be signposted to victim support, to rape crisis and to their domestic abuse charities so that women could be offered the opportunity to forge new connections, networks and prospects. They explained that this already happens sometimes—'so for victims, a conviction, a sentence [or a discontinuance] isn't the end'[103]—but such signposting should be taking place as a matter of course.

For prosecutors exercising their quasi-judicial role of deciding how to proceed with an unsupportive complainant, prosecutors might therefore endeavour to provide the victim with opportunities to regain control over their lives.[104] Focusing on the individual and their claim to prosper may seem at first to be at odds with Fineman's vulnerability theory outlined above which guides us away from an individualistic appraisal of the self as atomistic and self-determining. Yet, Fineman's theory incorporates both ontological vulnerability and individual resilience factors. Relational autonomy might therefore be incorporated into the theory as an aspect of resilience. Sketching the relationally autonomous subject is a richer, more nuanced account of autonomy which takes into account the part that self-determination plays in affording control, meaningfulness, motivation and healthy psychological and behavioural functioning in our lives.[105] It would be a mistake therefore to pit autonomy as the opponent of vulnerability theory and where autonomy has no place.[106] Rather, the fostering of autonomy in relational terms ought to be considered a key guiding principle of the responsive state prosecutor, where safety considerations allow.

---

[102] FG 2, Participant 4.

[103] FG 1, Participant 1.

[104] Sullivan et al. (n 64) 563.

[105] Beverley Clough, 'Disability and Vulnerability: Challenging the Capacity/Incapacity Binary' (2017) 16(3) *Social Policy and Society* 469, 477; Richard Ryan and Edward Deci, *Self-Determination Theory: Basic Psychological Needs in Motivation, Development, and Wellness* (The Guilford Press, 2017).

[106] Catriona Mackenzie, 'The Importance of Relational Autonomy and Capabilities for an Ethics of Vulnerability' in Catriona Mackenzie, Wendy Rogers and Susan Dodds (eds), *Vulnerability: New Essays in Ethics and Feminist Philosophy* (Oxford University Press 2014) 33.

3. Being 'Trauma-Informed': Lessons for Prosecutors

In each of the focus groups I conducted, support workers consistently showed awareness about the potential for survivors to be traumatised. Whilst governments have repeatedly stressed the centrality of the victim in the criminal justice process, a trauma-informed perspective has not been fully integrated into prosecutorial or, more widely, criminal justice praxis. Understanding trauma and its diverse effects on individuals would provide a useful lens to evaluate how well the criminal justice system is delivering victim-centrality.[107] Learning from the experiences of support workers in the primary research, it is clear that better prosecutorial appreciation of the effects of trauma on abused women would, again, assist prosecutors to draw a richer, more textured and multifaceted legal subject.

Trauma is defined by the emotional and psychological effect that an event can have on a person, rather than the event itself. Trauma is pervasive amongst women who have experienced domestic abuse (and when distressing events are prolonged or recur, trauma can become complex[108]). Psychological reactions to stressors will vary in magnitude and presentation in the person depending on their personal resilience (e.g. their prior exposure to traumatic events, their age, their economic and social resilience).[109] It is common for trauma to manifest as fear, uncertainty, shame and guilt.[110] Others experience depression, anxiety, a reduction in self-esteem or a sense of powerlessness or inequality (particularly in relation to an abusive partner).[111] Memory is often affected as a result of trauma; survivors may struggle to recall a neat linear order of events, may fail to recall specific details or may confuse or muddle their recollections.[112] Post-traumatic stress might

---

[107]Louise Ellison and Vanessa Munro, 'Taking Trauma Seriously: Critical Reflections on the Criminal Justice Process' (2017) 21(3) *The International Journal of Evidence & Proof* 183, 183.

[108]Melanie Randall and Lori Haskell, 'Trauma-Informed Approaches to Law: Why Restorative Justice Must Understand Trauma and Psychological Coping' (2013) 36(2) *Dalhousie Law Journal* 501, 504.

[109]Ellison and Munro (n 107) 185.

[110]Maria Scheffer Lindgren and Barbro Renck, '"It Is Still So Deep-Seated, the Fear": Psychological Stress Reactions as Consequences of Intimate Partner Violence' (2008) 15(3) *Journal of Psychiatric and Mental Health Nursing* 219.

[111]Lesley Laing and Cherie Toivonen, 'Bridging the Gap: Evaluation of the Domestic Violence And Mental Health Pilot Project' (2010) Joan Harrison Support Services For Women 28; Cathy Humphreys and Ravi Thiara, 'Mental Health and Domestic Violence: "I Call It Symptoms of Abuse"' (2003) 33(2) *British Journal of Social Work* 209.

[112]NHS Lanarkshire and EVA Services, 'Trauma and the Brain' (2015) mediaco-op available at https://www.youtube.com/watch?v=4-tcKYx24aA accessed 29 April 2020.

also provoke flashbacks or re-experiencing of the event, physical symptoms like headaches and nausea, negative cognitions or hyper arousal. Participant 15 described how she observed the effects of trauma on survivors:

> We normally see survivors that seem meek and mild and avoidant and nervous, but actually that is only one trauma response. Some people might [present as] really angry or aggressive or whatever. They are not seen in that perfect victim box. And then they get such a different service from all the services. Definitely.[113]

Participant 17 added that,

> Often people who are survivors of trauma have been diagnosed with borderline personality disorder [BPD] because they have these very extreme highs and lows and they come across as very challenging for all agencies to work with. They have very heightened responses and they are just very angry; they can be very dependent on [us, and from time to time] you are literally a hero or the worst person on earth.

Anecdotally, a number of other support workers commented that they frequently supported women diagnosed with borderline personality disorder. Participant 15 commented, 'I think a lot of people are just diagnosed with BPD, but actually, it's just trauma and how trauma has manifested'.[114] Participant 16 agreed, 'because if you are a woman and you are challenging and annoying, the men diagnosing you are like, "you are just BPD" [but] actually like, no, this is just a traumatised woman'.[115] Psychologists have identified a high prevalence of trauma, complex trauma and PTSD in those diagnosed with borderline personality disorder.[116] 'The essential nature' of BPD has been described as a sense of profound emotional pain often arising from trauma victimisation which produces mood instability, suicidality, disassociation and impulsivity.[117] A similar blurring exists between the effects

[113]FG 5, Participant 15.

[114]FG 5, Participant 15.

[115]FG 5, Participant 17.

[116]Patrick Luyten, Chloe Campbell and Peter Fonagy, 'Borderline Personality Disorder, Complex Trauma, and Problems with Self-Identity: A Social-Communicative Approach' (2020) *Journal of Personality* 88.

[117]Genetics (e.g. temperament) and formative developmental experiences (e.g. maltreatment) can also contribute to BPD. Julian Ford and Christine Courtois, 'Complex PTSD, Affect Dysregulation, and Borderline Personality Disorder' (2014) 1(1) *Borderline Personality Disorder and Emotion Dysregulation* 9.

of trauma and diagnoses of bipolar disorder (characterised by extreme mood swings such as mania and depression); bipolar-like mood symptoms might well be mistaken for or considered part and parcel of the neurobiology of trauma.[118]

Being trauma-informed would take criminal prosecutors beyond current criminal justice treatments designed to improve victim experience of the system. Existing victim-centred adaptations include special measures,[119] victim personal statements,[120] ground rules hearings,[121] provisions to restrict the introduction of a complainant's previous sexual history[122] and the CPS 'Speaking To Witnesses At Court' guidance.[123] But whilst introducing these measures has gone some commendable way in centring the victim in the criminal process and demonstrates an awareness of the potential for the criminal justice system to re-victimise participants, Ellison and Munro suggest that incorporating trauma-informed practice into the criminal justice system still 'require[s] a radical transformation of the norms, procedures and emotional cultures that currently frame [its] operation'.[124]

First and foremost, such an approach would mean prosecutors were alert to both the prevalence and the complexity of trauma amongst many who have experienced domestic abuse. Trauma reverberates in lives and survivor's presentations adapt to shield themselves from anticipated pain or harm. Prosecutors need to be psychologically literate, and in a sophisticated way.[125] Flowing from the adage that 'crime hurts, justice should heal' prosecutors

[118]Benjamin Levy, 'The Broad Relationship Between Bipolar Disorder and Disorders of Psychological Trauma–Time-Limited to Life-Long Need for Mood Stabilizers' (2008) 6.2 *Journal of Psychological Trauma* 99, 119. Levy's work indicates that once trauma-related disorder has been addressed in 'BPD' patients (often through psychotherapy) mood stabilisers, which are often prescribed for life for 'BPD', can be terminated.

[119]Special measures afford witnesses the opportunity to give evidence remotely (pre-recorded, live evidence from behind screens or via video-link); see s16-34 of the Youth Justice and Criminal Evidence Act 1999.

[120]Victim personal statements enable victims to provide a statement to the sentencing judge, or later the parole board, detailing the impact of the crime on them.

[121]Ground rules hearings take place before trial with the purpose of planning advocates' questioning; for example, reducing complex language, repetitive questioning and needlessly prolonged periods in the witness box. The case of Lubemba [2014] EWCA Crim 2064 also permits rules being established regarding the general care of the witness; how the parties intend to introduce themselves, the frequency of breaks and the nature of the questions to be asked.

[122]S41–43 Youth Justice and Criminal Evidence Act 1999.

[123]Crown Prosecution Service, 'Speaking to Witnesses at Court' (revised 2018) available at https://www.cps.gov.uk/legal-guidance/speaking-witnesses-court accessed 30 April 2020.

[124]Ellison and Munro (n 107) 185.

[125]Randall and Haskell (n 108) 521.

should do everything within their reach to prevent survivors from being re-traumatised during the criminal process, being aware that their interactions could actually aid recovery and wellness.[126] Explaining court processes and procedures and educating the survivor about the potential for proceedings to retraumatise, whilst being able to signpost survivors to supportive services, would demonstrate being trauma-led. Showing the victim understanding, addressing her safety concerns, being culturally sensitive and helping the victim identify the nature and the impact of the trauma on her everyday life would all assist in the endeavour of supporting her recovery.[127]

Working with existing criminal procedures and the adversarial system, trauma-informed prosecutors might therefore adapt their working practices in a number of more concrete ways. Firstly, when exercising their pre-charge advice role, where witness statements lack precision, prosecutors might be more reticent to reject the case on that basis. Instead, bearing in mind the potential for trauma to impact memory, prosecutors might request further supporting evidence or ask the police to prepare an additional victim statement to address any inconsistencies or gaps in information. When speaking with the victim at court, a prosecutor who is trauma-led would endeavour to find the right words with the right tone. When presenting evidence at trial, prosecutors would endeavour to behave with witnesses and conduct themselves in a way that demonstrates expertise in trauma. If it proved tactically advantageous, prosecutors could call expert evidence to explain to the jury what the impacts of trauma might be for the witness. Participant 17 summed up the approach that many of the support workers considered the CPS should be adopting:

> It should be a trauma-informed or trauma-led approach - from a CPS perspective - it's important to think about how trauma will manifest in terms of [the quality of] their evidence and their witness statement... how they might engage with you... how they will present on the stand... how trauma effects memory. How will I help everyone else [working on this case] understand trauma? [If] the CPS don't have this approach, it's kind of terrifying because, for me, that's quite fundamental.

Trauma-informed practice should also pay attention to the effect on prosecutors of their exposure to graphic descriptions of distressing events and the potential for prosecutors to experience vicarious trauma. Learning about

---

[126] Ibid., 504.

[127] Sullivan et al. (n 64) 563.

abuse may raise painful images and emotions in the prosecutor or they might experience what has been termed 'compassion fatigue' where prosecutors over-identify with the survivor, lose confidence in the world, feel cynical or disillusioned and are increasingly sensitive to the potential for violence or abuse in their own lives.[128] For that reason, trauma-led lawyering must also include educating prosecutors in the ways that they can employ modes of self-care to counterbalance the effect of the traumatic experiences of others. Such techniques might include being educated about vicarious trauma, balancing and limiting traumatic caseloads, creating safe spaces for practitioners to talk about the effects of working with traumatic stories, journaling and encouraging institutional transparency about how to take care on oneself through, for example, regular exercise or mental health counselling.[129]

Chapter 5 introduced therapeutic jurisprudence—a school of jurisprudence that seeks to influence legal rules, procedures and processes to produce 'healing' potential for participants, and also urges law's *legal actors* to recognise their capacity to work in ways that can produce therapeutic or anti-therapeutic outcomes for those who come into contact with it.[130] The approach brings a humanising emphasis to legal practice.[131] The ambitions of therapeutic jurisprudence as a 'therapeutic agent',[132] therefore, naturally extend to working with a trauma-informed perspective with the aim of achieving 'thrivership' for victims.

Support worker 13 said that she did not expect lawyers to demonstrate empathetic emotional intelligence with survivors; 'The barrister will probably have only picked up that case that morning or a couple of days beforehand. They don't have the time or the emotional capacity to support the victim from that perspective…We [support workers] take the time to get to know them and to understand their case and to help them through it… They do need that'.[133] Distinct from sympathy (reserved for the identity-based anti-discrimination approach where 'they' not 'us' are targeted), empathy is an approach that draws out commonalities between individuals, rather than defining domestic abuse victims by their experience. This need

---

[128]Sarah Katz and Deeya Haldar, 'The Pedagogy of Trauma-Informed Lawyering' (2015) 22 *Clinical Law Review* 359, 359.

[129]Ibid., 390–393.

[130]Bruce Winick, 'The Jurisprudence of Therapeutic Jurisprudence' (1997) *Psychology, Public Policy and Law* 184, 185.

[131]Christopher Slobogin, 'Therapeutic Jurisprudence: 5 Dilemmas to Ponder' (1995) *Psychology, Public Policy and Law* 193.

[132]David Wexler, 'Applying the Law Therapeutically' (1996) *Applied and Preventive Psychology* 179, 179.

[133]FG 4.

not, I suggest, be beyond the scope of a lawyer's role. Rather than thinking of empathy as surplus to requirements, prosecutors ought to consider empathy as integral to their role, recognising our shared universal vulnerability, acknowledging shared experience, expectations and needs. Extolling empathy gives prosecutors permission to engage with the question of: what would *I* want and need the state to do for me? By advancing an empathetic approach, the prosecutor could not help but engage with the question of how their interpersonal interactions, the decisions they make and how they are communicated could best be implemented to support and empower the woman concerned. From this locus, the prosecutor signals good intentions and not the coerciveness associated with victim dissatisfaction and psychological stress.[134] Using the therapeutic technique of empathy improves the likelihood of the victim turning to the police and criminal justice in times of future need.[135]

Conclusion

I began this chapter by accepting the claim that the state has a duty to respond to our ontological vulnerability by ensuring that its institutions support our capacity to be resilient.[136] The current presumptions to arrest and to prosecute domestic abuse offenders, prima facie, meet the state's responsibility because they begin to challenge the conditions in which domestic abuse occurs. Yet, when a woman resists state intervention, the corresponding prosecutorial presumption that her particular vulnerability will require the matter to be pursued is unsophisticated. The application of the standard assumptions about the liberal legal subject in this context is misleading; we are not either free-standing, independently acting agents on the one hand, or on the other, dependent, incapable and vulnerable. Looking beyond vulnerability theory's well-founded demand for a 'responsive state'

[134]In fact, the CPS has produced policies designed to reduce the effects of 'secondary victimisation'. Measures include timely notification to victims of hearing outcomes, applying for special measures where victims are in fear, applying for appropriate 'non-contact' bail conditions and treating victims with 'respect and sensitivity'. See Crown Prosecution Service, 'Guidance on the Care and Treatment of Victims and Witnesses', available at http://www.cps.gov.uk/legal/v_to_z/care_and_treatment_of_victims_and_witnesses/#pledge accessed 10 May 2020.

[135]Janine Zweig and Martha Burt, 'Effects of Interactions Among Community Agencies on Legal Systems Responses to Domestic Violence and Sexual Assault in STOP-Funded Communities' (2003) 14(2) *Criminal Justice Policy Review* 249.

[136]Martha Fineman, 'The Vulnerable Subject: Anchoring Equality in the Human Condition' (2008) 20 *Yale Journal of Law and Feminism* 1.

by way of guidance for prosecutors facing the decision how to proceed in the face of victim withdrawal, I proposed that prosecutors should always be mindful of the survivor's 'thrivership'. Whilst this is indisputably an end goal for the woman, the prosecutor's end goal—as I outlined in Chapters 3 and 4—appears to be to meet CPS key performance indicators and targets. Yet, the two end goals need not be opposing; for, when prosecutors develop modes of praxis that put the survivor's healing and 'thrivership' at the fore, increased numbers of survivors will 'buy in' to the criminal process as being beneficial for them and the system's efficiency will improve.[137]

A holistic account of the 'thriver-subject' would replace the incomplete construction of reluctant survivors being 'vulnerable' and 'at risk' and therefore requiring their case to be tenaciously prosecuted. The concept of the thriver-subject recognises that each survivor has their own unique story and subjective lived experience, understanding how the criminal justice system could assist them in ascribing value to their lives and to thrive would inform prosecutorial action.[138] Thrivers are safe, have recognised and come to terms with the abuse that the perpetrator inflicted, have reclaimed their sense of self and a control over their lives, have supportive social networks and have improved confidence, mental health and well-being.

Support workers in the primary research explained that when they work with survivors, they are 'trauma-led'—meaning that the traumatising effects of the perpetrator's abuse are at the forefront when they engage with a client. They adjust their practice approach according to the individual client's trauma response. Support workers described being sensitive to the multiple presentations of trauma of the women in their care. Learning from this, prosecutors conceiving a thriver-subject, might also aim to recognise the effects of trauma on women's behaviours and actions and make adjustments to their practice accordingly; in particular, they would endeavour to reduce the secondary victimisation that can be experienced by victims as a result of passing through the criminal courts, by deploying empathetic and respectful interactions and decision-making. Being trauma-informed reminds us that inflexible interventions can be detrimental and paternalistic and can have

[137]See, for example, Avail Consulting, 'No Witness, No Justice (NWNJ) Pilot Evaluation Final Report: Crown Prosecution Service and ACPO' (2004) available at www.cps.gov.uk/publications/docs/NWNJ_pilot_evaluation_report_291004.pdf accessed 10 April 2018.

[138]An approach which accords with Michael Dunn, Isabel Clare and Anthony Holland, 'To Empower or to Protect? Constructing the "Vulnerable Adult" in English Law and Public Policy' (2008) *Legal Studies* 234–253.

the paradoxical effect of increasing vulnerability whilst intending to diminish it.[139]

The atomistic autonomous liberal subject might be a fallacy, but nevertheless I argued that autonomy has significant value for human growth and developing a cohesive sense of self. Autonomy is a capacity which can be fostered over a life-course; it does not emerge in a social vacuum and there is a debt owed to others. Autonomous decision-making and the ability to be self-determining can have important therapeutic consequences for survivors and are key building blocks to thrivership.[140] Support workers in the study advocated the gains that can be made for abused women from being 'client-led'. The desire to be able to make autonomous choices for ourselves is, at some level, a universal and inescapable human impulse and I drew out its benefits for survivors.[141] A woman's relational context and the therapeutic advantages of making choices are aspects that prosecutors might bring to bear when deciding whether or not to pursue a criminal prosecution absent the victim's support. Ultimately, I suggest that considered prosecutorial decision-making when a woman withdraws her support for a prosecution—even if it goes against the victim's stated wishes—when combined with a sensitive, trauma-informed communication of the reasons why the action has been taken, can enhance women's sense of agency which can have positive impacts on the physical, mental and emotional health of survivors that is vital for thriving.

References

Anderson P, 'Autonomy, Vulnerability and Gender' (2003) *Feminist Theory* 149.

Avail Consulting, 'No Witness, No Justice (NWNJ) Pilot Evaluation Final Report: Crown Prosecution Service and ACPO' (2004) available at www.cps.gov.uk/publications/docs/NWNJ_pilot_evaluation_report_291004.pdf accessed 10 April 2018.

Brown K, '"Vulnerability": Handle with Care' (2011) *Ethics and Social Welfare* 313.

Brown W, *States of Injury: Power and Freedom in Late Modernity* (Princeton University Press 1995).

[139]Or 'pathogenic vulnerability' as outlined in Catherine Mackenzie, Wendy Rogers and Susan Dodds, *Vulnerability: New Essays in Ethics and Feminist Philosophy* (Oxford University Press 2014) Introduction.

[140]Bruce Winick, 'On Autonomy: Legal and Psychological Perspectives' (1992) *Villanova Law Review* 1705.

[141]Morgan Cloud, 'More Than Utopia' in Martha Fineman and Anna Grear (eds), *Vulnerability: Reflections on a New Ethical Foundation for Law and Politics* (Ashgate 2013) 93.

Butler J, *Frames of War: When Is Life Grievable?* (Verso 2009).
Christman J, *The Politics of Persons: Individual Autonomy and Socio-Historical Selves* (Cambridge University Press 2009).
Clough B, 'Disability and Vulnerability: Challenging the Capacity/Incapacity Binary' (2017) 16(3) *Social Policy and Society* 469.
Crown Prosecution Service, 'Domestic Abuse Guidelines for Prosecutors' (2014) available at https://www.cps.gov.uk/legal-guidance/domestic-abuse-guidelines-prosecutors accessed 9 April 2020.
Deci E and Ryan R, *Handbook of Self-Determination Research* (University Rochester Press, 2004).
Dunn M, Clare I and Holland A, 'To Empower or to Protect? Constructing the "Vulnerable Adult" in English Law and Public Policy' (2008) *Legal Studies* 234.
Ellison L and Munro V, 'Taking Trauma Seriously: Critical Reflections on the Criminal Justice Process' (2017) 21(3) *The International Journal of Evidence & Proof* 183.
Erez E, Kichling M and Wemmers J, *Therapeutic Jurisprudence and Victim Participation in Justice* (Carolina Academic Press 2011).
Fineman M, *The Autonomy Myth* (The New Press 2005).
———, 'The Vulnerable Subject: Anchoring Equality in the Human Condition' (2008) 20 *Yale Journal of Law and Feminism* 1.
———, 'The Vulnerable Subject and the Responsive State' (2010) 60 *Emory Law Journal* 251.
Fineman M and Grear A, *Vulnerability: Reflections on a New Ethical Foundation for Law and Politics* (Ashgate 2013).
FitzGerald S, *Regulating the International Movement of Women* (Routledge 2012).
Furedi F, 'Fear and Security: A Vulnerability Led Policy Response' (2008) *Social Policy and Administration* 645.
Goodman L, Cattaneo L, Thomas K, Woulfe J, Chong S and Fels Smith K, 'Advancing Domestic Violence Program Evaluation: Development and Validation of the Measure of Victim Empowerment Related to Safety (MOVERS)' (2015) 5 *Psychology of Violence* 355.
Heller T, Sosna M and Wellberry D, *Reconstructing Individualism: Autonomy, Individualism and the Self in Western Thought* (Stanford University Press 1986).
Heywood I, Sammut D and Bradbury-Jones C, 'A Qualitative Exploration of "Thrivership" Among Women who have experienced Domestic Violence and Abuse: Development of a New Model' (2019) *19 BMC Women's Health* 106.
HM Government's 'Ending Violence Against Women and Girls Action Plan 2016–2020: Progress Update' (HMSO 2019) available at https://assets.publishing.service.gov.uk/government/uploads/system/uploads/attachment_data/file/783190/VAWG_Progress_Update_Web_Accessible.pdf accessed 10 April 2020.
Houston C, 'How Feminist Theory Became (Criminal) Law: Tracing the Path to Mandatory Criminal Intervention in Domestic Violence Cases' (2014) *Modern Law Review* 217.

Hoyle C and Sanders A, 'Police Response to Domestic Violence: From Victim Choice to Victim Empowerment' (2000) *British Journal Criminology* 14.

Humphreys C and Thiara R, 'Mental Health and Domestic Violence: "I Call It Symptoms of Abuse"' (2003) 33.2 *British Journal of Social Work* 209.

Kahneman D, Diener E and Schwartz N, *Well-Being: The Foundations of Hedonic Psychology* (Russell Sage 1999).

Katz S and Haldar D, 'The Pedagogy of Trauma-Informed Lawyering' (2015) 22 *Clinical Law Review* 359.

Laing L and Toivonen C, 'Bridging the Gap: Evaluation of the Domestic Violence and Mental Health Pilot Project' (2010) Joan Harrison Support Services For Women 28.

Levy B, 'The Broad Relationship Between Bipolar Disorder and Disorders of Psychological Trauma–Time-Limited to Life-Long Need for Mood Stabilizers' (2008) 6(2) *Journal of Psychological Trauma* 99.

Luyten P, Campbell C and Fonagy P, 'Borderline Personality Disorder, Complex Trauma, and Problems with Self-Identity: A Social-Communicative Approach' (2020) *Journal of Personality* 88.

Mackenzie C, Rogers W and Dodds S, *Vulnerability: New Essays in Ethics and Feminist Philosophy* (Oxford University Press 2014).

Mackenzie C and Stoljar N, *Relational Autonomy: Feminist Perspectives on Autonomy, Agency and the Social Self* (Oxford University Press 2000).

Madden-Dempsey M, 'A Response to Commentators' (2010) *International Journal of Law, Policy and Family* 24.

———, *Prosecuting Domestic Violence: A Philosophical Analysis* (Oxford University Press 2009).

Maslow A, 'A Theory of Human Motivation' (1943) 50(4) *Psychological Review* 370.

Miller A, 'Sexuality, Violence Against Women and Human Rights: Women Make Demands and Ladies Get Protection' (2004) *Health and Human Rights* 17.

Munro V and Scoular J, 'Abusing Vulnerability? Contemporary Law and Policy Responses to Sex Work in the UK' (2012) *Feminist Legal Studies* 189.

Nedelsky J, *Law's Relations: A Relational Theory of Self, Autonomy and Law* (Oxford University Press 2011).

Packer H, 'Two Models of the Criminal Process' (1964) *University of Pennsylvania Law Review* 1.

Poorman P, 'Perceptions of Thriving by Women Who Have Experienced Abuse or Status-Related Oppression' (2002) 26(1) *Psychology of Women Quarterly* 51.

Porter A, 'Prosecuting Domestic Abuse in England and Wales: Crown Prosecution Service Working Practice and New Public Managerialism' (2019) 28(4) *Social and Legal Studies* 493.

Randall M and Haskell L, 'Trauma-Informed Approaches to Law: Why Restorative Justice Must Understand Trauma and Psychological Coping' (2013) 36(2) *Dalhousie Law Journal* 501.

Richard Ryan and Edward Deci, 'Self-Determination Theory and the Facilitation of Intrinsic Motivation, Social Development and Well-Being' (2000) *American Psychologist* 68.

———, *Self-Determination Theory: Basic Psychological Needs in Motivation, Development, and Wellness* (The Guilford Press, 2017).

Scheffer Lindgren M and Renck B, '"It Is Still So Deep-Seated, the Fear": Psychological Stress Reactions as Consequences of Intimate Partner Violence' (2008) 15(3) *Journal of Psychiatric and Mental Health Nursing* 219.

Slobogin C, 'Therapeutic Jurisprudence: 5 Dilemmas to Ponder' (1995) *Psychology, Public Policy and Law* 193.

Sullivan C, 'Examining the Work of Domestic Violence Programs Within a "Social and Emotional Well-being Promotion" Conceptual Framework' (2012) National Resource Center on Domestic Violence 2014.

Sunstein C, 'Social Norms and Social Roles' (1996) *Columbia Law Review* 903.

Wacquant L, *Punishing the Poor: The Neoliberal Government of Social Insecurity* (Duke University Press 2009).

Wexler D, 'Applying the Law Therapeutically' (1996) *Applied and Preventive Psychology* 179.

———, 'Therapeutic Jurisprudence: An Overview' (2000) 17 *TM Cooley Law Review* 125.

Winick B, 'Applying the Law Therapeutically in Domestic Violence Cases' (2000) *UMKC Law Review* 60.

———, 'On Autonomy: Legal and Psychological Perspectives' (1992) *Villanova Law Review* 1705.

———, 'The Jurisprudence of Therapeutic Jurisprudence' (1997) *Psychology, Public Policy and Law* 184.

Zweig J and Burt M, 'Effects of Interactions Among Community Agencies on Legal Systems Responses to Domestic Violence and Sexual Assault in STOP-Funded Communities (2003) 14(2) *Criminal Justice Policy Review* 249.

7

Conclusion: Centring Survivors

The motivation to write this book was prompted by questions that arose for me regarding the CPS approach to prosecuting intimate partner abuse. When I joined the CPS in 2007, it was clear that the service was making every effort to address an apparent resistance on the part of the prosecution and police services to intervene in 'private' intimate partner abuse. The CPS was plainly trying to implement a significant and meaningful shift in approach and I had felt positive about being part of a concerted strategy to reverse past deficiencies and, in particular, the practice of automatically discontinuing cases at the stated request of the victim. I felt optimistic because, when I had been a defence solicitor, I like many others, had found myself advising defendants simply to enter not guilty pleas and then waiting to see whether the victim 'turned up' for trial. The prosecution would inevitably drop the case if the victim failed to attend court to give evidence. Yet, as the new policy played out in daily prosecutorial working practices—as outlined in Chapter 4—I began to regularly question my initial belief that routinely prosecuting cases in the face of an unsupportive victim would consistently contribute to progressive and affirmative action for them. Faced with a concerted management commitment to demonstrate the new priority, I increasingly found myself concerned that tenacious prosecutions should not always be considered preferable. Where my own assessment of the evidential and public interest tests led me to conclude that a case should be discontinued, my view was invariably being overridden by my line managers who would, more often than not, direct me to secure a court summons for the reluctant victim. I was concerned about these occasions of divergence between myself

A. Porter, *Prosecuting Domestic Abuse in Neoliberal Times*, Palgrave Socio-Legal Studies,
https://doi.org/10.1007/978-3-030-61369-3_7

and my managers and wanted to understand what drivers were steering the service's ambitions. I also wanted to know how such prosecutorial decision-making was affecting the women whose lives it touched and if the CPS priority to convict the perpetrator was always meeting the victim's needs and interests.

CPS domestic abuse policy expresses the service's commitment to prosecuting intimate partner abuse, and it sits within the wider government strategy to end violence against women and girls.[1] The CPS domestic abuse guidelines openly seek 'justice' for victims, and prosecutions are invariably to be considered in the 'public interest'.[2] When a domestic abuse survivor is no longer supportive of the prosecution, the guidelines encourage prosecutors to assess whether special measures might support her in giving evidence. Failing that, the guidelines indicate preferring victimless prosecutions where possible, or giving full consideration to 'the impact on the complainant's safety and wellbeing'[3] before deciding to issue a summons as a last resort. Discontinuance should only take place when the complainant's account is the '**only** evidence available, and a summons would not be appropriate'.[4] The presumption to prosecute and bring the perpetrator to account conveyed in these guidelines reflects the UK government's appetite for dealing with intimate partner abuse through the criminal law.

In Chapter 2, I examined how a strong preference for criminal justice in cases of intimate partner abuse arguably addresses the feminist account of the causes of domestic abuse as 'patriarchal force'.[5] This account understands that male privilege in the public sphere is reflected in private family dynamics where male supremacy manifests in male violence. Some feminists have expressed confidence in the value of processing matters of domestic abuse through the criminal courts as a means ending male violence in society. Their assertion depends on a particular assessment of the role and value of criminal prosecutions; specifically, that prosecutorial action has consequential and intrinsic (or expressive/symbolic) value in condemning social norms

[1]Crown Prosecution Service, 'Domestic Abuse Guidelines for Prosecutors' available at https://www.cps.gov.uk/legal-guidance/domestic-abuse-guidelines-prosecutors accessed 6 June 2020; HM Government, 'Strategy to End Violence Against Women and Girls 2016–2020' available at https://assets.publishing.service.gov.uk/government/uploads/system/uploads/attachment_data/file/522166/VAWG_Strategy_FINAL_PUBLICATION_MASTER_vRB.PDF accessed 6 June 2020.

[2]Crown Prosecution Service, 'Domestic Abuse Guidelines' (n 1).

[3]Ibid.

[4]Original emphasis in ibid.

[5]Claire Houston, 'How Feminist Theory Became (Criminal) Law: Tracing the Path to Mandatory Criminal Intervention in Domestic Violence Cases' (2014) *Michigan Journal of Gender and Law* 217.

that permit intimate partner abuse.[6] The CPS has affirmed this evaluation and, in their annual violence against women report, cites the United Nations special rapporteur on violence against women who asserts that '[f]or a state action to realize… intrinsic value [of prosecutions], it must not be a one-off instance of condemnation, but in fact it must systematically engage with domestic violence and condemn it'.[7] From this perspective, the criminal law and—what I have called—'tenacious prosecutions' offer the potential to challenge patriarchal norms, ideologies and structures by consistently denouncing the societal attitudes and behaviours that support them.

Tenaciously pursuing prosecutions also responds to second-wave feminist analysis that domestic abuse ought not to be considered a private matter left to be resolved between intimate partners. Rather, considered as a public crime, domestic abuse takes on the status of being a crime against us all, *requiring* that the behaviour be condemned through the criminal courts accordingly. Current CPS working practices therefore address the past charge that the criminal justice system suffered 'institutional indifference'[8] with regard to matters of intimate partner abuse in the private sphere. The current commitment to pursue convictions is then, ostensibly, a victory for the feminist and community groups that sought strong state condemnation of the behaviour as a crime and for those who took part in CPS policy consultation processes to effect that end.

At the same time, as Chapter 3 explored, the CPS presumption and commitment to achieving domestic abuse convictions accords with the neoliberal understanding of society as individualistic. In this conception, citizens are responsible for their successes, failures and criminal transgressions because they have been afforded the free market conditions to make successes of themselves. Criminalising gender-based violence champions victims' freedom (from abuse) whilst holding perpetrators individually responsible. As neoliberal governments roll back welfare provision and divest themselves of the traditional redistributive efforts of the state and of the role of provider of social and economic certainty, governments of the right have found public perceptions about state legitimacy destabilised.[9] Neoliberal

[6]Michelle Madden-Dempsey, *Prosecuting Domestic Violence: A Philosophical Analysis* (Oxford University Press 2009) 60.

[7]Yakin Erturk, '15 Years of the United Nations Special Rapporteur on Violence Against Women (1994–2009)—A Critical Review' (United Nations 2009) 27 cited in Crown Prosecution Service, 'Violence Against Women and Girls' Report' (10th edn, 2015–2016).

[8]Rebecca and Russell Dobash, 'Love, Honour and Obey: Institutional Ideologies and the Struggle for Battered Women' (1977) *Contemporary Crisis* 403, 410.

[9]Emma Bell, *Criminal Justice and Neoliberalism* (Palgrave Macmillan 2011) 206–207.

efforts to retrieve that legitimacy and to repair the 'broken society'[10] (that has resulted from years of centring the 'individual' and pushing competition between them) have relied on strengthening a punitive culture. In the context of the recent decades of neoliberal governance, bringing the perpetrators of intimate partner abuse to justice therefore sits within an overall expansion and 'hardening of the criminal law'[11] which aims to steady the societal ship. Violence against women campaigners has thus seen their ambition of ending domestic abuse, which may otherwise have targeted sexual inequality and other structural causes of abuse, addressed primarily through the preferred neoliberal tool, increased criminal justice.

The neoliberal approach to intimate partner abuse illustrates a neoliberal paradox; in its desire to reduce the state's presence in people's lives in preference for market ordering, the state simultaneously manoeuvres to create the conditions of freedom through an enhanced state presence in the criminal justice field. Justified by the explanation that the criminal law can prevent crime and reduce the risk of harm to victims, intimate partner abusers are one category of offender who become 'managed' through the criminal process. In the past, probation officers, for example, had roles that were more akin to the role of social worker—advising, assisting and befriending offenders to address the root causes of their offending and to support their rehabilitation—but the role has been compromised by current expectations that the probation service will reduce crime rates simply by offering weekly monitoring and punishment in the community.[12] Preventing crime through the threat of increased criminalisation has been the preferred approach of successive neoliberal governments over other genuine preventative measures such as investment in school education programmes, working with perpetrators to enhance life skills or funding professionals to support victims and perpetrators with mental illnesses and substance use disorders. Social democratic governments associated with solidaristic notions of reciprocity between individuals, communities and the state might also have financed greater investment in women's shelters, refuges and support services. If neoliberalism has been the antidote to state welfarism, the violence against women's movement

[10]The 'broken society' was a term used by incoming Conservative Prime Minister David Cameron to describe the perceived high levels of crime, breakdown of families, poor housing and education and benefit culture; David Cameron, 'Fixing Our Broken Society' (2008) speech delivered in Gallowgate, Glasgow.

[11]Bell, *Criminal Justice and Neoliberalism* (n 9) 1.

[12]Ibid., 88.

has so often experienced its discourses and demands absorbed into neoliberal political and penal hegemony.[13]

Yet, in recent times, it has been argued that neoliberal hegemony is coming to an end and, in its stead, populism is in ascendance.[14] Fraser observes that increased demands for protection, social security, non-precarious and well-paid employment, all of which have been severely compromised by neoliberalism, have given rise to populism or, as Pratt calls it, the 'revolt against uncertainty'.[15] In the wake of the retreat from welfarism, the break-up of manufacturing communities (and their inability to reinvent themselves in line with neoliberalism's swelling service, tourism and finance industries) and for all those individuals feeling anchorless after this restructuring, punishment is being asked to play a role never before envisaged. Whilst neoliberalism has already harnessed the criminal law and the punishment of offenders to provide certainty, solidarity and social control, populism further drives the expectation that moral and social order will be reinstated through any law that prioritises public protection from further risks to uncertainty.[16] Criminal law is playing even more of an expansive role for populism than as it did for neoliberalism to claw back legitimacy and calm anxieties about social and economic insecurities. An acceleration in the trend towards populist punitive common-sense political discourse has been further spurred on by the rise of social media (notably Facebook from 2004 and Twitter from 2008) which has been at the expense of relying on expert assessment. Pratt argues that this development has taken news making and reporting outside of the paradigm of reason, rationality and truth in the democratic world, further eroding moral standards and fuelling reactionary politics. The conditions driving populism are likely to produce further demands on criminal justice and punishment as a means of providing public reassurance and security, to re-assert government legitimacy and to retain power. It is anticipated

---

[13]See, for example, Kristin Bumiller, *In an Abusive State: How Neoliberalism Appropriated the Feminist Movement Against Sexual Violence* (Duke University Press 2008).

[14]Jonathan Pratt, 'When Risk and Populism Collide' in Jonathan Pratt and Jordan Anderson (eds), *Criminal Justice, Risk and the Revolt Against Uncertainty* (Palgrave Macmillan 2020) 275.

[15]Ravi Kumar, 'Populism, Neoliberalism and the Contemporary World: Reflections for an Alternative Politics with Nancy Fraser' (2019) 5(2) *Society and Culture in South Asia* 340, 340; Pratt (n 14) 276.

[16]At the time of writing, this trend towards using criminal law to set and evolve norms and to deter offending through strong punishment is in evidence in the recently proposed 'Desecration of War Memorials Bill' which enjoys cross-party parliamentary support. Conservative MP, Jonathan Gullis, proposed the Bill in rapid response to the recent Black Lives Matter protests. The Bill received widespread media coverage and support. The Bill proposes increased sentences to those who cause summary criminal damage to war memorials (where the value of damage is less than £5000) from 3 months to ten years imprisonment and from a fine of £2500 to an unlimited fine.

that populist governments are therefore likely to extend their reliance on criminalisation as a means of tackling violence against women.

Chapter 4 illustrated that 'government' in the Foucauldian sense rightly recognises that governmentality is not simply a top-down apparatus but a rich complex of micro-powers or procedures of government. The carceral state, too, relies on professionals to apply and interpret central policy.[17] Chapter 4 described how decision-making and working practices of nine such professionals—Crown Prosecutors—are heavily influenced by one particular technique of neoliberalism, managerialism.[18] In the area of prosecuting intimate partner abuse, this has manifested in the operational praxis of 'tenacious prosecutions' where convictions are sought and pursued wherever possible, irrespective of the stated wishes of the complainant. Managerialism—particularly revered at times of austerity—and its effects include producing routinised decision-making within the confines of acceptable institutional objectives. The primary research in Chapter 4 lends weight to Garland's assertion that the effect of 'performance indicators and management measures [has been the narrowing of] professional discretion [within] tightly regulated working practice'.[19] Targeting resources into key crime 'hotspots' such as domestic abuse is also typical of managerialism's strategy to achieve long-term cost savings.[20] This confidence in criminal justice and penality to control crime seems to be shared then by both neoliberalism and, its subsidiary, managerialism.[21]

Confronting Domestic Abuse Through the Criminal Justice System: Gains and Losses

Feminists have long been divided over the extent to which the state should be called upon to improve the conditions of women's lives. The example of the state treatment of domestic abuse illustrates why. On the one hand, the

[17]Michel Foucault, in Michel Senellart (ed), *The Birth of Biopolitics: Lectures at the College de France 1978–79* (Picador 2004) 131.

[18]There are of course limits to Chapter 4's empirical findings in terms of the generalisability of the relatively small prosecutor sample (as discussed more fully in Chapter 1). The value of the research is to (a) stimulate CPS institutional reflection and (b) contribute to literature that explores neoliberal and managerial influences on professional decision-making.

[19]David Garland, *The Culture of Control* (Oxford University Press 2011) 18.

[20]Ibid., 19.

[21]Reference to managerialism here mirrors Packer's Crime Control Model in Herbert Packer, 'Two Models of Criminal Process' (1964) *University of Pennsylvania Law Review* 1.

state (criminal justice) strategy to end violence against women and to take domestic abuse seriously denounces male violence against women and holds perpetrators to account. On the other, feminists like Fraser have argued that, when neoliberal and populist governments co-opt the feminist movement in this way, they deflect feminists from seeking genuine economic and systemic redistributive resolutions.[22] At the same time, when criminal solutions are preferred, the *individual* circumstances of women are given insufficient attention despite, in our example, a CPS policy that deliberately leaves scope for tailored decision-making. The challenge for contemporary feminists is to remain attentive to how feminism's emancipatory and liberatory charisma becomes a legitimation tool or alibi for neoliberal penality, whilst all the while being attentive to the ways that the criminal law impacts the lives of the *individual* women it purports to serve (notably their safety and agency).[23]

When gendered violence is treated primarily as crime, it is swept up in and gender-neutralised by the routine work of criminal justice.[24] The ready recognition by the CPS that domestic abuse is a gendered crime—recognising the prevalence of male perpetrators and female victims—has been swiftly followed by public statements made by the CPS acknowledging that men can also be victims.[25] Yet, in the CPS' commendable endeavour to give voice to male victims, prosecutors can be left with the false impression that the offence is gender-neutral.[26] The prosecutors in my sample certainly presented as being at best indifferent to, or at worst oblivious to tackling intimate partner abuse as a gendered crime (as opposed to as a 'serious' crime). Just as Chapter 4 evidenced, Wykes and Welsh assert that the criminal law speaks in terms of ungendered victims and thus, 'even as the state takes on gendered violence, it has done so in a manner that has failed to see the violence as gendered'.[27] Prosecutors in the sample failed to acknowledge gender inequality as either the cause of domestic abuse or as a reason why particular attention needs to be paid when routinised decision-making that

---

[22]Nancy Fraser, 'Feminism, Capitalism, and the Cunning of History' (2012) *HAL* 2–4.

[23]See Christine Schickert, 'Feminism in Neoliberal Times: An Interview with Nancy Fraser' (2018) 8(3) *Global Dialogue: Magazine of the International Sociological Association*; Vanessa Munro, 'Violence Against Women, "Victimhood" and the (Neo)Liberal State' in Margaret Davies and Vanessa Munro (eds), *The Ashgate Companion to Feminist Legal Theory* (Ashgate 2013) 244.

[24]Annette Ballinger, 'Lesson for the Coalition' (2011) 85(1) *Criminal Justice Matters* 16.

[25]CPS, 'CPS Makes Commitment to Male Victims of Sexual and Domestic Abuse' (2017) available at https://www.cps.gov.uk/cps/news/cps-makes-commitment-male-victims-sexual-and-domestic-abuse.

[26]See comments made by prosecutors in Chapter 4.

[27]Maggie Wykes and Kirsty Welsh, *Violence, Gender and Justice* (Sage 2009).

disproportionally affects women takes hold. The practical effect for individual women of channelling complaints through the police and prosecution process is that what becomes prioritised is not women's immediate or ongoing protection (such as through the extended provision of shelters, refuges and support workers) but pro-prosecution initiatives that prioritise criminal justice targets, such as achieving conviction rates and expeditious processing of cases. Any victory feminists might claim from the state's stated commitment to ending violence against women, needs to ask why that pledge should have resulted in a turn to criminalisation at the expense of, amongst other things, community-based support.[28]

Having observed the readiness of neoliberal state to use the criminal law as a primary means of ending gendered abuse, Halley has called on feminists to 'defitishize the state as the sole source of governmental power' and to prefer 'efforts to resist taking the state on its own terms'.[29] As I have already argued, when feminists work with the (neoliberal) state and take part in public consultations, the government garners legitimacy for its policies. It is therefore strategically astute for the government to include 'the opposition'; it acquires them public approval and authority to prioritise the punitive neoliberal social control project. The fight against violence against women becomes couched in neoliberal rhetoric as the following Home Office quote illustrates:

> Violence against women and girls (VAWG) are serious crimes. These crimes have a huge impact on our economy, health services, and the criminal justice system. Protecting women and girls from violence, and supporting victims and survivors of sexual violence, remains a priority of this government.[30]

The integration of the violence against women's movement into neoliberal rationales and logics here is evident. Violence against women represents and risks financial losses and puts additional burdens on state institutions. Yet, when the government conducted its public consultation on 'Transforming the Response to Domestic Abuse' in Spring 2018, to inform the new Domestic Abuse Bill, what else should feminists and violence against women campaigners have done but engage in that debate? Naturally, as experts

---

[28]Mimi Kim, 'Challenging the Pursuit of Criminalisation in an Era of Mass Incarceration: The Limitations of the Social Work Response to Domestic Violence in the USA' (2013) 43 *British Journal of Social Work* 1276.

[29]Janet Halley et al., *Governance Feminism* (University of Minnesota Press 2018) 4.

[30]Home Office, 'Policy: Violence Against Women and Girls' available at https://www.gov.uk/government/policies/violence-against-women-and-girls accessed 4 May 2020.

working daily in the field, these organisations want to share their perspective and engage in a process that could result in tangible improvements to the state's treatment of domestic abuse.

The Women's Aid Federation, for example (which comprises 180 separate organisations working with survivors) made joint recommendations to government. They proposed legislative and regulatory changes—a separate offence of non-fatal strangulation, a duty to consult with the victim regarding bail decisions, the abolition of the 'rough sex' defence[31] and support for migrant women to access public funds, housing and refuge services—together with sustainable funding for specialist services.[32] The Federation's consultation response makes it clear that the Bill must improve protection, support and access to justice for all groups facing multiple disadvantage including for black or minority ethnic women, lesbian, bisexual and trans women, both older and young women, disabled women and migrant women. The federation's appeal to government mirrors the conclusions drawn in my primary research; that criminal justice legislation alone will not be sufficient to transform the response to survivors and that reform is needed across the public sector and wider society. The federation confirms that:

> The Bill, and supporting non-legislative package, must drive a shift in the national response to domestic abuse from managing a survivors' risk, to meeting her needs. A system focused on managing high risk victims alone can miss the most vulnerable, fail to deliver early intervention or prevention, and increase costs to the public sector. Systems that centre on a survivor's needs, in contrast, can provide earlier help to secure long-term recovery, independence and freedom for all women and children experiencing abuse.[33]

There is a clear attempt here to shift away from neoliberal/managerial rhetoric to a more welfarist/solidaristic approach. Yet, at the same time the

---

[31]In which a perpetrator can argue that a victim consented to her injuries during sex.

[32]Women's Aid Federation, 'Joint Recommendations for the Domestic Abuse Bill' https://1q7dqy2unor827bqjls0c4rn-wpengine.netdna-ssl.com/wp-content/uploads/2020/06/Joint-Recommendations-for-the-Domestic-Abuse-Bill-FINAL.pdf accessed 16 June 2020. The federation includes membership of 180 separate organisations. Contributors to the Joint Recommendations included from Imkaan, Solace, Southall Black Sisters, AVA, Surviving Economic Abuse and the Centre for Women's Justice.

[33]Women's Aid Federation, 'Transforming the Response to Domestic Abuse Consultation: Response from Women's Aid Federation of England' available at https://1q7dqy2unor827bqjls0c4rn-wpengine.netdna-ssl.com/wp-content/uploads/2018/05/Transforming-the-Response-to-Domestic-Abuse-Consultation-Response-from-Womens-Aid-31-May-2018.pdf accessed 16 June 2020.

Federation is also appealing to neoliberal sensibilities, such as costs to the public sector and the values of independence and freedom. The Federation are using the master's tools to dismantle the master's house. Despite the Federation highlighting the economic advantages of public education and meeting the holistic needs of survivors at the earliest opportunity, the extent to which these non-criminal justice recommendations will be implemented, rather than tokenistically nodded to, remains to be seen.

The survivors' stories in Chapter 5 also revealed how law and legal procedures are often experienced by them as a targeted (often short term) intervention, as superficial or even as damaging and dangerous. For some of the women interviewed, the law's presence was not worth the cost of exposing themselves to the emotional labour of drawn-out legal proceedings or to the risk of future physical harm—which either increased or remained the same during and after proceedings. Convictions for these survivors might only be considered a 'pyrrhic victory'.[34] Support workers in Chapter 6, whilst setting out the gains that women could experience—validation, justice and closure—felt only too compelled to express that criminal prosecutions are only ever a fraction of a woman's journey to living abuse free. Moreover, poor experiences of criminal proceedings have the potential to erode women's trust in the police, in the system to rehabilitate the perpetrator or in themselves to be capable of making decisions that improve their situation. Prior to engaging the criminal justice system, the risks, problems and potential disappointments associated with engaging the law should be made plain to survivors so that they can make informed decisions and manage their expectations about what a prosecution and restraining order may or may not achieve.

To summarise, the government's commitment to protecting women from violence derives from economic imperative and is illustrative of the 'interweaving of feminist ideas into rationalities and technologies of neoliberal governmentality'.[35] If the priority is to protect and support women from abuse, the recent erosion of refuge funding[36] (a service recognised as key in supporting women who do not report to the police[37]) seems at once antithetical, yet also in keeping with neoliberalism's rolling back of the state.

[34]Carol Smart, *Feminism and the Power of the Law* (Routledge 1989) 49.

[35]Elizabeth Prugl, 'Neoliberalising Feminism' (2015) *New Political Economy* 614.

[36]Sally Lipscombe et al., 'Funding for Domestic Violence Refuges' (House of Common Library December 2017) available at file:///C:/Users/User/Downloads/CDP-2017-0250.pdf accessed 17 May 2020.

[37]Annette Ballinger, 'Lessons for the Coalition' (2011) 85(1) *Criminal Justice Matters* 16.

When feminist discourses become gender-neutralised in criminal justice priorities, when women's bodies, autonomy and mental health become monetised and when domestic abuse victims are constructed as 'particularly vulnerable' to provoke attentiveness in the criminal justice system, opportunities to contest such outcomes and argue for alternative, material resources for women are lost. Feminists should be alert to these potential drawbacks of engaging with the state.

Within the criminal justice system, I have argued that the turn to criminalisation within the neoliberal context can have the effect of crowding out alternative and diverse theorisations of survivors' subjectivities. Moving away from simplistic binaries such as the victim/agent dichotomy is necessary and requires recognition that victims of domestic abuse can practice agency in various ways to keep themselves safe, perhaps making micro 'movements to create freedom within a context of oppression'.[38] My hope is for the alternative frames I propose in Chapter 6 is to guide and improve the support that can be offered to women who find themselves within the criminal justice system; for ease of reference, I refer to this as conceiving a 'thriver-subject'.

Conceiving a 'thriver-subject' requires prosecutors to obtain full information about the survivor's situation and her reasons for not wishing to pursue a prosecution. When a woman retracts her support for the prosecution, the presumption that prosecution will be pursued must be moderated; prosecutors must sensitively weigh up the safety and well-being costs of proceeding. Prosecutors must be mindful not to engage 'in any conduct which supports the position that the complainant is complicit in perpetrating the abuse they are suffering'[39] meaning that any emotional, financial, social and physical abuse must not be reinforced by case discontinuance and that undue pressure from the perpetrator upon the victim ought not to dissuade prosecution. Such pressure cannot be condoned. Men must not be able to manipulate the prosecution outcome through threats or intimidation of the victim. However, in practice prosecutors know that a woman's safety cannot be assured through prosecution. Alternative accommodation cannot be offered to victims nor can prosecutors ensure perpetrators adhere to bail conditions or orders not to contact her. Until sufficient safeguarding is made available either within or outside the criminal justice system, then a woman's request to terminate proceedings needs to be taken very seriously by prosecutors on

---

[38]Nancy Hirschmann, 'Freedom, Power and Agency in Feminist Legal Theory' in Margaret Davis and Vanessa Munro (eds), *The Ashgate Research Companion to Feminist Legal Theory* (Ashgate 2013) 59.

[39]Crown Prosecution Service, 'Domestic Abuse Guidelines for Prosecutors' available at https://www.cps.gov.uk/legal-guidance/domestic-abuse-guidelines-prosecutors accessed 20 June 2020.

a case-by-case basis. This is the unsatisfactory reality prosecutors find themselves in.

Supporting the 'thriver-subject' also requires prosecutors to practice sensitive and empathetic interactions with survivors in line with therapeutic jurisprudential practices. Using law as a 'therapeutic agent' can help to support women's mental health and 'resilience'.[40] More specifically, and learning from support workers' accounts, prosecutors should deploy a 'trauma-informed' approach to every domestic abuse case, recognising and anticipating the multiplicity of ways trauma may or may not present in survivors.[41] Moreover, in striving for survivors' 'thrivership', prosecutors would be mindful of 'self-determination' theory and the value for survivors of being able to make and effect their own choices.[42] Being autonomous, I have contended, is integral to self-worth, self-respect and satisfaction. Yet autonomy must be understood relationally (recognising our connectivity to and dependency on others) and will help to contextualise women's decision-making, for example, the decision to remain with a violent partner. Social relations are both constitutive of the individual and a precondition for autonomy; a woman's experience of state actors can foster her autonomy provided the inherent quality of relationality is understood.[43] Crucially, conceiving a 'thriver-subject' means that each survivor should be regarded as an end in themselves and no-one merely as a tool for the ends of others (in contrast to no-drop style practices).[44]

In drawing out the potential limitations of the state's 'constraining logic of criminalisation',[45] I do not wish to undersell the great achievements of the women's movement in raising the profile of female victims of domestic

---

[40]In Chapter 6, I explore Fineman's vulnerability theory which encourages actors to see others as themselves. See also David Wexler, 'Applying the Law Therapeutically' (1996) *Applied and Preventive Psychology* 179.

[41]See also, for example, Louise Ellison and Vanessa Munro, 'Taking Trauma Seriously: Critical Reflections on the Criminal Justice Process' (2017) 21(3) *The International Journal of Evidence & Proof* 183.

[42]In Chapter 6, I explored how self-determination theory explains how individuals who are able to make their own choices, go out into the world in a more vigorous and 'effective' fashion: Richard Ryan and Edward Deci, *Self-Determination Theory: Basic Psychological Needs in Motivation, Development, and Wellness* (The Guilford Press, 2017).

[43]Rosemary Hunter, 'Contesting the Dominant Paradigm' in Margaret Davis and Vanessa Munro (eds), *The Ashgate Research Companion to Feminist Legal Theory* (Ashgate 2013) 16–17.

[44]Martha Nussbaum, *Women and Human Development: The Capabilities Approach* (Cambridge University Press 2000) 5.

[45]Kim, (n 28).

abuse. In practical terms, the presumption to prosecute secures safety for some women when their assailant is remanded or sentenced to custody or probation. This is because the separation enables her to make arrangements to leave, to conceal her location or to reach out for support. Her victimhood, as outlined in Chapter 5, is acknowledged, her experience validated and this may form part of a crucial path to her making sense of his behaviour and its unacceptability. Women may also find their way to feminist groups and organisations by engaging criminal justice.[46] Nor do I seek to undermine the norm producing potential of consistent and committed denunciation of intimate partner abuse. Recall also the automatic drop practices of the early CPS which gave scope to offenders to manipulate women into retracting.[47] The current presumption to prosecute must be considered a great advance in terms of reducing the expectation that perpetrators can affect case outcomes. Moreover, whilst my empirical research indicates that prosecutors routinely appeared to prefer summonsing a victim who had withdrawn her support for the prosecution, my research in Chapter 4 also revealed promise, from a survivor-defined perspective, that the CPS might be drawing back from the practice (with victimless prosecutions being encouraged).[48] Thus, the concern that that one type of patriarchal domination (the perpetrator's) might simply be replaced with another (the state's through criminal justice) is potentially being addressed within the CPS.

The Feminist Legal Project

The project of feminist jurisprudence has long been to excavate the claim that the law is gender-neutral and to render visible the gendered content of law and its processes where it exists. The feminist legal scholar's task is to uncover how gender is 'both ignored and enshrined in legal theory and practice'.[49] This is not academic folly, contesting the truth claims that law is ungendered reveals the assumptions that laws are built on and the way legal

---

[46]Heather Douglas, 'Battered Women's Experiences of the Criminal Justice System: Decentring the Law' (2012) *Feminist Legal Studies* 121–134.

[47]Antonia Cretney and Gwynn Davis. 'Prosecuting Domestic Assault: Victims Failing Courts, or Courts Failing Victims?' (1997) *The Howard Journal of Crime and Justice* 146–157.

[48]As Chapter 4 revealed, 3 prosecutors identified a shift followed training in 2016/2017 that promoted use of the victimless prosecution in preference for summons wherever possible.

[49]See Joanne Conaghan, 'Reassessing the Feminist Theoretical Project in Law' (2000) 27 *Journal of Law and Society* 351, 359–363.

procedures can differentially impact men's and women's lives. This endeavour therefore contributes to feminism as a political movement; Rackley, for example, has referred to 'academic activism'.[50] It is right then, that by exposing how law often fails to live up to the standard of applying equally to all in a neutral way, feminist legal scholars have inherent normative ambition.[51] After interviewing women survivors and their support workers and after placing women and their unique yet shared experiences at the fore, the conclusions I have drawn inevitably have normative aspiration as far as existing criminal law and prosecutorial decision-making is concerned. I have called for theoretically informed and empirically grounded prosecutorial praxis, to support survivors to reach 'thrivership'.

Throughout, I have been mindful of the critique of essentialism and of not wishing to overstate how 'women' as a category should be thought about by prosecutors. I have tried to use women's standpoint and diverse material realities as a way to unsettle how prosecutors have routinely come to think about victims of intimate partner abuse; as particularly vulnerable women deserving of a strong state response and in need of protection through prosecution. To that end, I answer Conaghan's call to 'reinstate women-centredness as a political strategy'[52] and use woman-centred epistemology to displace and destabilise an identified prosecutorial working practice. Conscious of the critique of essentialism, I am also concerned with the dangers associated with deconstructionism—that it sacrifices feminism's political energy because of its focus on women's diverse characteristics rather than their shared experiences (of subordination). To overcome this 'blackmail of essentialism'[53]—the either you are 'for' or 'against' it[54]—I attested to the strength of Munro's Wittgensteinian adoption of 'family resemblances'[55] and Schneider's encouragement to recognise that the 'particular' exists within the 'general'.[56] To that end, Chapter 4's analysis of women's particular and

[50]Erika Rackley, 'Why Feminist Legal Scholars Should Write Judgments: Reflections on the Feminist Judgments Project in England and Wales' (2012) 24.2 *Canadian Journal of Women and the Law* 389, 389.

[51]See Conaghan (n 49), 351. See also Rosemary Hunter, 'The Power of Feminist Judgments?' (2012) 20(2) *Feminist Legal Studies* 135.

[52]Ibid., 384.

[53]Vanessa Munro, 'Resemblances of Identity: Ludwig Wittgenstein and Contemporary Feminist Legal Theory' (2006) *Res Publica* 137, 145.

[54]Ibid., 145.

[55]Ibid.

[56]For a fuller discussion, see Chapter 5; Elizabeth Schneider, *Battered Women and Feminist Lawmaking* (Yale University Press 2000) 5.

unique legal consciousnesses recognises difference but also the intersecting and overlapping similarities (the Wittgensteinian approach) between women *before, with* and *against* the law, whilst all the time appreciating broader structural aspects that render their disadvantage contextualised according to gender (per Schneider's feminist law-making).

The approach I have taken stands in contrast to Madden-Dempsey's essentialist philosophical knowledge claims about women and the part patriarchy plays in the commission of certain domestic violence. Madden-Dempsey's feminist motivations lie in her goal of reconstituting the state as less patriarchal thereby eradicating the means of female oppression. Whilst Madden-Dempsey purports to accept the impact of intersectionality on women's disadvantage, she rejects post-modern deconstruction of womanhood because, she says, 'there are always other aspects to women's identity and bases other than sex for their oppression'.[57] Madden-Dempsey's grand ambition to eradicate 'patriarchy' or as she describes it 'wrongful structural inequality' arises from the grand or meta-narratives that are foundational to her understanding of women's systematic disadvantages and the part they play in intimate partner violence.

I have shown that the 'patriarchal force' theory is present in government strategy and the CPS policy to end violence against women. The theory describes how men's domination of women in society has led to the gender asymmetry of domestic abuse. Much has been gained by deploying a readily understandable and charged account of 'patriarchal force'; the state now actually, figuratively and systematically condemns domestic abuse and recognises its gendered nature. The 'patriarchal force' account of domestic abuse has been used in support of and to justify the disproportionate use of the criminal law as a means of addressing intimate partner abuse. The 'patriarchal force' thesis uses essentialism in a strategic way,[58] to motivate the state into action. Yet the 'patriarchal force' thesis must be deployed in a way that recognises that it will intersect with other social, psychological and structural trigger factors. I have therefore attested to Heise's ecological framework that also recognises factors including at the macro (e.g. cultural), situational (e.g. past personal experiences) and individual (e.g. pathology and substance

[57]Michelle Madden-Dempsey, *Prosecuting Domestic Violence: A Philosophical Analysis* (Oxford University Press 2009) 131.

[58]Gayatri Spivak, 'In a Word: Interview' in Naomi Schor and Elizabeth Weed (eds), *The Essential Difference* (Indiana University Press 1994).

misuse) levels to explain why, for example, the majority of men are *not* abusive and, conversely, why some women *are*.[59]

Finally, I want to position my findings with reference to the work of Carol Smart who, in 1989, cautioned feminists against the siren call of the law to end women's inequality because in accepting law's terms and masculinist knowledge, feminism would always concede too much.[60] Yet I have shown how current prosecutorial approaches to intimate partner abuse have in fact adapted to societal expectations and, inter alia, feminist demands and consequently have offered women recognition and progressive reform to a degree not witnessed or anticipated when Smart wrote her influential work.[61] Nonetheless, by using the example of prosecuting intimate partner abuse, I have endeavoured to respond to Smart's original appeal for feminists to engage with the way that law operates for women in practice[62] and continues to influence our personal lives.[63] Through a careful questioning of the ideas and values that underpin prosecutorial working practices, I have exposed neoliberalism's enveloping of feminist ideas as a means to bring more perpetrators to justice through the criminal law. The effect has been the de-funding of social support arrangements that could otherwise have offered genuine safety and therapeutic ameliorations for survivors. What flows from the findings—particularly those in Chapters 5 and 6—are the gains that could be made from de-centring law by expanding holistic non-legal strategies for survivors (and, indeed, perpetrators) in the manner Smart contemplated. However, Smart never wanted feminists to abandon law as a profitable site of discursive struggle. To that end, my engagement with the processes of criminal law and prosecutorial practices has also provoked conceptualisation of the 'thriver-subject', a subject that prompts the prosecutor to think beyond criminal justice goals and to the fundamental needs of the survivor/thriver.

[59]Lori Heise, 'Violence Against Women: An Integrated, Ecological Framework' (1998) 4(3) *Violence Against Women* 262.

[60]Smart, *Feminism and the Power of the Law* (n 34) 5.

[61]Rosemary Auchmuty and Karin Van Marle, 'Introduction: Special Issue: Carol Smart's Feminism and the Power of the Law' (2012) 20(2) *Feminist Legal Studies* 65–69.

[62]Smart, *Feminism and the Power of the Law* (n 34).

[63]Carol Smart, 'Reflection' (2012) *Feminist Legal Studies* 161–165.

References

Auchmuty R and Van Marle K, 'Introduction: Special Issue: Carol Smart's Feminism and the Power of the Law' (2012) 20(2) *Feminist Legal Studies* 65.

Ballinger A, 'Lesson for the Coalition' (2011) 85(1) *Criminal Justice Matters* 16.

Bell E, *Criminal Justice and Neoliberalism* (Palgrave Macmillan 2011).

Bumiller K, *In an Abusive State: How Neoliberalism Appropriated the Feminist Movement Against Sexual Violence* (Duke University Press 2008).

Conaghan J, 'Reassessing the Feminist Theoretical Project in Law' (2000) 27 *Journal of Law and Society* 351.

Cretney A and Davis G, 'Prosecuting Domestic Assault: Victims Failing Courts, or Courts Failing Victims?' (1997) *The Howard Journal of Crime and Justice* 146.

Crown Prosecution Service, 'CPS Makes Commitment to Male Victims of Sexual and Domestic Abuse' (2017) available at https://www.cps.gov.uk/cps/news/cps-makes-commitment-male-victims-sexual-and-domestic-abuse accessed 20 June 2020.

———, 'Domestic Abuse Guidelines for Prosecutors' available at https://www.cps.gov.uk/legal-guidance/domestic-abuse-guidelines-prosecutors accessed 6 June 2020, accessed 14 June 2020.

———, 'Violence Against Women and Girls' Report' (10th edn, 2015–2016).

Davies M and Munro V (eds), *The Ashgate Companion to Feminist Legal Theory* (Ashgate 2013).

Dobash RE and Dobash RP, 'Love, Honour and Obey: Institutional Ideologies and the Struggle for Battered Women' (1977) *Contemporary Crisis* 403.

Douglas H, 'Battered Women's Experiences of the Criminal Justice System: Decentring the Law' (2012) *Feminist Legal Studies* 121.

Ellison L and Munro V, 'Taking Trauma Seriously: Critical Reflections on the Criminal Justice Process' (2017) 21(3) *The International Journal of Evidence & Proof* 183.

Foucault M, in Michel Senellart (ed), *The Birth of Biopolitics: Lectures at the College de France 1978–79* (Picador 2004).

Fraser N, 'Feminism, Capitalism, and the Cunning of History' (2012) *HAL* 2– 4.

Garland D, *The Culture of Control* (Oxford University Press 2011).

Halley J et al., *Governance Feminism* (University of Minnesota Press 2018).

Heise L, 'Violence Against Women: An Integrated, Ecological Framework' (1998) 4(3) *Violence Against Women* 262.

HM Government, 'Strategy to End Violence Against Women and Girls 2016–2020' available at https://assets.publishing.service.gov.uk/government/uploads/system/uploads/attachment_data/file/522166/VAWG_Strategy_FINAL_PUBLICATION_MASTER_vRB.PDF accessed 6 June 2020.

Home Office, 'Policy: Violence Against Women and Girls' available at https://www.gov.uk/government/policies/violence-against-women-and-girls accessed 4 May 2020.

Houston C, 'How Feminist Theory Became (Criminal) Law: Tracing the Path to Mandatory Criminal Intervention in Domestic Violence Cases' (2014) *Michigan Journal of Gender and Law* 217.

Hunter R, 'Deconstructing the Subjects of Feminism: The Essentialism Debate in Feminist Theory and Practice' (1996) *Australian Feminist Law Journal* 135.

———, 'The Power of Feminist Judgments?' (2012) 20(2) *Feminist Legal Studies* 135.

Kim M, 'Challenging the Pursuit of Criminalisation in an Era of Mass Incarceration: The Limitations of the Social Work Response to Domestic Violence in the USA' (2013) 43 *British Journal of Social Work* 1276.

Kumar R, 'Populism, Neoliberalism and the Contemporary World: Reflections for an Alternative Politics with Nancy Fraser' (2019) 5(2) *Society and Culture in South Asia* 340.

Madden-Dempsey M, *Prosecuting Domestic Violence: A Philosophical Analysis* (Oxford University Press 2009).

Munro V, 'Resemblances of Identity: Ludwig Wittgenstein and Contemporary Feminist Legal Theory' (2006) *Res Publica* 137.

Nussbaum, *Women and Human Development: The Capabilities Approach* (Cambridge University Press 2000).

Packer H, 'Two Models of Criminal Process' (1964) *University of Pennsylvania Law Review* 1.

Pratt J and Anderson J (eds), *Criminal Justice, Risk and the Revolt Against Uncertainty* (Palgrave Macmillan 2020).

Prugl E, 'Neoliberalising Feminism' (2015) *New Political Economy* 614.

Rackley E, 'Why Feminist Legal Scholars Should Write Judgments: Reflections on the Feminist Judgments Project in England and Wales' (2012) 24(2) *Canadian Journal of Women and the Law* 389.

Schickert C, 'Feminism in Neoliberal Times: An Interview with Nancy Fraser' (2018) 8(3) *Global Dialogue: Magazine of the International Sociological Association.*

Schneider E, *Battered Women and Feminist Lawmaking* (Yale University Press 2000).

Smart C, *Feminism and the Power of the Law* (Routledge 1989).

———, 'Reflection' (2012) *Feminist Legal Studies* 161.

Spivak G, 'In a Word: Interview' in Naomi Schor and Elizabeth Weed (eds), *The Essential Difference* (Indiana University Press 1994).

Wexler D, 'Applying the Law Therapeutically' (1996) *Applied and Preventive Psychology* 179.

Women's Aid Federation, 'Joint Recommendations for the Domestic Abuse Bill' (2018) https://1q7dqy2unor827bqjls0c4rn-wpengine.netdna-ssl.com/wp-content/

uploads/2020/06/Joint-Recommendations-for-the-Domestic-Abuse-Bill-FINAL.pdf accessed 16 June 2020.

———, 'Transforming the Response to Domestic Abuse Consultation: Response from Women's Aid Federation of England' available at https://1q7dqy2unor827bqjls0c4rn-wpengine.netdna-ssl.com/wp-content/uploads/2018/05/Transforming-the-Response-to-Domestic-Abuse-Consultation-Response-from-Womens-Aid-31-May-2018.pdf accessed 16 June 2020.

Wykes M and Welsh K, *Violence, Gender and Justice* (Sage 2009).

Index

A. Porter, *Prosecuting Domestic Abuse in Neoliberal Times*, Palgrave Socio-Legal Studies,
https://doi.org/10.1007/978-3-030-61369-3

The manufacturer's authorised representative in the EU is Springer Nature Customer Service Centre GmbH, Europaplatz 3, 69115 Heidelberg, Germany. If you have any concerns regarding our products, please contact ProductSafety@springernature.com

Printed and bound by CPI Group (UK) Ltd, Croydon, CR0 4YY
30/09/2026
02225451-0020